W9-AWV-401

The Whiting Foundation congratulates *Conjunctions* on their 2020 Literary Magazine Prize!

From the judges:

"Every issue is a feat of curatorial invention, stitching together work by storytellers and scholars to create a fluid and expansive survey of our most pressing human concerns."

And congratulations to the full cohort of this year's winners:

One Story Print; New York, NY

Conjunctions Print; Annandale-on-Hudson, NY

Foglifter Print; San Francisco, CA

Kweli Digital; New York, NY

Nat. Brut Digital; Burlington, NC

The application window for the 2021 Prizes is open through Nov 30, 2020. Five prizes will be awarded across print and digital categories to journals with budgets of up to $500,000.

Visit **whiting.org/litmags** for eligibility information and to apply online.

whiting
FOUNDATION

COMING UP IN THE SPRING

Conjunctions:76
THE FORTIETH ANNIVERSARY ISSUE
Edited by Bradford Morrow

The price of a first-class stamp rose from fifteen cents to twenty that year, and a dozen eggs cost less than a buck. Ronald Reagan was inaugurated as president in January 1981, a couple of months before John Hinckley Jr. attempted to assassinate him. It was the year MTV started broadcasting, the year Andrew Lloyd Webber's *Cats* debuted in London, the year the first space shuttle, *Columbia*, was launched. The AIDS virus was identified that year, Sandra Day O'Connor became the first female Supreme Court justice, and, for better or worse, Lady Diana Spencer became Diana, Princess of Wales. Three-and-a-half-inch floppy disks, Jared Kushner, and the first American test-tube baby were born, as were Britney Spears, Skittles, and Post-it Notes. Elias Canetti won the Nobel Prize in Literature, Rick James released "Super Freak," *Raiders of the Lost Ark* topped the box office, and Hoagy Carmichael, Bob Marley, and Natalie Wood left this world.

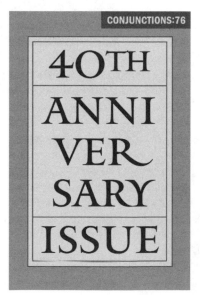

Nineteen eighty-one was also the year that Robert Creeley, Denise Levertov, Octavio Paz, Josephine Miles, Tennessee Williams, John Hawkes—all sadly deceased now—along with dozens of other writers, came together to contribute to the first issue of a literary journal called *Conjunctions*. Founded and edited by Bradford Morrow with the encouragement of poet and translator Kenneth Rexroth, *Conjunctions* has now published over one thousand writers, some at the beginnings of their careers, some avowed masters. Deemed a "living notebook" by its editor, *Conjunctions* continues to forge ahead some three decades after Bard College became its publisher, and four after it first saw the light of day.

This celebratory anniversary issue will feature new work by Can Xue, Rosmarie Waldrop, and many others, including a previously unpublished story by Isaac Bashevis Singer.

One-year individual US subscriptions to *Conjunctions* are only $30 (two years for $50) for today's most innovative fiction, poetry, and narrative nonfiction. To read dangerously, subscribe or renew at conjunctions.com, or mail your check to *Conjunctions*, Bard College, Annandale-on-Hudson, NY 12504. For e-book editions of current and selected past issues, visit openroadmedia.com/conjunctions. If you have questions or wish to request an invoice, e-mail conjunctions@bard.edu or call (845) 758-7054.

CONJUNCTIONS

Bi-Annual Volumes of New Writing

Edited by
Bradford Morrow

Contributing Editors
Diane Ackerman
Martine Bellen
Mei-mei Berssenbrugge
Mary Caponegro
Brian Evenson
Peter Gizzi
Robert Kelly
Ann Lauterbach
Carmen Maria Machado
Dinaw Mengestu
Rick Moody
Fred Moten
Karen Russell
Joanna Scott
David Shields
Peter Straub
Quincy Troupe

Published by Bard College

EDITOR: Bradford Morrow
MANAGING EDITOR: Evangeline Riddiford Graham
SENIOR EDITORS: Jedediah Berry, Benjamin Hale, J. W. McCormack, Edie Meidav,
    Michael Sarinsky, Pat Sims
COPY EDITOR: Pat Sims
ASSISTANT EDITORS: Sarah Ahmad, A. D. Lauren-Abunassar, Kate Monaghan,
    Magali Roman
PUBLICITY: Darren O'Sullivan, Mark R. Primoff
EDITORIAL ASSISTANTS: Michael Blackmon, Emily
    Giangiulio, Danielle Martin, Brian Araque Perez,
    Alexi Piirimae, Nik Slackman

CONJUNCTIONS is published in the spring and fall
of each year by Bard College, Annandale-on-Hudson,
NY 12504. This project is supported in part by awards
from the National Endowment for the Arts, the New
York State Council on the Arts with the support of
Governor Andrew M. Cuomo and the New York State
Legislature, and the Whiting Foundation.

SUBSCRIPTIONS: Use our secure online ordering system at conjunctions.com, or send
subscription orders to CONJUNCTIONS, Bard College, Annandale-on-Hudson, NY
12504. Single year (two volumes): $30.00 for individuals; $50.00 for institutions and
non-US. Two years (four volumes): $50.00 for individuals; $80.00 for institutions and
non-US. For information about subscriptions, back issues, and advertising, contact us
at (845) 758-7054 or conjunctions@bard.edu. *Conjunctions* is listed and indexed in
JSTOR and Humanities International Complete and included in EBSCO*host*.

Editorial communications should be sent to Bradford Morrow, *Conjunctions*, 21 East
10th Street, 3E, New York, NY 10003. Unsolicited manuscripts cannot be returned unless
accompanied by a stamped, self-addressed envelope. Electronic and simultaneous
submissions will not be considered. Do not send work via any method requiring a
signature for delivery. If you are submitting from outside the United States, contact
conjunctions@bard.edu for instructions.

Cover design by Jerry Kelly, New York. Cover art by unidentified American artist:
(*Underpass—New York*), ca. 1933–ca. 1934, courtesy of Smithsonian American Art
Museum. This painting was created for the Federal Art Project, a branch of the WPA,
which was developed to give financial and moral support to Depression-era artists.

Conjunctions e-books of current and selected past issues are distributed by Open Road
Integrated Media (openroadmedia.com/conjunctions) and available for purchase in all
e-reader formats from Amazon, Apple, B&N, Google, Indiebound, Kobo, Overdrive, and
elsewhere.

Retailers can order print issues directly from *Conjunctions*.

Printers: Maple Press, GHP

Typesetter: Bill White, Typeworks

ISSN 0278-2324

ISBN 978-0-941964-27-2

Manufactured in the United States of America.

TABLE OF CONTENTS

DISPATCHES FROM SOLITUDE

Edited by Bradford Morrow

We wish to express our gratitude
to the

Whiting Foundation

for its generosity in naming

Conjunctions

a winner of the

Whiting Literary Magazine Prize

EDITOR'S NOTE

WE HAD PLANNED another issue for fall 2020, *States of Play*, whose theme would be centered on the complex, often dangerous world of games—risk, chance, winning, losing. Our announcement was written and typeset, a few writers had expressed interest in contributing, preliminary cover images were chosen.

Then the coronavirus took over. Our offices were forced, like those of countless others, to go remote. As hundreds, then thousands, began to die—among them dear friends of mine, such as *Conjunctions* donor Jay Hanus and longtime contributor H. G. Carrillo—New York and other cities were forced into lockdown. COVID-19 became the daily and nightly shadow that fell across our lives. Most of us who weren't essential workers retreated into some form of isolation, whether sheltering in a metropolis, a town, or the country, where rural life, at least in the beginning, seemed safer.

Amid this harrowing outbreak, another, more urgent theme for the fall *Conjunctions* became imperative, one in which we might gather writings from those who were compelled to change their daily routines, even reevaluate what their work and lives meant to them. Contributions didn't necessarily have to be *about* the pandemic, as such, but shaped by its constraints, by the terrors and courage it has provoked.

Dispatches from Solitude came into being under these circumstances. With COVID-19 having taken over 200,000 American lives and a million worldwide, the end seems no more in sight now than when this issue was conceived. I would like to extend my gratitude to everyone on our editorial staff—including our former and new managing editors, Nicole Nyhan and Evangeline Riddiford Graham—and in our production family, who worked under such unforgiving conditions to help bring this issue to fruition. And to every writer who sent work and every writer whose contributions are in these pages, as well as all our readers, we at *Conjunctions* hope you stay healthy, safe, and inspired.

—Bradford Morrow
October 2020
New York City

Two Songs
Sandra Cisneros

BUEN ÁRBOL / A GOOD TREE
A Song for Guitar

Que a buen árbol se arrima,
Buena sombra le cobija.
Arrímate. Anímate.
Don't be afraid of me.

If you were smart
You'd know I'm a good good tree.
If you were smart
You'd know I'm a good good tree.

I'm the finial and flag of my own nation.
I'm the school of knocks.
I'm a little bit of comfort mixed
With a little bit of consternation.
I'm the waltz of reason
In the season of rain at last!

If you were smart
You'd know I'm a good good tree.
If you were smart
You'd know I'm a good good tree.

Sweet huisache, teach me.
Nourish me, *nogal.*
Cottonwood, fortify.
Mesquite, endurance please.

I've waited out drought.
Sprouted from my own fire.

Survived the hailstorm
Of desire. Desire.
If you only knew.

If you were smart
You'd know I'm a good good tree.
If you were smart
You'd know I'm a good good tree.

The flower and the fruit am I.
Butterflies breathing life am I.
Resurrection and redemption am I.
Pie in the sky am I.
Kid and wise guy am I.
The still and the gale am I.
Fever and frustration am I.
The evening tide am I.
The soup without the fly am I.
The whole *naranja* am I.

I've died and risen
From the ash of my own
Hesitation. I'm creation.
But you don't see.

If you were smart
You'd know I'm a good good tree.
If you were smart
You'd know I'm a good good tree.

I don't have time for attitude sickness
At this altitude.
I don't have time for percolators,
Nuclear reactors.

I don't need a flash-in-the-pan
Bit of ecstasy
When I've been struck by light.
I'm my own Las Vegas
Night with real stars
For the show. I'm in it

9

For the mystic. Stick
Around and I'll show you
A thing or two.

I'm a good good tree.
I'm a good good tree.
I'm a good good good
Good tree.

SQUINK

A Song

Squink,
Will you come out and play?

It's Sunday.
I'm tired of school.
I live in a big pink
House with dogs and cats and
Birds to here.

I've got friends from
Aquí to there
Who love me for me, they swear,
But they're always

There.

Not here.

Squink,
Will you arrive in the nick?

I've got no Rin Tin Tin to
Rescue me from me.
No Tin Tan to
Make me laugh.
No Evel Knievel to shoot

Himself out of a cannon
For my amusement. No

Body to
Buddy up to. I could
Use a buddy. No
Body gets me in this
Rinky-dink town.

Squink,
Will you arrive like rain?
Will you drive away my drought-struck life
And unstick me from myself?

I've got friends from
Aquí to there
Who love me for me, they swear,
But they're always

There.

Not here.

Squink,
I need a Cantinflas to Cantinflear with.
Someone who laughs in two languages.
Someone like you will do. To

Sing Beatle duets off-key.
Laugh till we pee.
Throw popcorn in the air
And almost put out an eye.
¡Ya mero. ¡Ay! No

Body gets me in this
Rinky-dink town. But
You.

Squink,
Is it the age of *susto*,
Or just *my* age?

11

Does everyone feel this way?
Afraid to admit they're afraid.
We're all honest-to-God deceivers,
Afraid of the dark.
Honest, we're just liars.

Squink,
They say close your eyes and
This too shall pass.
But love is a swift kick to the ass.
And grief is a midwestern winter.
Love is a swift kick to the ass.
And grief is February in Iowa.

Squink,
I need someone
To ride a bike along
Side me at night.
I need someone to moon the moon
And shock the uptight trees.
Please.

I know you're just
Un duende.
Un escuincle mocoso,
And I'm old
Enough to be your baby
Sitter. Baby,

But you're fun, and I'm funny.
You're wind, and I'm dandelion seed.
You're sunbeam. I'm gossamer
Thread hoping to catch somewhere,
Noiseless and patient as
Whitman's spider. Oh,
My soul. Oh,
My soul,
Oh!

Portrait of Two Young Ladies in White and Green Robes
(Unidentified Artist, circa Sixteenth Century)

Jane Pek

I.

A FEW HOURS AGO your last descendant died. She held only a whisper of your essence—or, as one would say in this scientifically rigorous present, only a minuscule percentage of her genetic material was derived from yours—but, of them all, she was the one who reminded me most of you.

She was a documentary filmmaker, the third generation of your descendants to be born and raised in America. Her work examined ways in which the technologies of her era shaped people's lives. In her twenties and thirties she lived in China, where she made a series of films about the state's electronic surveillance system, the tools used by the government to monitor its population, the balance to be struck between security and personal freedom. Her documentaries were as fair as they could be, in my view, taking into account the inherent biases of her Western upbringing and education. The Chinese government, which after all this time remains deficient at accepting criticism, disagreed. After they revoked her visa she returned to America and settled in San Francisco.

You would have enjoyed San Francisco, I think. Its pastel hues and precipitous slopes, its anarchic spirit, the lapping glitter of water all around.

I befriended her later in her life, when it became clear she would have no children. I presented myself as an admirer of her work and a student of Chinese history; also, an immigrant from Hangzhou, where I knew her own family was originally from. We grew close. I made myself indispensable to her. At the end of her life, I was in the hospital room when the lines jagging up and down across the screen of the vital-signs monitor subsided. Humans have developed the custom of measuring the distance a person stands from the border between the living and the dead. They watch each step their loved ones take toward that one-way crossing, count down every last breath.

13

*

I suggested to your descendant once that the technologies highlighted in her films were really no different from what people living during the Ming dynasty or any other historical period of China would have called magic. Then, they had been watched by ghosts and demons and deities, their sins recorded, their actions influenced; now it was the turn of facial-recognition software, online-history tracking apps, predictive algorithms. She smiled and said that I was in the company of brilliant minds: a famous writer and futurist had proposed a similar idea many years ago.

I didn't tell her that I'd met this writer on a beach in Trincomalee, Sri Lanka, even more years ago, or that he and I had struck up a conversation while sipping lukewarm beers and waiting for the waves to settle. At one point he was describing his vision of the future to me, space elevators and communication satellites and personal devices that contained near-infinite reserves of information, and I said all that sounded much the same as the way things had always been, Chang-er floating to the moon, texts charmed to display whatever knowledge the reader sought, an enduring invisible world overlaid upon the physical one.

"Magic, you mean?" he said.

"That's one word for it," I said.

Mostly we had talked about what we were both there for, which was to go diving. He asked why I had chosen this relatively obscure beach. I told him I had heard that the remnants of a medieval Hindu temple lay submerged in the vicinity (the work of Portuguese colonial forces, which, after looting the complex and killing its priests and pilgrims, had gone above and beyond to lever it over the cliff edge into the bay). Later, when the sea had calmed, I swam between broken columns and poised bronze goddesses, over inscriptions of faith splintered across the rocks. Now and then I still search for such relics, even if I don't bother documenting them. Nostalgia, I suppose. In the green silence of the water I could sense the shimmer of the eternal. I hoped that when the writer found these ruins—I might as well have drawn him a map, with all the hints I provided—he would as well.

*

II.

The night before your wedding, the last night I would have with you, I surrendered my pride on the altar of desperation and asked you why in all eighteen hells you were doing this.

"I want to have a child," you said.

"Wait," I said, "seriously? Since when?"

"Since Xiangyang, maybe," you said. "It's hard to tell, these things."

Back then we didn't think in terms of time. Our references were geography and action, places we had been, things we had done. In Xiangyang we had talked a jilted, impoverished artist out of jumping into the Hanshui River, and spun a pretext to give him a hundred taels of silver: we would ask him to paint our portrait. We wore our best dresses for it, you in white and I in green, tinted our cheeks and lips, put pins in our hair. We never collected the painting from him. We prided ourselves on traveling light, and, anyway, we saw no use for it, a record of things that would never change.

Xiangyang was several Ming emperors past, a hundred stops ago in our travels through China. We looked for enchanted artifacts, analyzed and cataloged them, sought to understand the wondrous within the human realm. Until we stopped in at West Lake to follow up on rumors of a jade bracelet that could heal its wearer (a fake, it turned out) and you met the man you decided would do for a husband, I had never considered that we might not live like this always. For a moment I thought that I must not know you at all.

You had been hoping it would pass, you said, like a thunderstorm, or an inept dynasty. "Also, children frighten me. They need so much, and they are so easy to lose."

I placed my palm on your stomach, between the twin ridges of your hips. "All right," I said. "A child." I imagined your belly swelling the way those of human women did, the creature that would tear its way out. Yours; and not yours. "You don't have to marry him for that."

"It wouldn't be fair to him. Or to the child."

"What about to me?" This was why I hadn't wanted to ask. I'd known I would succumb to self-pity, and that it would make no difference.

You told me you had calculated the fate of the man who would be your husband based on the ten stems and twelve branches of his birth. He had a delicate constitution. He would pass in twenty-four years, before his fiftieth birthday.

I didn't say anything.

15

You said, "What is twenty-four years to you?"

I said, "What will twenty-four years be to *you*?" I wasn't thinking twenty-four. I was thinking fifty, sixty, your skin drying to parchment, your hair thinning and graying, your frame stooping ever closer to the ground in which you would—if you did this—someday rot.

You touched my face. I waited for you to ask if I would give up my own immortality, if I was willing to step with you out of the wilderness of myth and into the terraced rice fields and tiled roofs of history.

"You don't have to stay," you said.

I told some version of this story to a man I met in a tavern in rural Shandong. A spirit trading in her immortality to have a child with a human, asking her companion to wait twenty-four years until they could be together again. I was on my way north to Beijing, to bring your son back home following his placement as top scholar in the imperial examination; the boy might have excelled at composing eloquent Confucian nonsense, but he would have been picked apart by bandits the moment his horse trotted beyond the city walls. This man was traveling south, returning to Suzhou after visiting a friend. The tavern was empty except for the two of us. We ended up drinking together, probably for much longer than we should have, talking over the noise of the torn paper windows flapping in the wind.

When I was done, the man said, "But so . . . what happened? When the twenty-four years were up?"

I laughed. "Nothing." Seen in a certain light, now, I could appreciate the glinting, mocking edges of our story. The wine probably helped. It felt potent and tasted foul. "She died within two years. The birth was difficult for her and she never recovered." Neither of us had thought to calculate your fate, in addition to your husband's. After all, we had walked through fires and dived off waterfalls, dismembered demons, batted away the assorted Buddhist monks determined to save us by destroying us so we could reincarnate as lovely, pliant daughters and wives and mothers. What could possibly happen to you while ensconced in domesticity, running a medicine shop with your constitutionally challenged husband? It turned out you were fucking terrible at being a human.

My fellow traveler poured me another cup of wine from the jar we were sharing and told me a story as well, of a young man who had been in love with a prostitute but lacked the wealth to redeem her from the brothel. Instead, she was acquired by a textiles merchant and he took her away with him to another province. The young man expressed his sorrow through any number of histrionic poems. Twenty-four years later, no longer young, he was visiting a friend in a town in that province, and found out, by chance, that the no-longer prostitute lived close by, and also that the merchant had died and she was now a widow.

"Twenty-four years!" I said. "Really?"

He smiled. "Don't you think that's why we met today?"

"What did—," I almost said *you*, since it was obvious he was talking about himself—"he do?"

"Nothing."

I said, "He no longer loved her?"

"He did," said the man. "He chose his love over her."

Nine days after your son and I arrived back in Zhenjiang, your husband collapsed while in his shop. At the funeral I heard your voice beneath the drone of the Taoist priest reciting his interminable scriptures, asking: *What is twenty-four years to you?*

Quite a while later I read a story about two snake spirits in human guise. The white maiden and the green maiden, they were called. It's part of a collection of folktales by a late-Ming writer and poet from Suzhou. In this story the white maiden lives in the depths of West Lake and attains immortality from ingesting some magical pills that a human boy accidentally swallowed and then vomited out again. The green maiden's equally immortal state is never explained. The boy grows up to become the white maiden's husband, their early sharing of bodily fluids a portent of compatibility. A turtle spirit in the form of a Buddhist monk has it out for the white maiden—he was also in that lake, and wanted those pills for himself—and traps her in a pagoda. The green maiden, her faithful companion, hones her skills for twenty-four years and succeeds in breaking the white maiden out of her prison. After which, the white maiden returns to her husband and her son, their medicine shop, her bucolic life. Nothing further is said of the green maiden.

III.

At some point between your death and your husband's, I returned to Xiangyang to look for our artist. Age had petrified him; I barely recognized him beneath its encrustation. When he saw me he told me I bore a remarkable resemblance to someone he had met long ago. "I painted their portrait," he said. "That girl and her sister."

17

I imagined how you would have smirked at that, the notion of us as sisters, and for an instant it was like I was standing at the bottom of a very deep well, its lid skewed to expose a hallucinatory glimmer of sky. "That's so funny," I said, "because that's why I'm here." I explained that I worked for an art collector who had heard of the painting and was interested in acquiring it.

"You're sixty years too late," he said. "I gave it away. Couldn't stand to look at it."

I said, as calmly as I could, "Why?"

"I couldn't get it right." His arthritic hands curled open and then closed again. "There was something about the two of them. The way they were. I couldn't get that into the portrait." He stopped painting altogether shortly afterward.

"I'm so sorry," I said.

He shook his head. He told me his friend—the same one he had given the painting to—got him a position at a trading house, and within ten years he had made enough money for ten lifetimes. "Best decision I ever made," he said, "after not drowning myself over a whore."

It took me almost three hundred years to find that damn painting. From Xiangyang I followed the mercantile route that the cotton trader who had taken the painting would have, floating south and east on overladen barges down the Hanshui. By the time I located a branch of the man's family he had been dead for decades, his possessions scattered across his three concubines and fourteen children. Meanwhile, your son sold the medicine shop, returned to Beijing, rose to become a senior official in the Ministry of Justice, and—in what he must have thought of as a personal political coup, but with less-than-ideal timing—married your granddaughter into Ming nobility right before the Jurchens stampeded into the capital. I was in Changsha, checking on a lead from an art dealer, and I had to hustle to Beijing to extract her and her newborn from that shitshow. (I left her husband behind, which was better for all concerned.) I parked them in Hangzhou, the last place we had lived before I lost you, and there your family remained until the final act of the Qing dynasty, a modest clan of tea growers on the slopes surrounding West Lake, safely hidden in the undergrowth of history.

My search led me, eventually, to Guangzhou, the port city on the Pearl River where the Qing had consolidated all maritime trade.

There I learned of an English missionary who fancied himself a guardian of Chinese culture and how he had convinced the painting's erstwhile owner, a recent convert to Christianity, to give it to him for safekeeping. In our great capital of London, he said, we have a special building that stores treasures from all over the world, to make sure they won't be lost, or ruined, or stolen. He had fled for England on the last clipper ship out of Guangzhou before the British navy began bombing the city during the Second Opium War.

And that's where our portrait is. Room 33 of the British Museum, in the company of a red lacquer box depicting a spring landscape and a commendable forgery of a Jingdezhen porcelain vase. The placard beneath the painting highlights the delicacy of its brushstrokes and the insights it provides into female friendship during the Ming era. Our artist was too harsh on himself. He might not have understood us, but he did manage to set down what he saw. You are smiling at me. It was something I said, I don't remember what. I used to think that as long as I could make you smile, the world would be a fine place. The colors of our dresses glow against the dun background and behind us the clouds swirl like at any moment they could lift us away.

There's something I must confess. When I finally saw the painting, I might have—sort of—cried. I never had, previously. They brought you away in the bridal sedan, and again in the coffin, and both times I watched you become the centerpiece of their human rituals, composed and costumed, almost unrecognizable to me. So then, three hundred years later, to be undone by patterns of ink on silk, swatches of white and green paint, a memory of an unmemorable day: it was quite alarming, actually. Thankfully, the man standing a few feet away from me in the gallery said, no doubt after observing me sniffle for far too long, "You seem like you could use a drink."

He could have suggested a dagger through my eye and I would have taken it. "Do you know a place?" I said.

He looked startled, which might have been for any number of reasons: my forwardness, my speaking English—I had picked it up from the sailors on the long voyage over—or the accent with which I was doing it, which must have made me sound as if I had grown up scuffling for survival on the docks of London. Then he laughed, and offered me both his arm and his handkerchief.

The establishment where he took me was gold trimmed and gaudy, with mirrored walls and fat, winged babies painted across the ceiling. He salvaged my opinion of him by ordering me an enchanting drink. It was a translucent green, as if lit by a hidden flame, and when I sipped it I could taste anise and fennel. After the first glass, he told me, I would see things as I wished they were; after the second glass, as they were not; and, finally, as they truly were.

As we drank he asked me what I had seen, looking at that painting. Beauty, I said, and how it passed.

"Young people are supposed to defer such dour thoughts to the old," he said.

"Oh," I said, "I just look young for my age."

"The ephemerality of beauty is indeed a tragedy," he said, "but surely not in art. The painting will preserve those women's beauty forever."

"While they grew old and died," I said. "That's even worse. It should have been the other way around."

He and I were both well past our third glasses by then, so I told him the story of the hermit on Taishi Mountain who would remain alive for as long as his portrait was intact. The version I told was the one you and I had followed from village to village throughout Henan Province, seeking to determine its authenticity: a scholar official, fallen out of favor with the first Ming court, who begged his portrait to assume the burden of aging for him so he could serve as a historian of the dynasty from its founding to its fall.

"Fascinating," said my drinking companion. "The Ming dynasty ended in . . . what was it, the seventeenth century? What happened to him then?"

"I don't know," I said. "The story doesn't get that far."

We had found him, this hermit, and you coaxed him into showing us the painting. The person depicted in it looked like some ill-tempered ancestor of his who at the time of the portrait sitting was still alive solely to spite all expectations to the contrary. Once he was done with this history of the Ming, the hermit told us, he would burn the portrait. He had no wish to live forever. On our way down from Taishi Mountain I said to you that I was sure he would come up with another reason for living before he laid down his ink brush. You don't think being eternal can start to feel tiring, after a while? you said. It hasn't yet, I said, and we have several hundred years on him. We made a wager: the loser would procure a water dragon's pearl for the winner. But then you died, long before the last Ming emperor did, and I never went back to Taishi to check.

I spent the rest of that day walking through London, admiring, despite myself, its gardens, its cathedrals, its prosperity, its purpose. It reminded me of the grandest days of the Ming, when lantern displays ignited entire mountainsides and Zheng He's treasure fleet measured the breadth of the oceans. In King's Cross Station I saw the twentieth century roaring toward us, all steel and smoke, insatiable, and I thought of how the Summer Palace had burned for days after British troops set it ablaze to punish the Qing government for outlawing the import of opium. When I returned to Hangzhou I put your great-great-grandson on a ship that landed in California shortly before the Chinese Exclusion Act was signed into law. He hated America, the vast and relentless otherness of it, but he never once tried to go back to China.

Quite a while later I read a story about an Englishman and a magical portrait, written by an author as noted for a controversial lifestyle as his literary skill. This Englishman's wish to remain young and beautiful is granted: his portrait will age in his place. He spends his days and nights seeking pleasures and indulging them. While his physical appearance remains unchanged, his painted likeness grows increasingly old and hideous. The Englishman believes this reflects a cosmic judgment being levied on his personal moral choices. He doesn't consider the possibility that the painting is simply showing him, as such a magical artifact does, what he would have become had he continued to age in typical mortal fashion, or that even his most callous acts are nothing out of the ordinary for a person of his breeding and his means, or that the cosmos has never noticed what humans do to themselves or to each other.

Imagine a *qilin*—you were always partial to those annoyingly pious creatures—which lives in an enchanted garden. The keepers mandated to care for this *qilin* feed it delicacies, brush its mane, polish its rainbowed scales, and all the while, these keepers, they're also secretly siphoning away the *qilin*'s magic for themselves, because they can. Visitors from beyond the garden are permitted in so they can gaze upon the splendor of the *qilin* and applaud the keepers for how well they are tending to their charge. The visitors bring stories of the *qilin* back with them, and that's how, over time, poachers come to learn about this remarkable animal, the grace of its antlers and its jeweled brilliance, an irresistible challenge.

When the first poachers scale the wall of the garden, the *qilin* is outraged. It puffs up its chest to scorch them with its righteous breath of fire, and . . . nothing. Nothing at all, except the emptiest, most embarrassing wheeze; and the rest of the poachers, waiting outside the walls, hear that sound as well, and they understand what it means.

21

They overrun the garden, wound the *qilin* with their arrows, entangle it in their nets. The *qilin*'s keepers try to stop them and are either killed or persuaded to acquiesce. Once the *qilin* is on the ground the poachers carve away its ornamentation with their knives. There's something for each of them to take away and sell: the antlers, the mane, the dragon scales, the cloven hooves. They leave the *qilin* alive, though. This way the *qilin*'s ornamentation can grow back and they can return and cut it away again, and again, until this arrangement settles into normalcy, until the *qilin*'s purpose becomes, in the very first place, to bring the poachers wealth.

Now a horde of children crowd in. They see the garden as their playground, the *qilin* as their amusement. It will be fun, they think, to play at being keepers. They dress up in the uniforms they have stripped off the keepers' corpses and argue over what they should do with the *qilin*, flopping about in its own blood and excrement, until someone gets the idea of opening it up because who knows what treasures it might hold? The children rush to rip open the *qilin*'s belly and start grabbing at what's inside. The kidneys, the entrails, the liver, the heart. Because they can.

So you can see how what I did to your great-great-grandson, for him, seemed the obvious choice. Certain exile versus probable extinction. But I've come to suspect all I did was stretch the thread of your lineage tighter, and thinner, and in the end it broke anyway.

IV.

You know, I used to think about all the questions I would ask you if I could. Whether you had indeed run the numbers on your own fate but decided not to share, and if so whether it was to spare me or because you thought I would try to stop you. (Of course I would have.) Whether, if you could have seen how this would go down, one brief fuse of a human life lighting another until everything went dark, you would still think it was worth it. (You'd probably have said yes regardless of what you truly thought; you could never bear to be wrong.) Whether you didn't ask me to join you because you were afraid I would say no, or, maybe, that I would say yes. (I still don't know what I would have said. But you should have asked, you should have.)

This morning, though, I have no questions left. I leave the hospital and take a walk through the city. Up and down its hills, past the swaddled homeless on its sidewalks, along the reclaimed curve of its bay, under its gray-scale sky. The fog drifting in across the water is the Pacific Ocean's marine layer cooled to dew point, and also all the ghosts waiting to be remembered before the morning sun burns them away. You're gone now, six hundred years gone, but guess what: I did stay after all.

Luna

H. G. *Carrillo*

THE TOUCAN FLIES UNENCUMBERED.

Not the rainbow species that comes to mind. Mostly black, yellow-, and white-faced with a rim of green around each eye. Its breast yellow with a red crest as if to make the bottom loop of the end of a bib. Its half-mustard, half-mahogany-colored bill, striped black on each side, opens in midhiss. After months of not having had its wings clipped, it is either the sound or the current created by the large wooden doors that set it in banking, screeching circles around the vast, open room before it lights for purchase on one of the dozen aquariums that rest on a waist-high ledge, running along the farthest wall.

The polished cement floor with its inlaid brass accents is marked with droppings. As are the Chagall rug, the Italian leather-and-chrome settee, and the walkway leading to the dining room.

It is difficult to tell how it found purchase on the plexiglass case that covers the large Motherwell collage above the aquariums—at what angle had it been able to turn its beak, head, and tail—to create the two wide streaks down the front. It would have needed to perch on the shoulders or red top hat of the ten- or eleven-foot papier-mâché Día de Los Muertos puppet that hangs from the center of the ceiling by a noose to have made the circles around the floor underneath its dangling feet.

Two hundred and thirty-eight thousand three hundred and sixty-eight 4.5-by-6.5 cards are housed in a teak, ebony, and jumu case or portable desk with ivory inlays and ivory-and-silk drawer pulls. A fifteen-year standing order has existed directly with Amatruda la carta di Amalfi for one hundred boxes of fifty one hundred–pound text weight, Bombax, flat cards delivered on the first business day of the year. There is no date or provenance for the chest. There is, however, a receipt in a file in the office for it from a Boston antiques dealer that seems to have gone out of business. There is no forwarding address or Internet listing. It is an assumption.

The case is composed of two rows of five long drawers that are approximately two feet deep. The expert tongue-and-groove fittings are European—clearly an Italian cabinetmaker, eighteenth century, who may have wanted to be or may have studied with a luthier; very much like the work done in Cremona at the time—so the use of jumu is confusing.

Despite its age, there is no sign of warping or distortion. The boxes move in and out of the case as if in warm oil, though the tasseled silk pulls appear to have been replaced within the last century. The cards—made the same way since 1289 AD—may have been the inspiration for the precision of the fit. There is just enough room for the cards to sit upright in the drawer boxes.

Each card was produced without error on the Royal Quiet Deluxe Gold that sits in the center of the desk in the office. The only typewriter in the house, lab, or outbuildings, a gold-plated machine circa 1947, produced in limited edition, and it is said that Ian Fleming had owned one just like it.

It is the distance of the case from the typewriter—some sixty or so feet from the office to the lighted niche at the end of the living room, where it rests on a low table as if to both highlight as well as to present it—that suggests a life's work on display. The Italian marble top is closely fitted to the case; it couldn't have been an afterthought the bevels fit so perfectly. Another object in the niche—the wall above it is bare and like the rest of the room is painted ocher—is a hand-thrown John Kusman lily vase in a rouge flambé that the toucan sends teetering before it defiles it with a long white-gray and green issue.

The first evidence of the acquisition and observation of the appearance of the toucan reads:

```
38,310.01.20020123.202.01
-----------------------------------------------------------------
Ramphastos toucanus
Ramphastos swainsonii
Chestnut-mandibled toucan, or Swainson's toucan

Purchase:        Michael Guzman Soto, DVM, San Diego,
                 California
                 AVMA member
                 (see: 56,982.03)
Inoculations:    (see: 17,676.01)

Price:     25,00
Gender:    Male
Age:       56 days
Length:    62 centimeters
Weight:    339 grams
Fledged:   50 days
Markings:  None
```

The succeeding cards record its daily temperature, heart rate; it seems its blood was drawn and tested every other week. Yet there are records indicative of methodology, less historic and significantly more personal. The card that tells the story of the toucan's introduction into the environment in which it will be observed reads:

```
38,310.05.20020123.3428.05
-------------------------------------------------------------
— Pear, banana, aguacate, apple, melon, mango, papaya.
         > No grain, or feed.
         > Won't touch cooked rice.
— Frightened at night; high-pitched screaming, sometimes until
  sunrise. "Let me out, let me out, I don't belong here," it
  seems to say. "Wake up and let me out, goddamn it!"
— Hates to be handled:
         > Pecks and scratches when its cage is
           approached.
— Unpredictable, as if moody:
         > Responds to both recorded and simulated calls.
         > Gives no indication if it can hear other
           birds; i.e., in lab or cages in house, or the
           calls that come in from the outside. Though,
           outside its cage, freed, will attack other
           birds, the cat.
```

Two hundred and thirty-five parakeets, 1,100 parrots, and 3,428 toucans have been on display, observed, experimented on, dissected, and discarded over a fifteen-year period. Of the 211 hummingbirds, only four were sent to a taxidermist for preservation, and rest under track lighting, arranged, as if suspended in flight, on a very high shelf in the office. They are reflected in a wall of preserved *Papilio gundlachianus*, *Phaloë cubana*, and *Phoebis avellaneda* mariposas: orange, black, pink, green, purple iridescence under glass. Also under glass, covering the wide desktop, are 4,263 canceled eight-, twelve-, fourteen-, and nineteen-cent Cuba Aereo stamps with Felipe Poey etchings of the same butterflies that are on the wall.

But all of that is easy information to find. The cards in the box under the light in the living room tell you.

The first set of numbers on each—for example: 38,310—identifies things as they are. In this case, 310 is a reiteration of species, and 38 is the sequential number assigned to the particular bird, therefore indicia of the thirty-eight birds that have passed through here before it. A small tab affixed to the back of each stamp, and the butterflies,

26

typed on the Royal Quiet Deluxe Gold also corresponds to a card in the file, as do the tabs pasted to the black metal stands that hold the hummingbirds aloft.

The second set of numbers once again is indicative of something more aesthetic about the object, the bird, a movement. A list of regards, views, or glances that can move through a wide range of looks or surveys as curiosity begets new curiosity. The number 01, bracketed between the first set of decimal points on the card marked 38,310.01.20020123.202.01, for example, divides seconds into that instance when two, three, five things are observed at once: wing and neck positions are given the same value of perception as what the bird is thinking, whether it likes or dislikes grapes, and that which becomes a call or a flutter has been translated into lines rather than full sentences that, much like the encryption of a poem, unveil as much as they conceal. Therefore hundreds of birds speak in voices, in both English and Spanish, that tell of their days, their appetites, their distractions, their nervousness, and their loves. A mynah of indeterminable age sang, Como si fuera esta noche la última vez, where a forty-year-old parrot would repeat the word fuck over and over until it had been given grapes.

And where figuring the second set of numbers proves to be much more complicated in its variables and possibilities as individual as fingerprints, the third, fourth, and fifth—year/month/day, hour/minute, point second—seem banal, and rather simple until you realize the sheer number of thoughts, ideas, suppositions, pinpointed and anchored to a precise moment that they occurred.

Even I find it stymieing, and for years, my livelihood has been dependent on my ability not to be dazzled and to retain value and authenticate genius.

Two master's degrees—one in chemistry, the other in art history—along with the completion of a PhD and several articles on Northern Renaissance painting, and a particular interest in Juan de Flandes, in which, to some acclaim, I postulate the effects of a Hispano-Flemish identity—what it might have meant to the sixteenth-century master's work to suddenly show up one day in Spain. And my own wonderment about forgetting snowfalls and the sun one grows under, learning new words that feel so strange in the mouth when found in songs for national celebrations that remind him of his foreign birth, and how these all give him what appears to be a fresh, new vision of light compared to his contemporaries landed me my brief tenure at el Museo del Prado.

And I suppose I could have been happiest there, asking questions for which I theorized a multiplicity of answers in even more papers, consulting with the curatorial board, nearly a celebrity with the museum trustees, until mounting debt from what it took to train for that job—qualify for the position—sharply reminded, only the rich have time to think, and brought me back to the States, and Chicago. And what I find myself asking more frequently now—instead of the kind of What is it? that would make my heart jump at each viewing of a painting, that kept me up nights thinking which chemical tests, which X-rays will reveal what truths—gives way to the much more lucrative How did you come by this?

It's my experience with both art and science that secured my position as a sort of generalist. My knowing—specifically, my knowing more than two of the Egyptologists associated with our New York or London offices—which carbon testing would authenticate without harming and therefore devaluing an ibis ossuary as both Egyptian and contemporaneous with *The Book of the Dead* attributed to Seshat is still talked about around the office even though it happened nearly seven years ago. When I started. Had it just been an interesting find or my assumptions simply been accurate, I'm sure the story would have died years ago. It's the record price the ossuary—something that, for years, held hairpins on a North Shore lady's vanity—brought at auction that has kept it alive.

And where I've seen very little of the Northern Renaissance since coming to work for the auction house outside of museum visits—and once, in a film that seemed to be about cigarettes and talking about the lack of sex while sitting in coffee shops, a poster of *Christ appearing to the Virgin with the Redeemed of the Old Testament* is crookedly affixed above the bed of an actress who has played a wacky waitress on two television sitcoms—I have seen more diamonds than I had ever thought I would see in my entire life, and I was on the floor in London to see a rather uninteresting Picasso turned into millions of dollars. The name of the auction house uttered at a cocktail party could turn heads in a way de Flandes's never did. In fact, I was never invited to that kind of cocktail party before—the kind where baby lamb chops are served and champagne and there really is a string quartet—the ones held by museums are often a grimier version, on a budget with wet canapés stuck to paper doilies, and a sound system.

As much as I miss the autonomy of life inside museums, I like the prestige that gets me inside a house like this one—well-appointed houses, where art and artifact tell you something about those who lived there—and the assurance given me that I will be able to find something that will reveal a secret held fast without disturbing the murk of patina.

More often than not, it is a representative retained by the family who lets me in the door and shows me around, points to the objects, paintings, and furnishings that are to go up for auction. They tire of me when they see I already have information they can provide—copies of provenance, bills of sale, documented anecdotes, photographs of the items—and eventually tell me they can be found in some adjacent room or elsewise out of the way. An ancient cat may move under a dining table as slowly as ideas, a continual drip in a distant sink might overflow a teacup, as I work through lists of who in our offices will verify and authenticate each item on the list, what sorts of tests will be needed, and what can be moved directly to the storage warehouse, prepared, photographed, and cataloged for auction, and what needs to be shipped elsewhere. The expectation is that I know something and will deliver on what I know.

Of course, I let myself in here. And certainty is another thing altogether.

I could have driven up the mountain blindfolded in the dark though I haven't been here in three or four years. As certain as I am that though the finch cage is bamboo it is Victorian, the water and feed pots and ivory inlays are genuine chinoiserie. And where it could be assumed that the finches inside—*Gorrión azafrán*, tagged 78,940.01, 78,940.02, 78,940.03, 78,940.04; *Sicalis flaveola* according to their corresponding cards—might have died of thirst and lack of food, despite the stiffness of rigor mortis, it's clear the neck was broken on each and they had been arranged as if turning—beak resting on the breast of the one before it—in a circle on the floor of the cage. Yet I have no idea what's kept the toucan alive, what it has eaten these past several weeks, and the cat seems to have disappeared.

Getting to El Yunque is fairly simple. Though, say mountain or rain forest to someone who has never been here, to anyone stuck underneath a foot or so of snow that fell in Chicago this late March morning, and you may as well be talking make-believe instead of easily had. There are cards in the case that for the last fifteen years give a quarterly accounting and breakdown of the typical flight schedule to the island by airline. They detail a rate of accuracy, and variations from published schedules, and are not all that different in the kind of information they give from an Edwardian lady's daybook that I was once given to assign to an appraiser who could make no sense of the entries, which were sometimes simply single words or briefly phrased accounts—neuralgia, ennui, hysterical . . . hands clutched so tightly I thought I should break them—in a tidy, florid script.

Thirty-six years of entries, I had pointed out to the appraiser, though we had been told by the seller that her great-grandmother had died at seventy-three. The seller had also given us the year of her grandmother's death. Subtract two ten-month gaps for when the woman's two children were born; add to each four-day grouping of entries the tiny notes we are given about days of sobbing, somnambulism, doctors' visits, cold compresses, fainting spells—*There will be no end of the shouting that will take place when Walter finds out that I had to be carried off of the main boulevard,* she writes—and then their sudden disappearance—suddenly nothing for twenty-three years as if a great hand came out to wipe her brow—the same way that my brother, Diego—as if in similar epiphany—stopped charting flights, the length of plume left behind them, as they landed in San Juan.

This house and the acre and a half behind it just cuts into the perimeter of the rain forest off the road. From Luis Muñoz Marín International, signs begin to point approximately fifty kilometers south, east and up the mountain. Highway turns to road as San Juan in your rearview mirror looks as if it will collapse on itself and fall backward into the ocean. Your ears will flood and you'll begin to smell the air thinning. Halfway, you'll pass an open-air cantina and you may have to occasionally break for a rooster or a goat before you get to the pink wall with the cobalt wooden gate.

Though you can't tell from the road, it is more than one house. Diego used the building by the pool, closest to the main house, for guests. Much like the skinny buildings in Amsterdam—four rooms stacked on each other—with walls made of ten-inch-by-ten-inch-square windows that provide a 365-degree view of the mountain and the forest preserve due south. A cement path marks the steep downward defile into a valley covered in over 237 varieties of trees, according to cards 11234–11507, which leads to another building, which although larger than the first outbuilding looks very much like a miniature version of the kinds of buildings built for the sciences on university campuses during the forties.

Diego took his lunch with him down to his lab, ran experiments there during the day. Late afternoons, he would strip all of his clothes off and walk past where the path turns to nothing but mossy soft earth, ferns, bejucos with their pink flowers, cupays, mocas. Deeper into the basin the tips of the flamboyants around the main house peek out over the lip, and he would have seen them from the pond and waterfall during his daily swim. Weather permitting, he would sun himself dry on a rock before making his way to the smallest of the three outbuildings—a shack, really, that he would laugh and speculate to be whirling away during hurricane season—where he painted the green *Amazona vittata* in the air above it: 22861.073–22861.7993; 7,920 drawings, paintings and sketches of the green Amazon parrots, in flight, brooding, feeding, bathing, nesting, cataloged and each detailed with a cross-reference and more numbers that make me wonder what had happened to numbers one through seventy-two. But that's how Diego worked; in this highly articulated and monitored life, there were always moments of explosion obliterating everything in their path.

I have been here frequently enough to know that in the evenings, with the first shift toward darkness in the sky, he would make his way back up to the main house—typical Spanish hacienda style—with his clothing thrown over his shoulder, shoes in hand. He would make himself dinner, then read or listen to music—but never at the same time—before going to bed. Never once, and I have known him my entire life, had I any idea what he could be dreaming about, or what he was thinking for sure.

There were weeks in the past when I would come to stay with him that there seemed to be a shuttle of twenty or thirty people—artists, scientists, exotic dancers—coming and going up and down the mountain, back and forth in shifts between here and the airport, the grocer's, the liquor store in San Juan. He would dance, play the guitar, and sing until the sun came up. The next visit we would barely speak; there were times he would barely move from a deck chair without explanation. I remember someone simply saying, Genius, every time it was noticed that he had a tendency to stare off into space, leave the planet in the middle of conversations. A group of us were at an outdoor café in Old San Juan and Diego's eyes were fixed on something none of us could see—neither ship nor bird—above the bay. He had not even so much as looked in the direction of the woman in an orange jumpsuit we had all been sneaking glances at, making fun of—something about air traffic control—when all of sudden Diego said, Pearl's a singer. Nothing more; just, Pearl's a singer, as if we all should have known better. His expression never changed. It was a while before he came back to the table and to us and the conversation. And it was he who had to resume it, as if he had never left. We listened as he talked about the water and gulls and that he never really cared for Puro coffee, and had shamed us all into silence. But it would be years later—in a bar in Manhattan—that I would come to find out he had referenced the title of a song that none of us knew.

A man once loved Diego so much that he knew to love Diego was also to leave him alone. Make sure that he was someplace warm and humid, and not unlike the environment where he was born, but more importantly, leave him alone.

According to letters spanning over ten years and cataloged as 962.03–962.11, it was unrequited or, if not unrequited, simply enough for him to watch Diego from the distance of a letter; Diego distrusted computers, and though he would answer messages left for him, I never once—even when we were children—saw him pick up a ringing phone.

It seems that it had been enough for a Dr. Carlos Ginestera—to buy this house and fund its upkeep from a distance of somewhere outside of Hanover, New Hampshire—to remember Diego as the bright-eyed boy in a graduate environmental sciences course whose only questions were about survival and migration: You asked as you always ask why members of the same species, same class, same genus, and at times the very same brood thrive when transported while others perish, Dr. Ginestera once wrote.

Mi Vida, all of Dr. Ginestera's letters begin. Mi queridisima vida, Dr. Ginestera—who had a wife and children and a granddaughter, who wrote in letters cataloged 985.07–985.11 of their collective surprise at Diego's existence after the good doctor had died at seventy-two of a stroke, and a sizable fortune from his estate had been settled on Diego—mi queridisisisisisisisima vida, he closed his letters.

It is the toucan's shadow, like a caress, passing over me that pulls me from sleep. Its sawlike call and flapping from perch to perch had integrated themselves into parts of a dream I can't recall but for the flying and falling and slow circles of a funnel and the stone set in the center of my chest that yanks me upright on the couch.

My eyes open as the toucan lands on the Fornasetti trifold screen in the corner and eliminates down the center wooden panel where the city of cards towers from the floor into a flagged turret. It has also mucked cards that I had left on the coffee table. Lined chronologically from the top down—the most recent past at the bottom—are rows of doctors' visits, sixty-three twentieth-century paintings, blood tests conducted on fifty-three cocos rojos as well as a card for each of the measurements of their right leading edge, lesser coverts, scapulars, middle coverts, tendrils, and the distance between the primaries and secondaries along their trailing edges. And though the toucan had missed them, three years of new moons—the day, the hour, the minute, the second they came into view, and the thunder in his ears that made him write, So this is what people mean when they say they were overcome with joy—are splattered with mucousy stuff clotted with white chunks so acidic it has burned a hole into the paper and through to the table in places.

It started in the uterus, then her spine and lungs, said a woman wanting to rid herself of her sister's rather valuable collection of Frank Lloyd Wright furniture and Teco vases. One of the few times that I had had to talk to an actual relative rather than an intermediary, and I remember thinking how horrible for her as her face creased and her eyes watered.

Now I wish I had what she had. Knowing that it had been an irregular cell with an agenda that had suddenly placed her in the middle of the middle of her sister's life and all of the things that she had collected around her had seemed great comfort.

Diego's Mercedes, for example, was impounded after it had sat in the parking lot at the airport for over ninety days. Yet even after I pay the fine and the towing fee, I don't have any of the busywork that the woman with all that Frank Lloyd Wright made. The car—00621—and each repair and oil change have been cataloged and classified in detail along with spare parts and new tires. Two days before he left the car at the airport, he had had the brakes checked. The card describes the day as very hot and sunny. Though there are no cards that describe the eighty-three days between it and the icy evening he filled his belly full of Seconal and Welch's grape juice, took all of his clothes off, and fell asleep on the banks of the Huron River. Rather than in handfuls like all of the other boys that we knew, M&M's had to be lined up—dark browns next to light browns, moving toward yellows, the oranges, ending at reds—and eaten one at a time, and when we were in middle school, I found our canary frozen to the bottom of its cage outside our bedroom window after it had failed to survive the second of a series of exposures he had planned to adapt it to Michigan winters. But neither of these is as specific or as soothing as having an irregular cell with an agenda at which to point.

The failure to thrive in 003798–004210—guinchos, *Pandion hali-aetus*, a series of ospreys that were brought in from Cuba by a source kept so secret there are no records, merely the letter or symbol x; in a succession of four three-month periods they were kept in a makeshift wire-mesh cage on the terrace until what is described as untimely deaths—was attributed to a virus that eleven labs were unable to identify, though Diego had isolated on over three hundred slides. There had only been two flamingos, together, living in the pond at the waterfall and he seems to have had no idea if they flew off together or perished, no sign. He wrote often that there were many nights he would train his binoculars on the sunset, looking for years after they had disappeared. And the kettle of magnificents, *Eugene fulgens*, hatched in an incubator, but all born with the same genetic defect; had they not been euthanized, none would have been able to fly. No matter how closely you follow their history, there's a history you never know, he wrote on the last card that mentions the magnificents.

The floors in the main room and the hallway leading to the kitchen are slick with morning condensation. And the toucan follows, but it will not eat cooked rice. Responds, calls out as if in acknowledgment, to each short burst that the coffee grinder makes. The fifty-pound bag of feed that I brought up from the lab has been chewed by rats and spills a line up the path and across the patio and terrace, but the toucan turns its head to the sound, flaps and calls, but nothing more. I empty the contents of the refrigerator into a large plastic bag, tie it, and set it aside to take down the mountain later. In four seventeenth-century English delftware bowls tagged 9873–9876, I mixed combinations—feed and red banana from the terrace garden, rice and yellow banana from the pond, rice and green banana that grows outside the front portico—but the toucan won't touch them. It drinks water out of the aquariums on the wall in the main room rather than the bowl on its perch in the study. And I think perhaps it is inhibited by my observation, and leave it be.

There are lists that list the lists. Cross-references that reference references that all lead back to the box in the main room. Walking through—checking off paintings, turning over pieces of pottery and looking for the tag that corresponds to the number on the list—it is hard to imagine, even for me, who had watched him measure the width of the dresser in our childhood bedroom, mark it, and then dust only his half, to imagine the kind of mind that does this sort of thing.

Each sock is marked with a tag that has been sewn into it that gives an associative reference for its mate. There are twenty-five of the same gray vicuña sweater, all the same size, all purchased through a series of cataloged letters—a correspondence, really—in which the London haberdasher answers questions about the farm, the animals, the location, and climate, as well as the processing of the fibers and the ethics of the manufacturers that made them. Eleven are folded neatly; nine still have the original store tags on them. There is a ticket from a San Juan dry cleaner—cataloged 07722—that accounts for two of them. Two are in the bag that he left at our parents' house. He folded the one he was wearing and piled it onto his other clothes.

Two days before he departed from San Juan he wrote:

```
6725.01.20031221.19.07
------------------------------------------------------------
Hanes Classics V-Neck T-shirt
Size:  Large (42-44)

— Measurements seem to be off by 3.67 centimeters.
— Fibers tested: (C₆H₁₀O₅)ₙ polymetric polysaccharide
  carbohydrate of beta glucose with some questionable
  inaccuracies/impurities that may be accounted for in
  processing.
                — Quite lovely.
                — Breathable.
                — Nice.
                — Danced all night around the main room to test
                  tensile strength and absorbency.
                — Very fine.

Future Inquiries: Stripping process; Insecticides; Sibelius
Symphony no. 2; La Lupe singing Puro Teatro; accurate
measures of absorbency.
```

Because they come three to a package, there are five additional cards, and corresponding labels sewn into each of the shirts.

The phone, labeled 399.01, the only phone in all of the estate, rings in the study, and the toucan calls back from the kitchen at the other side of the house in between its short, clipping chirps.

Our mother wants to know if I'm OK—¿Como esta, mijo? she asks with a tender tenderness in her voice so strong it is delicate to the point of breaking—but with as much concern as there is fear in her voice that asks about what I might have found without asking it. She asks about the weather and says that it's still snowing there. Lots of snow, she says, you can't even see the steps of the gazebo from the kitchen window.

She wants to know but doesn't. Doesn't want to ask at the same

35

time, but at the same time, wants to ask, so she asks, When do you think you're coming home? Home? I ask. Back to Michigan, home to Chicago? and she changes the subject and tells me, Your father and I finally got around to taking down the Christmas tree. I walk past where I have opened the rolling corrugated metal doors that protect against hurricane or theft, open the walls of the back of the house, and overlook the pool, as she describes how careful my father was about wrapping each ornament in tissue paper. Such care, she says, and for the first time ever I think that he's not our father.

Never before has it been important to think that this man has been nothing but kind and generous and caring and supportive and encouraging of the woman he met while on sabbatical who was fresh off one of the last planes out of Havana with a two- and three-year-old in tow. But there are 1,133 cards detailing the way that the first of the *Ramphastos toucanus, Ramphastos swainsonii*, Chestnut-mandibled toucans pecked and pecked at the sides of their own bodies until there were enormous holes in them.

Our mother says that Papá says there are to be at least three more inches here, it's coming down now, you can barely see out into the ravine. There are snow demons, she says. Papá says, snow demons like giants. And as she describes how hard it was getting someone to come up and plow, I look through the items tagged as 23339–23347 in which Diego and I look like Michelin Men, up to our waists in snow.

¿Por cierto? Papá asks, his voice barely audible when he asks again if I'm sure I don't want them to come down; it is warm and calm, secure as a blanket that makes you think nothing can ever happen, everything is safe. I'm sure when the snow breaks, we could be down there with you, helping you, before tomorrow night, he says. And I know that he has turned his back to our mother and cups the receiver with his hand—he does this when he doesn't want to hear her protests, when he's trying to protect her or all of us; he did it last New Year's morning when the call came—and as if they might see, might suddenly turn around and see me steal into Diego's bathroom and begin to empty the contents of one of three medicine chests into the wastepaper basket. Twenty-two doctors over thirty-three years according to 226–3118, five different diagnoses, regulating sleep, waking, eating, dreaming, controlling the need to laugh and the urge to cry or shout or lash out: Lithium, Depakote, Carbamazepine, Lamotrigine, Neurontin, Topiramate, Clozaril, Zyprexa, Quetiapine, Geodon, Clonazepam, Ativan; Zolpidem. . . .

All this snow here, our mother says, as if seeing it for the first time, as if it were a spill of something she has no idea how to clean up. Snow for the first time, as if she hasn't kept a Cuban household, as if there hadn't been pork tenderloin for Christmas dinner this past year and we hadn't all swallowed grape seeds New Year's Eve night. We're just staying in, she says, just staying home. And I imagine them like the fifth and sixth *Ramphastos toucanus, Ramphastos swainsonii*, Chestnut-mandibled toucans huddled in the back of the cage—perfectly healthy, according to 38,306.05—him pressed tightly against his mate, barely moving, without drinking or eating.

I'm taking the wastepaper basket from the bathroom to the kitchen, and as we are about to hang up, she says, Cuídate, mi niño, Cuídate, and I've found the toucan has ripped open the side of the plastic bag I had left, found a container of take-out paella, eaten the rotting shrimp, sausage, and chicken, but has left the rice. It will not touch the rice. And I tell her, Soon, Mamá, vos vamos, soon.

Here—in a Victorian wrought-iron chaise numbered with a brass plate 29411—the evening light changes so that you could think you're anywhere. Anywhere, I remember a scientist who was visiting for the weekly marvel as the last of the sunlight gave way to the moon over the tops of palmas, Anywhere. The toucan shrieks and flaps as the sun disappears down the side of the mountain, flies circles in and out of the house, crests the mountainside, but for all the open windows, all of the open doors, does not fly away.

In all of the contents of the house, there is no record of any critical paper, no completed advanced degree, nothing that brings conclusive evidence, or gives authority to any findings, nothing that shows expertise or superiority of knowledge, yet hundreds of scientists—friends, ornithologists, biologists, veterinarians, would have been colleagues had Diego not, when he was a bright-eyed boy, climbed naked one winter to the top of a campus bell tower to ask why—responded to an invitation to see the moon, as described in letters, cross-referenced in the card case, in all its phases, glorious as could be seen anywhere in the world. And it was here on a very warm winter evening on this terrace the year that I moved back to the States that, I believe it was an ornithologist who told me, told me I was lucky to live in Chicago. And he told me of a little-known secret of green parrots—hundreds of them, he said—nested in Hyde Park. He told me it was best to see them in the winter, when the trees were bare and their green feathers were brilliant against the snow. I asked how did they get there, and he told me he supposed someone raising them as pets had simply opened a window. He sighed and rattled the ice in his glass at me, requesting a refill of his drink, when I asked him how they survived. They breathe, dear boy, they breathe, he said. And Diego, not turning his eyes from the darkening skyline, sat in this chaise that a card says he had had cemented into place so that it should never be moved, and asked, And you know that how?

Rexroth's Cabin

Forrest Gander

On the way to
to the site of his
cabin, his temple
refurbished from the plundered
temple of another religion
a religion of fishermen
on the Tokelalume aka
Lagunitas Creek in Devil's
Gulch, the path into the forest flagged
flagged on either side with orange
sticky monkey flowers
innumerable stubby, macho
fence lizards rush in bursts
ahead of you like heralds as
you come up the trail, but
half a mile in, a single
Western skink, its neon-blue tail hauled
   upright behind it
races diagonally cross trail and disappears
beneath thimbleberry brambles mantled
with shredded spiderweb

*

In the epic literature of India
which all those years ago
he was reading, lying
on this greywacke slab
above the ebulliently plashing
creek, his head in shade, his
lanky body warm

39

legs crossed in the sun's
maple light breaking through tree
limbs pajamaed in moss
and stretching awkwardly out
out over the gulch
from a steep hillside held in place
only by radial green explosions
of bracken, maidenhair fern, and
a pair of red-spiked black caterpillars
which crawl onto his leather boots
set side by side in the rampant pipe vine the
caterpillars have been devouring
in all that epic literature of India
no more than three colors
are mentioned

*

See? He is here and not here, not
unlike you yourself, or the water
striders in the creek
rowing in punctuated contractions
against the drift, what
you see in the clear absolute of the water
as you stand on some paleostump at the bank
under an electric insect whine
distributed perfectly throughout the canopy,
what you see below
in the pellucid water is a cluster of
six Gothic black shadowdots
cast onto the streambed
below the thin, sand-colored
bodies of the actual water striders
who are bowed all but invisibly above
the tensile surface of the stream

*

Not here, and here, and though you
you have hiked the dirt path through the forest
as he did before you were born
to the familiar place, the confluence
of two modest falls, to the ground truth
the little clearing where he snored
and fried two eggs for breakfast and sat
cross-legged on a slab of rock scribbling
into the future that holds you in it,
you are only still arriving
still
arriving
no trace of the cabin left, and yet
his presence is not
decomposable, your mind
merges with what is not
your mind, your happiness
is radiant and you squat, listening
in the tangible density of what is and isn't there
as you become your shadow fluidly contiguous
with the shadows of trees

Heliotropic
Meredith Stricker

> *I turned death's face to me like an oversized heliotrope . . .*
>
> —Odysseas Elytis, *With Light and With Death*

SALT

pelagic birds hurled in air
whose salt is our own *gnosis*
come into the darkened house
brightness outside like a torrent
when I whistle a black dog runs swiftly out of the dream
the frightening mother
her unreadable, dark eyes
fear of falling into the well
wakened by the rough coat of a horse's neck
lend me your abyss
one at a time, bees line up at the spring
falling drop by drop from sheer rock face
the narrow tree shakes as it is cut down
in the rasping breath of saw cuts
saints and sunflowers gather
pleated cloth over her shoulder
the clearing just beyond
rhythm of a shrine reclaimed
returning home past olive groves
windows with worn panes
darkened, contradictory
stained with the wind that heat stirs
my body aches with my mother's dying
bones brittle in their labor of resin
here in the shivering of leaves
love, requited or not, breaks through
grows wild as astral grass fields

THE SAINT'S DAY OF YOUR MOUTH

in the heat of perpetual naming
candles burn and burn
names fall apart and we are lost
all the calendars on fire
hands slant like sideways doves
wedding rings disappear
rim of sunset reflected in unearthly clouds
we watch the street go by our table
two men "all sex" in pink pants
life finds its ideal in unexpected gestures
birds get louder
my mother supplicating to be turned
pillows gnarl her dying
I don't know how to feed her
sparrow on a windswept branch
milk left out in a bowl
steadiness of the moon unpeeling its light
return to darkest water
the veins in trees and people

WINNOWING RING

if in the polyphonic
throats of red-winged
blackbirds, each word
is elegy to world's slow
dissolve into passengers
singing in a brightly painted
bus with beaded curtains
past oleanders & scant pines
if each world at each time
of its word is fluid
precipice of this day
my mother breathes in
her Hungarian coaches
with their prewar winter furs

then breathes out the river mouth
of pelicans where blue sea hospices
its rim of horizon incoherent
in many languages the wavering
voice insists "the most important point . . ."
then trails off into accidental
constellations that fall unmoored
into the flammable
names of things

WHAT HAPPENED

there was a mother
and now a box of ashes
there was a moon and streets full of people
now a moon and streets and contagion
wild, wet astonished green
laced through with social distance
shortages rain and sparrows
the sun acting normal
oak leaves no more bitter than before
every surface volatile, every innocuous
looking doorknob, a small bomb
how will we learn to forage seaweed
when every surface turns to memory and vigilance
that terrible moment when you realize there is no one
to blame for your life—no one
this bright rain-soaked week of quarantine
forests unwalled skies unflown
I receive delivery of my mother's ashes
in a small pine box while wearing nitrile gloves
I panic-buy lentils unsuccessfully
as there are no lentils available
though yerba santa grows freely on back roads
our one chance to notice these fast-moving
Orphic clouds with their transient
milk bodies and these leaves
with their dark inlets of fear and shine

WILD QUIETUDES

first contemplate

<THE WHICKERING OF BIRDS
IN CANDLED PINES
AS ANTIDOTE TO DEATH>

then notice there is no antidote
tree full of birds, blue blue sky
our arteries are preset fault lines
I am ready to swim out past the Artemis reef
return marsupial in warm coat
gathering ripe fallen fruit
white bowl undone by sunlight
her head thrown back on the pillow
eyes closed mouth open the body takes its time
we imagine a vigil as simple presence
a room and a candle, a body, a witness
this one has lots of laundry, visitors, many languages
roof leaks, there are comings and goings, a ratcatcher
a backed-up toilet and crows, squirrels on the roof
television tuned to music, sirens, bills to pay
a dying woman breathes bravely, we could be her
we will be—no, I don't believe it either
as the clock across from her bed stops ticking
time is pointless, we throw the clock away as though
time would also stop but the contagion of time does not stop
it hovers motionless my mother's head thrown back
in agony or thrall, the nose becoming skull the mouth
wide open staring into starry black eternal

INCARNATION

cattle lowing in woven night
for their calves taken away

my mother leaving this world
to go into this world

where I can no longer find her
last light edging pale yellow

into ultramarine rim of pine pollen
on rainwater, low voices expectant

waiting for the visitor to arrive at last
under a threshing of stars

The Dust of Pious Feet
Helena María Viramontes

ADDRESSED TO LEHNA SINGH, Gopal's biannual letters had arrived
like serial entertainment, dispatches from America that sailed across
the turbulent Pacific to Hindustan's Bay of Bengal, to Calcutta, then
onto an overcrowded train boxcar to Agra. From there each traveled
onward to Delhi, officially rubber-stamped here, smudged magenta
there. The envelopes collected various British bureaucratic signatures along the way, then continued by truck to Ludhiana, then by
boat down the Sutlej River to Ferozepur, and finally—miraculously—
between the bony messenger boy's dirty fingertips via water buffalo
cart. Lehna Singh had heard the jubilance with which the scrawny
boy hollered his name and looked up to see the white sun glaring on
the messenger. Stripped to the waist, the boy stood across the small
embankment of the flooded, terraced rice paddies, his hair pulled
into a topknot covered by a patka kerchief, waving the letter as if it
were a sickle.

Lehna planted the remaining fistful of rice seedlings, then carefully
slogged toward the boy, his movement gently crimping the surface
of the silken water behind him. His bare feet crusted with mud,
he scrubbed his soiled palms dry on his kacchera breeches and sat
cross-legged on the mat under the dappled shade of a tamarind tree,
its ripe pods pointing downward. The uninvited messenger joined
Lehna to hear the dispatch and sat across from him; after the boy's
harsh wheezing from dashing and hollering, Lehna didn't have the
heart to dismiss him. He tilted his face to favor a good eye, tore open
the left side of the light tissue envelope, then blew into it to spill the
letter into the palm of his hand, a magical gesture to the messenger.

Lehna never quite knew what to expect from his good friend's letters,
and since Gopal wrote in English, Lehna would have to translate to
Punjabi for the boy, an exhausting endeavor made more exhausting
because sometimes Gopal freely expressed difficult thoughts—*When
there is only one God,* Gopal once wrote, *why then are there so
many bloody religious wars?* And his private postscripted concerns
for Lehna's well-being were very personal—*I hear from a birdie you*

haven't an appetite and so I must ask you this: have the nightmares returned, dear friend? Gopal was like a baba to him and sometimes admonished Lehna's soldiering past, writing, *Were you blind not to see the paradox of an Indian sepoy in Mespot fighting the Sunnis and Shia united against the bloody British occupation? This was not ours to fight!* Lehna said nothing about Gopal's own paradox of writing to him in British English, the bondage between occupier and occupied being sutured in paradoxes. But mostly Gopal's letters were filled with entertaining tales, which pleased the messenger immensely. Lehna read aloud, attempting again to fit familiar Punjabi images with the foreign words, furrowing his brow with the effort, detailing a Tijuana border crossing on foot where everyone mistook Gopal *for a Mexico man and why not?*

—But he's not Mexico, the flummoxed boy said in Punjabi. His carmine-colored skin squeezed against his belly, revealing skeletal ribs. A Kamboj like him, Lehna knew malnourishment kneaded youth into age. The boy looked much older than his ten years.

—That's a point of good humor, Lehna replied. The boy clearly hadn't understood but leaned his head right to left in affirmation.

From Tijuana, Gopal would later take a tedious bus ride down the spiny peninsula of Baja California all the way to the Sea of Cortez by *"carretera" is what the road is called in Mexico language and it is as insufferable as bad poetry—hours, hours of bumps and joggles to the back of the neck.* The boy repeated the word *carretera*, testing the taste of the word. Sunlight pierced the shade of the tamarind tree, but both ignored its prickly heat striking their knobby backs.

Gopal described the spectacle of the landscape at his first sight of it. Baja's Vizcaino Desert captured his heart, and he underlined with extravagant vigor the words *"simply marvelous"*—especially the prodigious, uncanny, upside-down trees with roots twisting up to the air looking *like ancient arms reaching for Guru Nanak's grand embrace! Take note, dear cousin,* Gopal wrote, *Vizcaino is not like Mespot's dry, barren stone suckered in by desolation and destruction, nor does it clutch secrets tightly to its chest.* Nearing the end of the letter, Gopal once again predicted Lehna would *achieve a measure of solace,* the assertiveness of Alta California's fertile resources flooding with new opportunities *and who would not want to come to a new world that would make a world of difference?*

—I would like to go on a carretera, the boy said in a dreamy voice; he was not yet old enough to wear a dastaar as other Sikh men did but he was old enough to know he would never leave Ferozepur.

—I will go for you, Lehna uttered, folding the letter and tucking it in his kacchera's sash. He stared into the distance above the boy's head.

—Is that a point of humor? the boy asked.

Lehna rose to finish his rice planting and begin his planning. He dusted off the seat of his kacchera and salaamed directly into the boy's dark-colored eyes—My maharaja, he asked playfully, what is your name?

Lehna had to admit, there *was* something different about his nature once he was living in Holtville, California. He had found his English helpful in negotiating with farming contractors, his military service encouraging in a way that was contrary to his introvert demeanor, and his knowledge of British rule invaluable in grasping American caste customs. He quickly discovered that, for all its qualities, America had its own fault lines, and his greatest virtue was his ability to know he wasn't stupid about how these systems worked. From the Mughals to the Afghans to the British Raj, there was little love lost between the dominant occupiers and the people like him they used up, and upon his arrival in America he knew immediately to obey written signs that read, MEXICANS AND DOGS NOT ALLOWED or other strict instructions like WHITES ONLY. It was always a challenge, since his faith was based on principles of respect and equality, not always ideally observed but always worthy of attainment—the surname "Singh" meant to eliminate caste and align everyone equally. Yet he committed himself to doing all that was necessary to find peace in his new home. Although he would never give up his burgundy cotton dastaar, which had already attracted too much unwanted attention from people incapable of understanding that Sikh turbans were religious, Lehna chose to wear denim trousers and a pair of Mexican huarache sandals instead of his kurta and kacchera, his kes wrapped tightly in his dastaar.

Even with such misguided maledictions on gates and over doorways, the distance between Punjab and California had allowed Lehna some form of peaceful solace. He slowly returned to the ritual of reciting parkash karna in the mornings, the Gurmukhi script more legible as the morning light shone on the lyrical couplets of the sacred book, the Sri Guru Granth Sahib: *Nanak says, when the Name of God you hear / A meditative state is near . . . The Name of God is like a light / When hearing, the blind regain their sight.* He then

49

calmly restored the miniature holy book to the silver portable palki for safekeeping.

Lehna spent his years near the Mexico and California border, temporarily contented by the daily insularity of routine, which consisted of prayers and the seasonal migratory work he sought, sometimes on foot, sometimes under contract, other times hopping the Southern Pacific with a Punjabi or Chinese work crew, his holy book housed in his palki, his palki packed in his haversack, boxcars racketing northerly on the edge of the strange Salton Sea, sometimes arriving as far north as San Francisco, all the way to Sacramento once. He'd lose himself in the harvest of lettuce and cantaloupe, diligently working at forgetting, toiling away and keeping his mind on the immediacy of the present task. After a few seasons, he agreed to join Gopal in a tenant-farming venture along with three Hindustanis, one of them a young boy no more than twelve, by the name of Mohan, who reminded Lehna of the bony messenger back in Ferozepur.

The five men shared a two-room farmhouse a few miles outside of El Centro. It came with a hinged, black potbellied stove and a tipsy kitchen table, six chairs, an abused chest of drawers, and three windows left open to diminish the putrid, rancid stink of dirty laundry piled in corners, the overflowing night pails not taken to the outhouse, and the stubborn reek of bodily sweat and cooking ghee that hung in the stagnant air. When Gopal unwittingly discovered tiny maggots in food scraps between the unwashed dishes piled high in a tin bucket they used as a sink, he'd had enough. The men endured half an hour of invective about their filthy hygiene and ungodly ways, until young Mohan, shaken by the possibility that he might be assigned the chores, intervened and quietly—so quietly Gopal asked him to speak up like a man—suggested that they pool together money to hire a housekeeper.

Lehna strongly objected to the hiring of the Mexican American widow. He was fearful that a woman would diminish the peaceful restraint among the men, but his objections were overruled by sheer necessity. Because he tried to ignore her, his encounters with her became awkward and painful. He was forced to slightly nod an acknowledgment as she tied an apron around her waist, she slightly nodding in return. Lehna sometimes forgot that the housekeeper had arrived in the early mornings, and was startled to hear the clinks of pots, the creak of floorboard, the whistle of boiling tea kettle, sounds that made him feel as if ghosts sought asylum in the old farmhouse. No sooner would he step into the kitchen to prepare a cup of tea than he would bump into her, his disconcerted heart thumping, and then there she was again, suddenly appearing on the porch while he waited for the other men, holding the handle of a broom as if she anticipated his movements, always surfacing on the periphery of his bad eye like a shadow. By evening when the men returned from work, she vanished. Her apron was hung on a hooked nail near the door like shed skin remnants of her presence in the swept and dusted house, in the washed crockery pushed against a small counter, in the row of overalls and trousers drying, white dhotis and undergarments stiff from blue rinse on a makeshift laundry line, in the jelly jar filled with wild lavender on the table, in a stack of fresh flour tortillas as thick as naans wrapped in a dish towel and placed near a pile of clean bowls for serving, in the stewy fragrance of frijoles de olla lingering throughout the house.

At the table, Gopal ate with ravenous delight, spooning the home-made chile rojo still sitting in the mouth of the molcajete into his pinto beans, the other men noisy in dedicated bean-soup slurping, and except for Mohan, who had no facial hair, they swiped their whisk-broom mustaches with the backs of their hands, all of them refusing to hear Lehna's customary complaints about the house-keeper's intrusions. Today's was his discovery of a crocheted doily placed under his silver palki, and what right did she have to handle the sacred Sri Guru Granth Sahib he rested on the beets crate? The men gazed at one another over Lehna's head, bewildered at his fidelity to misery. Gopal sighed and met his friend's complaint with silence as he smeared a piece of tortilla over the last residue of beans, chewed with carious teeth, then pushed back his rickety chair to leave his bowl in the basin—trustful that it would be washed by the house-keeper in the morning—his steps purposefully heavy on the floor-boards leading in the direction of the porch. Shortly after, the others followed suit and went outdoors, too exhausted to do anything but listen to one another's breathing. They cherished the long daylight hours as they relaxed in the cooling breeze, having left Lehna alone at the kitchen table with his miserable face in his miserable hands.

He had no words to explain to them that just when his content-ment had reached a lackluster exactitude of predictability, the house-keeper arrived, the housekeeper took over, the housekeeper reigned, the housekeeper haunted him, and Lehna couldn't help but feel a resentment toward her mixed in with a sense of betrayal toward the men. He was shocked at the fact that he hadn't gotten used to her

51

even after all these weeks, nor had he the ability to muster gratitude for her work. In the lonely outskirts between El Centro and Calexico, his insomnia returned shortly after her arrival. The moonlight poured through the open window, outlining the slumbering bodies of his roommates, and gifting a small trapezoid of light on the silver palki. On the lumpy mattress dampened by terrible night sweats, Lehna came to understand that the housekeeper deeply frightened him.

On the dozy border between sleep and wakefulness, his nightmares warped the incessant din of nocturnal insects into a louder, menacing, sonic droning of Royal Air Force propellers overhead. His quickened breathing constricted, moistening the goggles of his insect gas mask, and slowly his attention moved skyward to the planes and then to the discharging incandescent bright streamers from their metal underbellies, unfolding swiftly toward the earth, the blue beams almost beautiful in their sparkling phosphorescent glow, until the impact and the massive, deafening explosions, the impenetrable clouds of yellow, and suddenly his ears felt as if he were underwater. The luminous yellow rose before him, geysers and geysers of dust and stones, and the long sleeves of his khaki drill tunic turned yellow, his gas mask, his dastaar powdered with grit. Before him the ancient Mesopotamian roads were being pulverized into powdery bones and sand, and his hearing became a frozen frequency of nothingness as he grappled almost blindly through the long, labyrinthine silences of the narrow streets. On and on the explosives blasted, and he began to stumble on bodies charred from liquid fire, bodies sprawled one on top of the other. He fell over them, back-crawled in fear, and then his vision slowly returned, one eye, at least one eye, and he pulled out his kirpan sword for whom? For the dead? Many of them so small, so shocked quiet in death, their white lips forming holes, open mouths hollow, powdered white, eye sockets shriveled, the results of mustard gas after ten minutes of excruciating suffocation.

Other times the nightmares involved endless chases through Mesopotamian cobblestoned streets in the middle of a parched landscape where escape was hopeless. A wailing woman shrouded in a black abaya and hijab pursued him in order to avenge her murdered children, her niqab veil covering her facial features except a pair of fierce, terrible eyes. Through the ruins of a condemned city he ran for his life and he could feel her lunging, felt her fingertips, her breath on his neck, his chest unable to support another step.

And then Lehna startled awake, heaving and confused, his heart swollen and constrained, and he knew now, in his thirty-eighth year on this earth, that the pull of despair would drown him without mercy. He sat up in one room of the two-room farmhouse, amid the reassuring buzz-saw snoring of his roommates and the angles of morning light upon the floor, and he touched the wet split that was his bad eye. A glistened sweat encrusted his face and he could not quiet the nightmarish weeping, for it took full minutes to realize that the deep mournful circle of grief-stricken wailing came from him.

Weeks of restless nights began to produce exhaustion that spawned a series of day fevers, sickly calenturas, as his Mexican American neighbors called them, and he suffered bone aches and backaches, his knees creaking like snaps of twigs such that Gopal sent him home to rest one afternoon, worried about his friend's upset stomach, hazy vision, and difficulty breathing. Lehna had to use a sturdy wooden stick for support to amble back to their rented house, each step an extreme struggle. The rows of oak trees had created a tunnel-like path to the house, and once he cleared it Lehna discovered the housekeeper sitting uncomfortably on a stool on the front porch, the curve of her back, her daisy-patterned housedress over her knees, whispering prayers with her beads. Legs crossed, one sandal swinging and swaying from her toes, she crossed herself and continued fingering her rosary, head bowed, lips moving with each prayer bead. The sun was high in an avalanche of light. He saw loose strands of hair escaped from her pulled-back long braid and lifted his chin to feel the winds blowing stronger—his bones felt like kindling burning inside the furnace of his skin—and when he stopped to listen to the treetops slowly spluttering and the crow's lonely cawing, she looked up as if she felt a heated gaze, then stood, slipping the rosary in her apron pocket. Rail thin, his face rust colored like oxidized iron, he approached her in a daze, here and not here, caught between the roof of the sky and the floor of the earth, together and completely alone. Light-headed, almost faint as she glanced at him, he lifted his walking stick like a kirpan sword, confused by all this witchery. She placed her hand on his forehead to test for a fever and Lehna was paralyzed by her touch, so thankful for the coolness of her palm. Grateful for her tenderness, he released the walking stick, and another world swirled in front of him with dizzying speed.

The Holtville County court clerk, who looked up from his steaming morning porridge and judged Mercedes Jesusita Alvarez's surname to be strictly Spanish and therefore white, denied the marriage license.

He shook his head regretfully, the middle part of his sparse, greased hair crooked as an unkempt country road.

—Under the Statutes of California Chapter 61, Section 69 in the year of 1934, no license may be issued . . . the man uttered between mouthfuls. Lehna gazed at him, a fearful premonition proving real, his hope fugitive. Mercedes Jesusita stood beside him in a rosette-patterned, pleated cotton hooverette dress she had sewn herself in preparation for their nuptials, worn over her only pair of beige stockings and street-dusty Oxford heels, a veil attached to a hat with a velveteen bow pinned tightly to her coronet of black braids. She fisted a pair of white gloves at the judgment.

—Listen here, the clerk said. A spoon stuck in his bowl of oats on the counter in front of him as he swiped an arm over his mouth to complete his sentence—I'm not a bastard, least as far as I know, least don't ask my wife, but I ain't paying no hefty fine for you twos. The steam generated by his porridge clouded his vision, and he removed his glasses, which left red marks on the bridge of his nose. —You do understand, the clerk continued, wiping his specs with the corner of his striped vest. He glanced at Lehna, then at Mercedes Jesusita. —This match ain't natural.

Under her veil, Mercedes Jesusita's cheeks flushed, and the determined force by which she pulled on her white gloves inspired another plan in Lehna. It disturbed him mightily to see how they were scorned and dismissed, a reception long expected but surprising in the pain it still evoked. Lehna motioned for them to leave, but before departing, Mercedes Jesusita slapped the bowl off the counter, and they exited to the sound of a string of expletives as the gummy porridge crashed on the clerk's shoes.

The timetables showed a train scheduled to arrive from San Diego in El Centro at 10:07 a.m. If they hurried, Lehna could purchase two round-trip tickets to Yuma, Arizona; they could embark at El Centro with plenty of time to cross into Arizona, a state without a three-day waiting period for marriage licenses, get married, return that afternoon, and not lose another day of work. His haversack strapped across his chest, he helped Mercedes Jesusita up the wrought-iron stairs of their designated passenger car, one he was sure had once contained livestock; its seats were makeshift removable hardwood benches and the freight windows were mere slits between reinforced plywood.

Mercedes Jesusita carried a sewing purse containing her embroidery and a canteen of manzanilla tea, and when they found a seat, she rested the purse on her lap. Passengers followed in an orderly chaos, filling the overhead netted pouches with bundles and bags and valises, finding spaces under the benches for a small cage of frantic chickens and a crate cradling two whiny puppies. A din of excited voices rose as young girls dressed in Sunday-best blue pinafores, red cotton ribbons in their braids, and boys in black slacks, starched shirts, and suspenders readied themselves for their special excursion. All the seats having been taken, Lehna immediately offered his to a mother, her baby wrapped in a rainbow shawl. He checked his pocket watch again because their train was stalled, waiting for a tardy Southern Pacific transfer at El Centro. After a few hours of nerve-racking delay, the locomotive whistle blew and the train finally departed, bellowing and hissing fumes from beneath the huge grates. Everyone, standing or sitting, felt the pull, crank, and clackety-clacking of the ten-wheeler straining around the mountainous ridges toward Yuma. The train's momentum was disrupted again, slowed, and then halted altogether; coal shovelers jumped off the engine car, cursing, hollering for volunteers to help them remove the Quechans' blockades, which had been piled on the tracks in protest. From where he was standing, Lehna could barely see the shovelers dismantling a stack of Bureau of Reclamation signs broken off their posts and mud-caked boards bearing the name of the All-American Canal company. Another hellish two hours plus passed before the train jolted forward.

The stagnant heat, lack of real windows, the two delays, the increasing hunger and thirst had made the journey all the more disconcerting; gurgling children coalesced in a complicated game of cat's cradle and boiled over into a disagreeing gaggle. In the shifting of light and time, the young mother's face was lacquered in perspiration and as she leaned her head back to doze her woven shawl slipped to reveal a breast, her suckling baby fast asleep. Mercedes Jesusita mantled the shawl so as not to disturb the modesty of the sleeping woman. By midafternoon a toddler's cries kept the passengers on edge, and by late afternoon the locomotive slowed and squealed, its brakes jerking everyone awake.

Disembarking, the passengers found themselves standing on the small platform of the train depot amid cages and crates, valises and baskets, in semidisbelief that they had finally arrived in Yuma, and in one piece. Back in British India, the Raj had decreed an ordinance banning leave-taking or welcoming of loved ones at train stations, a cruel ordinance meant to punish, to remind them of their place, which was why Lehna momentarily paused on the platform of Yuma's depot. He had not witnessed in years such melancholy farewell caresses or merry homecoming embraces, the wave of a hand, a name called out: *My son, darling, Abuelito, can you see me? Mija, over here! Here I am!* Above the station's rooftop a stationary weather vane awaited a greeting from a breeze.

With so little time to calm the bone jitters, Lehna looked at his pocket watch as the train's platform emptied of people. The same porter who had assisted an older woman off the train, her feeble steps careful and regal under a long, flowing, colorful skirt, informed Lehna that they had no more than twenty minutes before the Yuma County courthouse was set to close. Worse yet, even if it wasn't closing time, the porter continued, Mrs. Wilmerine Jackson, the county clerk, was known to leave the office early if the day proved uneventful or if the neighbor's roosters woke her up too soon that day and she needed a nap, or if there was a mail haul to sort—she was also the postmaster of Yuma County and the post office was not exactly a stone's throw from the courthouse. Drained by daylong pocket-watch anxiety, Lehna simply took hold of Mercedes Jesusita's sewing purse, his own haversack strapped over his chest, and at once began to sprint toward Main Street in the direction of the porter's finger. He barely heard Mercedes Jesusita's oxford heels battering the plank porches behind him; she simply could not keep up, the pleat in her flowered hooverette dress splitting open and displaying her knees. His satchel flapping against his ribs, Lehna darted across the cement of the highway without looking, and an Oklahoma City Transport Company truck honked at him loudly.

Out of breath, Lehna spotted the United States flag on display and swung open the courthouse door beneath it. The room had the heavy scent of ancient scrolls, of brittle documents in creaky binders: land deeds, maps, mine claims, lawsuits, wills, birth notes, death certificates, citizenship papers, freedom papers, divorce proceedings, marriage licenses. He was shocked the courtroom was completely empty, deserted of sound except for the pendulum ticking of a wall clock. His sudden appearance startled the presiding clerk, who stood on the other side of a barred window clutching her purse; she shook her bolls of gray hair at having been caught red-handed in the business of departing.

He gasped for air, placed the sewing purse down, braced his palms on his knees, and bent over between breaths.

—It's already too late and time to close shop! Mrs. Jackson said as stiffly as a schoolmarm, irritated at herself for not having locked up a smidgen sooner.

56

Lehna never quite knew how to read these old American women like Mrs. Jackson. They reminded him of overripe fruit with jowls that looked like soft peach fuzz; some had double-chin wattles while others looked so emaciated and sad he thought the wind could toss them to the next county with hardly a gust. Sometimes they could be very kind, other times threatening, even incredibly cruel, and they unsettled him because of their unreliability. Behind him, the door hinges squeaked open and Mercedes Jesusita entered, breathless, her slouch hat tilted so far to the right that the huge bow hung right over her forehead, and a light veil of dust clung to her dress. Her breasts heaving, she did not look pleased at being left behind, and she removed her gloves, straightened her hat, redirected the pleats at the waist of her dress with mindful tugs. The right heel of her shoe had loosened and she hobbled to join Lehna in front of the county clerk's barred window, ready for the civil ceremony.

—Lord, now I seen it all, Mrs. Jackson said in a private murmur. She returned to her desk to replace her purse and a clunky ring of metal keys. Her wide backside moved sluggishly toward one cabinet, and she pulled open a drawer, ran two fingers over some folders, removed a large envelope, and withdrew two forms. She then replaced the envelope and closed the drawer, the clock beating like a dholak drum, as crazy loud as Lehna's heart. Grabbing a magnifying glass from her desk, she returned to her window, dislodged something from her throat, and began to recite, eyes bugged big through the magnifying glass, the rote script that concluded in the words "by the power vested in me." Writing *"Mexican"* color or race here and *"Black"* there, the county clerk of Yuma County slipped the sheets of paper under the barred window and jabbed an index finger for their signatures here and here. Mercedes Jesusita bent to pen her name with a slow measure of focus. The clerk blew the wet ink of their signatures dry, stamped and signed the documents, delivered a copy to the couple.

—Best of luck, Mrs. Jackson said—You'll need it.

The weight of the marriage certificate in Lehna's haversack was a wisp of breath against the weight of the occasion and the day's anxiety. At least now they were married, and he set himself to ponder why Mercedes Jesusita had agreed. Left with an eviction notice and doctors' bills in El Centro, she had taken on a job as a housekeeper, and the rest, as they say, was history, but he entertained the belief that perhaps it might have been something else, and in his mind Lehna recited Sri Guru Granth Sahib:

Helena María Viramontes

> *The ache of love, beloved. The king*
> *My friend the Guru to me brings*
> *Awakened is the mind within*
> *What mind and body crave therein*
> *Is stilled; of wedded bliss does sing*
> *My mind, the bliss that union brings.*

On the narrow sidewalks of Yuma's Main Street, Mercedes Jesusita limped on her broken oxford heel. Incredibly hungry, they followed the aromatic trail of meatloaf emanating from the town's crowded homespun diner. A woman's loud laughter erupted inside, a subdued lullaby faded as many a truck driver sat at the counter forking hot chicken potpies while other white folk and family ate platters of enchiladas or potato fries in the checkered booths. To be safe, Mercedes Jesusita ordered from the back-alley kitchen door: four sopapillas dipped in honey, scrambled eggs and beans wrapped in corn tortillas, and water to be poured into her canteen. She leaned on the doorframe, dusted off the lap of her dress, refusing to feel wounded at being forced to wait near overflowing garbage cans, swaths of black flies rioting above. She inspected with a sad inevitability a small rip in her stocking, removed her broken shoe, and Lehna studied her oxford heel as if it were an alien contraption.

Lehna used his kerchief to swipe away the sweat beads on his forehead. For him, it had been both the worst day *this ain't natural* and best day *of wedded bliss does sing / My mind, the bliss that union brings*, although the day was hardly over. Oxford shoe in hand, he returned to Main Street. People tramped along, unknowing of their futures, uncaring of their legacies, the strange beautiful desert terrain surrounding the horseshoe outskirts of downtown Yuma. In front of the Apothecary and DrugStore, several Quechan makers displayed their miniature clay animal talismans and pottery, and weavers hung their blankets. Lehna admired the geometric patterned blankets as being as perfect in color and design as the phulkari designs of Punjab. His hunger intolerable, he chewed on a date, allowing the exquisite sweetness to roll on his tongue, and then he purchased another for Mercedes Jesusita from the date vendor, an old Quechan. The elder wore a tall hat and Lehna instinctively knew that the man's unshorn silver hair was that of a warrior, a tribute to virtue; the elder's dust residue–covered coat was absent lapels and buttoned up to his Adam's apple and the sleeves of his coat ended in threadbare cuffs inches short of his wrists. The old vendor met Lehna's inquiring stare and Lehna recognized in it his own face ravaged by a capacity to persevere, the old man's features chiseled like sunsetting light sharpening the Yuma hilltops.

All his life he had lived in paradoxes: he had fought for the British Raj in exchange for land promised to Punjabis and a degree of self-governance for his countrymen, then the occupiers continued their rule, breaking their sworn words, slaughtering family picnickers, peaceful protesters in Jallianwala Bagh in Amritsar, the holy city of the Sikhs, with unapologetic and unforgivable malice. Once when he attended a San Francisco gurdwara, a Sikh follower of the Ghadars by the name of Udhan Singh had urged Lehna to return to their motherland to revolt against the Raj, and, yes, avenge those murdered in Amritsar since the passing years did not heal. But in the end nothing survived vengeance: no humans, no plants, no animals, no victors, no earth no air no water, only fire, and after that nothing save fossilized souls. To withstand the violence inflicted by the occupiers, to adapt the same methods, was to become them. Lehna's intuition told of something much more: a sustainable and transgressive practice of refusal, a new and different place in mind and body, between earth and sky.

Jolted out of his reverie, Lehna felt the old Quechan offering him a jarra cool to the touch. He pressed his lips to the rim and gulped the clay taste of water, not realizing how thirsty he had been, and returned the jug with a shake to make sure he hadn't completely emptied it. A dusky fuchsia brightened the sublime oasis of date palms—but how could these date palms grow such luscious dates from desert soil unless they had willful roots and plenty of sky? Lehna salaamed the man's intimate sharing; the water had refreshed him, eased his anxiety, and he entered the checkered floor and blue painted shelves of the Apothecary and DrugStore without reservations.

At the end of a long glass counter, a small stall given over to the brine scent of leather goods was decorated with ex-lax and Rx prescription posters. Lehna allowed himself to explore under the watchful eye of the shopkeeper, to loiter inside the store. Clutching the damaged shoe, he inspected a crate of socks to see if he could find a pair of women's stockings. Behind the counter, the shopkeeper held on to a flyswatter so as to warn the frenzy of buzzing flies what was in store, and behind his shoulders stood ceiling-to-floor shelves of blue, green, and clear elixir bottles, bags of herbs, and concoctions by the tin—the sheer abundance of remedies meant that the region was afflicted with illnesses aplenty. The shopkeeper's curiosity overcame any polite discretion, and he pointed to Lehna's dastaar with his flyswatter.

—What you got under there?

Lehna's attention was snarled in Burma-Shave pics, an advertisement announcing, "So He Learned about the 5 O'Clock Shadow from Her." A swat smashed a fly; the corpse was swept off the glass counter to the sawdust on the floor.

—You gonna spill the beans?

—Sir? Lehna knew there was only one way Americans understood those who wore turbans: as exotic "raghead" fortune-tellers who wore heavy kohl around their eyes and massaged a crystal ball in the picture shows. He considered at length a cautious reply.

—Well, what you got under that head rag of yours?

—Love, Lehna replied.

The shopkeeper exhaled a whistle of awe as if he had tried to guess but had come up with the wrong answer. He placed the flyswatter on the counter, trying to hide his bewildered delight—Does that shoe there need fixing?

Lehna surrendered the shoe for repair and waited for the shopkeeper. He leaned so close to the glass counter that he had to palm off his moistened breath several times in order to view an assortment of GEM razors and Colgate Rapid Shaving Cream larva-shaped tubes arranged slapdash next to the array of Mac Gregor Men's Toiletries.

Later that evening, her shoe repaired, Mercedes Jesusita carried their warm meals, and the two walked to the West Side Auto Court Hotel to inquire about a room. Twilight's split-peach glow cast strange shapes from the scrub oaks and sage bushes against the red bluffs and buttes. On the small hotel porch facing Main Street, the couple sat on old rocking chairs to eat, sharing the canteen between them. Coupledom an unknown country, Lehna delivered a date, its papery skin cracked by the sweet meat, and Mercedes Jesusita thanked him politely. Except for the sound of jaunty laughter from men playing poker in the Court Hotel lobby, and except for a bus or produce truck that zoomed by as if speed were an essential commodity, the evening passed quietly. As twilight fell into darkness too swiftly, Lehna followed Mercedes Jesusita into Room 125, farthest from the lobby, which the manager used for storage. A car's sharp headlights spliced through the windows as Mercedes Jesusita closed the paisley curtains and turned on the sole electric lamp, which illuminated old bedsprings and mattresses and stacked chairs, the discarded furnishings a barricade against the outside world.

With her back to him she removed her hat and, standing in front of the cracked mirror, unpinned her coronet of braids and shook the black cascade of hair loose. All day, today, tonight, Lehna was nervous, and yet as he watched her pull her belt from the waist loops of her dress, his doubts diminished. Untucking an end of cloth, he unwound his dastaar, deliberately leaving the piles of cotton wraps on the quilted coverlet of the bed. A knot on top of his head was fastened by the kangha comb, and Lehna pulled the comb out and undid his topknot of unshorn hair, fingers trembling. He let his hair scroll down his shoulders into a length longer than hers—and, by her gaze, he surmised that she had never seen a man with that length of velvet black and gray hair before.

Inside the Apothecary and DrugStore, the expectations of this matrimonial terrain had become as clear to him as the Granth depicting devotional guidelines on how to conduct one's life. From the haversack, Lehna removed the silver palki containing the Granth and placed it on a bed stand, then removed a small wooden bowl and brush, a paper-wrapped bar of soap, a used razor and strop. Mercedes Jesusita studied the items, at first perplexed, then more confused as he sat on a chair waiting. A few heartbeats later, she looked serious, removed her good pair of scissors from her sewing purse, unfolded an embroidered bridal pillowcase partially stitched and cloaked him with it, then touched the soft mesh of lengthy beard.

Lehna knew she was a practiced woman; she had shaved her first husband, and he pondered whether first husband had admired the strands of black hair loosened into a free-fall cascade, revered the outline of her nose silhouetted against the lamp's soft glow, her face now the same color as Lehna's. When the beard was no more, Lehna grasped thin air, so accustomed was he to stroking it during his baths, his face baring a youthful lightness he had forgotten existed, and then he narrowed his brow as she cut the back of his hair, her waist pressed against his shoulders with intimate ease, the whoosh of timeless hair locks falling and scattering on the darkened floor. The scissors chilled against his neck and he winced in sudden shock, the steel reminding him of oft-repeated history where the Mughals had guillotined the Sikhs.

She had nursed first husband until his passing, and Lehna appreciated such loyalty, but the brief thought of another man touching her, caressing her with kisses, fueled his jealousy, inflamed a strange concupiscence, and he grimaced, heard movements, a fumbling, and opened his good eye to critically appraise her. She first whetted a

61

straight razor with the strop. His new wife, Mercedes Jesusita Alvarez Singh, who now gazed down with determination, poured a dash of water from her canteen and then lathered soap in a wooden bowl like someone whisking meringue, her breasts slightly quivering at the feat. He hadn't noticed until now that the pillowcase cloaked around him like a cape was beautifully embroidered with her same trained, deft hands, the married name Singh in baroque letters, the S's sewn in swirls a color that reminded him of cumin, cloves, and turmeric. With bristle-brush froth, a simultaneous sensation of warmth and coolness on his face, Mercedes Jesusita Alvarez Singh began to shave him tenderly and without hesitation, proving her willingness to explore for him this new place unafraid, the foam curling against the razor blade. She raked the curve between his jawline and Adam's apple, dipped the razor in the bowl of water, tapped off the excess soap, dried it with a hotel hand towel. He was relieved to feel her fingers quivering as she arrived closer and closer to his skin, arrived at the virginal shaving that uncovered a set of dimples. Of course it must have been love because they both acknowledged that without one another, loneliness would bury their lives, so Yes, she had nodded, Yes, to a serious and crucial pact, Yes to an acceptance of each other's curious mysteries.

A lonely train whistled in the distance, an isolated truck roared past and receded into the silence of solitary highway. The lamplight pierced the darkness of the curtain-drawn hotel room and the pile of furnishings cast shadowy clusters on the ceiling like constellations of stars above the West Side Auto Court. Mercedes Jesusita switched off the lamp, and a slice of moonlight illuminated from between the curtains; a bit of his soap on her cheek, her lips on his, Lehna finally grasped Gopal's description of the Vizcaino Desert's boojum marvel, the upturned trees with roots held up high, ready for Guru Nanak's grand embrace.

Sunday had arrived—*Six days shalt thou labor, and do all thy work; but the seventh day is a Sabbath unto the Lord thy God*—and brought with it a collective exhale that breezed over various harboring labor campsites of the San Joaquin Valley. In the labor camp, the Sunday handheld altar bells chimed faintly through the orchards. Mercedes Jesusita Alvarez Singh tried to explain to Lehna that the bells were signaling the miracle conversion of wine into the blood of Christ, and that when the sound of bells chimed again, it was to announce that the Eucharist had become the body of Lord Jesus Christ. Flames poked from between the fire grates of the Singh campsite and smelled thickly of the lemon wedges Mercedes Jesusita had used to divert the residue of morning sickness by sucking them and then discarding the rinds into the fire. From their wedding day until now, she had shaved him every Sunday. Today, an enamel bowl of water on the rim of the firepit to rinse the razor, Lehna felt his wife's bulging compact belly, buried his face in her apron to swipe away the soap, the apron heavy with the scent of lemons. Mercedes Jesusita pulled away to trim his thick, graying mustache and then clasped her husband's face with both hands to inspect the quality of her work, squinting one eye for better study, tilted his head this side and that, said his side-whiskers were uneven but ni modo.

—Only God is perfect, her husband replied.

Minds of Winter
Bennett Sims

1.

BLIZZARD THIS MORNING. I sipped coffee alone at the window, watching the snow fall. It was ten out, overcast, and the glass was ferny with frost. Fat, frantic flakes were being buffeted around in broken circles. A game I liked to play when it snowed this hard was to isolate a drifting flake within the window frame, somewhere near the top of the pane, and try to keep track of it as it fell. While it veered left and right I would follow its descent, careful not to lose sight of it amid the visual noise of the pointillist flurry, until finally it had disappeared beneath the sill. Concentrating now on the upper frame, I let several rows of snow pass, then picked a flake more or less at random. It was crumb-like and evidently weightless, staying aloft a little longer than the rest. Whenever I focused on a flake like this, I found that it ended up seeming more animate than the others. Whereas most of the snow drifted down lifelessly, in mindless free fall—no more volitional than the motes of dust that rose like bubbles through the window's shafts of champagne sunlight—whatever flake I happened to be focusing on at the moment seemed to be flying of its own accord, charting a safe route through the blizzard. It was no different with this flake. I watched as it hovered, swerved, chandelled, and dove, with what seemed like the motivated agency of a moth, as if evading birds or bats, or else like a spaceship in a dogfight, a miniature Millennium Falcon navigating this asteroid field of white crises. And the longer I followed it in its zigzag, erratic path, the more sentient it seemed. When a fatter flake drifted toward it, for instance, threatening to collide head-on and subsume it through their mutual fusion, the smaller flake juked left and flew free at the last moment, to all appearances "eluding" the larger one. It really was as if there were some preservation instinct inside the snow, guiding it away from the dangers of melting or merging: some will to survive or individual identity that this single flake—the white shell of a slight self—was careful not to forfeit to absorption. What was odd about this illusion of consciousness, to me, was that it could be maintained only if I concentrated on the snow. If I were to merely glance out the window, I knew, then the seething, staticky activity of the blizzard would seem uniformly inanimate and randomized again. That discrepancy fascinated me. It was interesting that paying attention to a flake should imbue it with any more personality—any more inner life—than a passing glance would. What it reminded me of was the different levels of deadness in a doll, the way that play could bestow degrees of personhood on a piece of plastic. In childhood, when my Kenner Han Solo action figure lay discarded on the carpet, it was utterly devoid of life. Not just dead but inorganic: inanimate matter that had never been alive. But as soon as I picked the toy back up, it became Han Solo again. I could march him across the bedspread and mash him into a grappling match with Boba Fett, and for the duration of this play he would seem conscious and agentive, filled with plans, desires, conflicts. Even if Han Solo "died," vanquished in mortal combat with Boba Fett—even if I went *Pew! Pew!* in imitation of the bounty hunter's laser blast and spun the hit, stiff-limbed Han Solo around in the air—even so, the "dead" Han Solo would still be less dead in my hand than the toy had been back on the carpet. As long as he was in play, he was a person: he *had been* alive and was therefore still a he, rather than an it. Only when I tossed the toy aside, turning my attention elsewhere, would Han Solo revert to objecthood, sinking deep into the catatonia (the carbonite) of his nonconsciousness. By holding him in my hand, I animated him: I transmitted some vital spark from my own mind to his body through the jumper cable of my touch. Perhaps that was what was happening with the snow right now, I thought, watching my flake pendulate through the air—like a spider swinging down its thread—as it drifted toward the windowsill. Merely by looking at one flake in particular, I could summon it from out of the depths of its crystalline insentience, animating it not with my hand but with my eye. Through this act of concentration and play, my own consciousness was rubbing off on the flake. For as long as I focused on it, it came to seem creaturely and vibrant, because it was stirring inside of—being stirred to life by—the ray of my paid attention. The same way that a doll will seem to walk when you manipulate it, or the way that a dead moth's wings will flutter when you blow on them, beating with borrowed vibrancy. That was what was happening when I watched the snow falling beyond my window. From out of the white totality a tiny whiteness had individuated itself: one flake in particular had emerged from the flurry as a fleck of awareness. It was like watching mind emerge from matter, the coming to consciousness of one monad within matter's white mindlessness. This was why you needed a theory of mind when watching snow, I thought. An epistemology of the blizzard. Just before the flake finally disappeared beneath the sill, it lingered a little on the air, as if to give me a parting glance, and when it had passed out of sight I imagined it landing somewhere on the ground below, its thinking extinguished in whatever cold heap absorbed it.

2.

In the blizzard's lull, the pine tree by the street was left crusted with snow. I studied it through the window. Thick powder had amassed on the flat upper surfaces of its branches, resulting in a precise two-tone color-field: each bough was divided into a white band above, and, below, greenish bark. The snow was so consistently applied across the bark that, in grasping for the exact contrast that it called to mind, I found myself visualizing cupcakes, doughnuts, cookies: that stark border where the pale glaze gives way to dark pastry. And for the first time I understood, after using the terms unthinkingly all my life, why sugared glazes were called icing, or frosting, in the first place. Staring at a dusted branch, I thought, "The snow looks just like icing" or "It's like frosting," and it was only by routing my mind through the dumbness of that redundancy—the snow literally *was* ice, *was* frost—that I was able to travel backward through the metaphor, recovering its source. I had inadvertently applied the image to its origin, reproducing in reverse the exact same process of phrasemaking that some baker must have gone through centuries before, when, meditating on a new confection one winter morning and searching for a term to coin for the technique, he glanced out the window and saw the white coating of snow spread evenly over earth or over the bark of a branch and thought to call the sugar paste "icing." I took out my phone and checked Wikipedia: this sense of "icing" dated back to at least 1683, according to the OED, 1750 for "frosting." In this way, I thought, a three-hundred-year-old thought had just escaped from the snow. It was as if the pâtissier's perception—that moment of insight at the bakery window—had been frozen in the snow as much as in the figure of speech. And I had now glimpsed that same perception in the snow outside this window. Just as a thawing block of Arctic ice will sometimes release some ancient illness—a Precambrian flu, preserved for millennia in its pockets of trapped gas—it was as if the snow too had released in its slow melting this metaphor from the mind of that pâtissier, the posthumous point of view of a pâtissier, off-gassing into the winter air the wordplay of a pâtissier who had been dead now for three centuries. This must be what people had in mind when they described language as a virus. Frosting, I thought, as I studied the pine tree, and it was this dead pâtissier's thought that I was thinking, passing through my eye and into my mind, infecting my gaze with an other's word from another winter.

3.

The window's muntins divided the glass into a grid of squares, which gave the view outside the appearance of a split screen. This made the winter landscape seem discontinuous, fragmented, as if the window were broadcasting half a dozen video feeds of half a dozen different snowy streets simultaneously. In one, a sidewalk. In another, the pine tree. I had grown used to staring at split screens lately, since I had been spending more and more of my days videoconferencing on Zoom, which gridded its users into a matrix of mini squares. Now, at the window, I had the momentary sensation—a kind of afterimage of the application—that I was on a conference call with several snow-falls. And when the blizzard began to drive fresh flurries against the glass, whiting out each screen with static, it was as if every feed had gone dead at once. This whiteout reminded me—something I had found myself thinking often recently—that the split screen would be a good editing technique for representing the mind in mourning. In most films, I had noticed, the edit associated with mourning was usually montage. When a character is grieving, the viewer knows that this mental activity is taking place by the montage that plays, a carousel of three-second memory clips excerpted from the bereaved consciousness. Each memory is typically suffused with honeyed light and scored with swelling cello: the lost one laughing on a swing set at sunset; the lost one walking toward a dappled river, turning around to smile into the camera; the lost one running fingers through golden wheat. This rapid succession of imagery is meant to suggest the shuffle effect of mourning: the way that scenes of the lost one simply flash into consciousness, in no particular order; the way that you are not in control of what gets recalled, but have to endure these stray moments as they strobe over you. But what montage missed, I thought, was the simultaneity of these memories. In the most dif-ficult moments of mourning—when you were so overwhelmed with impressions of the lost one that you couldn't breathe—it didn't feel as if you were cycling through a string of linear memories, one after the other, distributed serially through time. Instead, it felt as if you were experiencing every memory at the *same* time. The image of the lost one laughing on a swing set would flash into consciousness alongside the memory of the lost one walking toward the river, alongside every other memory of the lost one, all of these discrete moments from your life flooding through the one-second-wide aperture of your time-bound consciousness. The memories may be distinct, discontinuous, but they were presented to the mind simultaneously. And it was the impossibility of processing all of these memories at once that inspired panic symptoms in the body—the inability to breathe, the ragged heartbeat—since for a moment it felt as if you were going to die, or go dead, as if more and more memories would keep filling your brain until, overloaded, it would white out. No montage, however rapid-fire and visually overstimulating, could quite approximate this feeling of congested recollection. If any editing technique could, it might be the split screen. Assuming that a cinematographer really wanted to represent the felt experience of mourning, I thought, the screen could be divided into a grid like this window, with each panel playing a different scene: the lost one on the sidewalk would play side by side with the lost one below the pine tree, just above the lost one on the snowy street. That way, the film's viewer would be placed in the same perceptual position as the film's mourner, since the mental effort required of the audience to make sense of this matrix of images (holding all of them in mind at once, synthesizing these dozens of different screens and processing them as a kaleidoscopic whole) would mirror the mental effort required of the mourner to make sense of grief's matrix of memories (holding all of them in mind at once, synthesizing dozens of different moments from a life and processing them as a single kaleidoscopic loss). Confronted with the perceptual impossibility of processing this, the viewer—like the mourner—would feel the imminent whiteout in their minds. Thinking about this again before the window, I recalled that passage from *Postmodernism, or, the Cultural Logic of Late Capitalism*, when Fredric Jameson describes a similar perceptual breakdown in the context of a video installation. In an art gallery, Jameson describes, a film is being played on different television monitors throughout the room, some on the ceiling, some on the floors, forcing the viewer to rotate in place in order to compass them all and construct a mentally coherent model of the fragmented film. It is a split screen that has been distributed through space. Standing in the gallery, Jameson writes, the viewer feels called upon to "do the impossible, namely, to see all the screens at once"; and since perceiving in this way would require a completely different sensorium (eyes in the back of the head, for instance), spaces like these seem to challenge viewers to mutate or evolve beyond their present bodies, to—in Jameson's phrase—"grow new organs." What the gallery seems to grant the viewer, then, is a kind of negative apprehension of these new organs: the fleeting sensation—through their felt lack or need—of what *it would be like* to possess them. In the same way that a small child, grasping at a cabinet just out of reach, is able to feel—in the gap of negative space between his fingertips and the handle—what it will be like when he is finally grown up and tall enough, thereby anticipating the potentials of this future self, viewers in this gallery are able to feel—through their very failure to perceive the screens—the optical possibilities of a future body. The video installation, as a design space, seems to be intentionally oriented toward this future body: every awkwardly angled television screen is an affordance for the viewer's future organs, just as the tall cabinet's handle is an affordance for the child's future fingers. Perhaps it was the same, I found myself thinking, with the experience of mourning. When that memory wall overwhelms the mourning mind, resulting in a crash of uncomprehending static, perhaps what we are meant to apprehend is the possibility of a future consciousness, a mind beyond our present mind, which would actually be able to contain all of these memories in their simultaneity, revolving the totality of the lost one's life inside itself—like a diamond held up to light—to consider its facets from every side. Isn't that what people meant when they described the deathbed experience of having one's "life flash before your eyes"? When characters undergo this process in films, it was also usually represented as a montage. But now I wondered whether it too could look more like (assuming it "looks" like anything) a split screen. For what you were supposed to be able to see in this instant was the wholeness and oneness of your existence—the adjacency of every moment on a single plane: your death already present in your birth, your children already present in your childhood—such that your entire life could be compressed into a millisecond of multifaceted or matrical remembering. And since this moment would contain inside itself every memory you had ever formed, it occurred to me, it would also have to include all your prior memories of mourning. The lost one on the sidewalk, the lost one below the pine tree, the lost one on the snowy street: every memory you had re-called long ago, in your bereavement, would be returned to you now on your deathbed. As you died, those memories would once again strobe over you, except this time, I imagined, you would experience none of the mental strain or sense of panic you had in mourning, since by now your dying mind would have expanded to the point where it could perceive these memories—alongside every other moment from your life—in serenity. You would now be capable of doing the impossible, of seeing all these screens at once. The earlier experience of your mind in mourning would be like a foretaste of this deathbed experience: when the lost one's life first flashed before you, it would be like a preview of your own life flashing before you, since the lost one would be one more panel in the split screen that would flash before you as you died (and perhaps that was why, in the most difficult moments of mourning, whenever your heartbeat in-tensified and you had difficulty breathing, it could feel as if you were about to die. In a manner of speaking you *were* dying: you were being brought closer than you were ordinarily capable of approaching to the vortex of your deathbed mind, when the one-second-wide aperture of your time-bound consciousness would split open to admit the split screen of every moment from your life). Just as Jameson's video in-stallation served as the negative apprehension of a future body, perhaps mourning was a negative apprehension of this posthumous body. Through your failure to process your memories of the lost one, you were able to intuit what it *would be like* to properly remember the lost one: in other words, what it will be like to die. Maybe all mourn-ing is an affordance for your deathbed self, I thought, as the blizzard withdrew from the window and the street came back into view. Maybe the whiteout helps prepare you.

4.

As it raked the ground outside, the wind gathered up loose grains of snow, molding them into sinuous spindrifts that helped to disclose the paths of its laminar flows. This was the only way I could tell that a hard breeze was blowing. Otherwise the world beyond the window looked still. Late afternoon and the sky already darkening. Along the sidewalk I watched these white lines slithering over the concrete, writhing in place like the ghosts of snakes. Each creature was a col-laboration of particle and wave, debris and current, holding together for seconds before the wind shifted again and they whipped out and disintegrated. Whenever a line vanished like this, an identical one would soon form to replace it, taking shape in seemingly the same spot. The same wind was blowing over the same bare place on the sidewalk, and it was possible to imagine that each spindrift was even composed of the same particles of snow: that the current was recirculating its flakes as quickly as the turbulence dispersed them, recycling them into new lines. It was difficult to describe. This dynamic disintegration and reincorporation of the spindrifts—the way that thousands of particles could converge on an invisible vector, shed away like spray, then rejoin it—put me in mind of the Large Hadron Collider, or those 3D animations of water droplets circulating in cough or sneeze columns, where primary-colored CGI spheroids are slowed down until their ostensibly stochastic trajectories can be mathematized and made imaginable. Like these phenomena, the spindrifts seemed to follow a chaotic process: something that could not be described in words, only modeled. But no sooner had this idea occurred to me than I realized that the gathering action of the wind was also, at bottom, syntactical. The wind was arranging its grains the way a sentence arranges its words, or a mind its thoughts, and each spindrift was as frangible as thought too, falling apart as easily as a sentence does. I watched the lines outside vanish and re-form. It was as if there were something the wind wanted to say and kept erasing. It was trying to get it right. It was difficult to describe. In a sense what I was watching was this very difficulty of description—the problem of indescribability—in motion. And so maybe the most faithful description of the spindrift would simply be to say that it resembled description itself. In any process of revision, the same sentence will need to keep being rewritten. The moment one version is erased— one wrong phrase—a minor variation will form to take its place. The same words keep occurring. Returning. They get caught in the current or breath of the sentence, drawn back into it, such that the line is trapped traveling the path of all its past attempts. Writing in place like the ghosts of snakes. Watching one spindrift slither, I wanted to say that the line writhes in place. Place was not quite right. I wanted to say that out of nothing, writhing, the line takes shape. I wanted to say the line writhes out of shape. The spindrift was soon erased, and the new line writhing looked like my own wanting to say. On the sidewalk outside, a wanting to say was taking place. What I wanted to say about its want to say was the way it was wanting to say in place. Even as I was watching this, the wind must have died down, or moved on, because all of the spindrifts disappeared together, and

71

the sidewalk went instantly white and flat, the surface smoothed like water calming. Along the curb, where the city's plows had shoveled up crusty mounds, I could make out faint striations in the hillocked snow, little ridges that the wind had carved and the cold had hardened. For a moment these scale-model sastrugi looked like spindrifts that had been solidified, frozen in time. The streetlamps ticked on just then, and all the snow beyond the window went neon in the orange light. It was difficult to describe.

Three Poems
Colin Channer

BUBBLE

Love from another time beneath me
in that new white cube house, mouth-water
from my brother's lip a dollop on my arm;

and the bed irks when he fidgets
in the wait-for-signal from the gap
between floor tiles and the ground;

not "the grounds" . . . ground . . . house bottom,
hush wilderness where short
unpainted pylons bear our house,

moral interstice of lizards, worms
and insects—where with keyholes
in our milk teeth we go crawling

with *jook* sticks to kill;
but not today, not now, not in this
drowsy interval, not with bellied

dog beneath us filled with pups;
expectant anguish, feels like advent
service at St. Mary's or the held-in

glee on card nights near Christmas
when big people leave red punch
with anise to the ferns and tip to mum's

barracks and we hear the *rip* of tape
in plastic sleigh beds getting pulled,
and we guess at gifts;

so, me and Gary sleepy-tangled-up this morning,
birth funk rising from the privates
of the house; *penny-wally* dust makes

helix in the light the louvers plane;
the pregnant dog sounds settled in the place
where she belongs, the crawly gap,

our dim far-fetching range,
and in bed my mind gallops,
my chewed fingers work, names coming

as I pick tufts from the blue chenille
we cover with, our inner sky, thought bubble,
holder of our wishes, gases, pissings,

bun crumbs, Milo, condensed milk,
the drowsy pleasure of being above new
life as it's ushered in not lost on me,

not lost because it's just too big to grasp;
this is six-year-old bare love,
just adorable distress as each

pup imagined is named, my mind alert
for big dog bray or jostle, or a sightless
infant chirp, and now it comes!

newborn's here-in-wonder cry on waking
in an outtabelly underworld;
the next sound comes to mind still

when I think *efficient*—
one growl all slaughtered runts,
and every time I hear the sound

and every time I hear the sound
and every time I hear the sound
the sound the sound the sound . . .

OREJA

Given time, I'd know the word,
but had I not done duty,
sight unseen agreed
to take Alberto's *madre* on a walk
I would not have learned the *clave*
beat of boots and Roman sandals
on our stone canal.

Blood beat, it stayed reliant
as a dog or cast shadow,
this sound of middle life unleashed,

and we rambled arms looped in summer's rush wind,
purposeful as migrants but willfully naive,
navel gazing neovatics
acting like tense did not matter,
like what-next was up to belief.

Sun-stunned by August Providence,
bruised town west from where Cape hooks brawl sea,
we moved in shook cloth, hair masque
and skin attar to the brink,
left downtown—sought art.

From the hump-emplaced museum
we looked down. Light slighted.
Canal turned zip in gathered frock
flung off.

By then discussion was finished.
I'd been humbled, embarrassed,
Spanish sputtered when Caracas came up.

    Oh, wrecked Caracas,
    Bolívar's sinking galleon,
    Chavismo's glowing tanker run aground.

The museum was chilly.
We caught breath in its smug café,
sat thigh-thigh, spangling
leftists bereft,
sipping thoughtful—tea then staring
past the basement of our cups.

Would know the word in time,
but if I'd not said yes to my friend,
gone for that walk,
in language made some rough wrong turns
I would not have been there
feeling tender to texture's proletariat,
the millions of slighted small words.

Started with redundance; Ana Maria indulged,

    eyes / ojos
    eyebrows / cejas
    lash / pestaña

I see her face on teacups now.
She taught tazas don't have handles.
In Spanish cups have ears

DUB

What I've come for in the house of dub
is cotched up in a corner, black and dented.

Through the dust that fogs it, slashes
where the faders used to be. The half door

claps; smells douse: old damp,
goat fur, guano, bats. The roof holes

mate the algae puddles; loss amalgamated
has clung. Hear me now and hear me good:

to shake dubroyal's console;
watch insects slush from it in seeped ocher,

feels at once minute and big, pint epic;
impulse comes to clean it, pay some vague penance,

or pray. The half door pries itself open;
there's wind rush as I note make—

student always—dun mattresses, dead leaves,
hen bones in slack boxes, a wad of condoms

going resin with each day. All this looked to
while I aggregate, re/aggregate, or try to,

what was here when *him bruk up* music,
made mash-ups, loopy instrumentals

flecked with chant snatches, fogged horns,
stridulant insects and echo, mountain ranges

hazing, far-repeating hills; these were my blues,
my hymns, my war songs, my lay psalms

in the epoch of *pants lent*, vicious Nixon,
Indira's starlet shades and what they promised;

DJ Castro live remixing history; Marley's ambush;
arson at the old-age home, 150 golden ladies

burned—mass grave for their remains like
charred idols—the cold war hot and local,

tribal killings like the Irish, gunmen
green and orange culling more in months

than all the Troubles, the melodica our bagpipe,
roots chanter, source of skirl, its sketching eerie,

chalking on the B side for the black exquisite corpse.
What I've come for—I leave.

Corvid Vision
Barbara Tran

one for sorrow

Forty days and forty nights And at last   Ararat
    Noah sent Raven forth
    Raven did not return
for all Raven needed
was all that remained   death

two for mirth

Raven calls *Grok* mocks me *grok*

how little I *grok*

three for a funeral

When something is said to come full
circle does this mark completion or make
                a new form

an O
through which another
could fly?

Barbara Tran

                              When Raven eats
                                  is it meat
                                  or flesh?

four for birth

    Lightning strikes
          birthing Fire   Raven fails
               to fetch it   Fire burns   rings round   Owl's eyes
                              teaches   Snake to dart

               Spider weaves   before she departs   a basket
          Over water she strides   an ember encased   on her back
               Into the world Spider releases the gift
                                             of Fire

              five for heaven

          Boon of a breeze Spider escapes

    Raven's eye   Her thread

          carried   to a new shore

    If the thread   sticks

          the first bridge   is formed

                    80

six for hell

Wind carried
a feather and my father
to the island

of Manhattan
My mother released
her wish   I

was born   A priest
had pity
on my mother

found
my father
a job

the second
bridge
We stayed

A sticky
web grew A new
home

seven for the devil, his own self

Around me all
I could see
was that

which was not   in fact
before my eyes
I tried to type *moon*

                  phase Auto-
   correct replaced it
       with *mom*

                 passed This morning
                    two crows on a rooftop
                          Tent rock

                  Fairy chimney
                  Earth pyramid
                      Alternating hard

           and soft
                rock Mineral
                    determines

       color Attention

eight for a wish

      Hoodoo residue

           If the shadow
     of an idea follows

       how clear
     can thought ever run?

How to drop a shadow past?
                 Apollo burned Raven black

  (failure to silence a truth)

nine for a kiss

Raven consumes Coyote's castoffs

the innards of rodents both large
    and swallowable flies off to shine

    before the silver morning moon
I go home and swallow the ligaments

tendons flesh whole On my back
    I carry fire and blood mother and

    father the war they left behind the
war they wage daily in their own minds

the moon the sun the leaves I want to
    lay across the page the ones I spill like

    lies like bread crumbs like stories for
some other creature desperate to

believe to weave into the web that
    holds her aloft traps her in the corner

she calls ~~safe~~ ~~home~~ ~~hers~~ here now

ten for a bird you must not miss

Self-portrait as carrion-
            eating crow

The dead enter
    my body

Barbara Tran

and not only rise
but sing as they do

I am the color
of all things

On my one eye
sits the world

Pages from *The Plotinus*
Rikki Ducornet

AGITATED AND PRESSED FOR TIME, I grabbed the knobby stick—a harmless memento of the footpath—now long gone—that had for a time provided access to the woods (such as they were) and ran into the street unprepared for the inevitable encounter (such a dope!) with the Plotinus. A shriek later and my knobby stick was reduced to dust along with my shoes and socks, my coveralls—these losses accompanied by a blinding light, ear pain impossible to articulate, and my arrest.

Secluded in a closet, its air vent accessible on tiptoe, I relate this in code using my knuckles against the grid to whoever will listen. (Very few can possibly decipher my desperate rappings, but the one who does will be the right one. Even in good times, when we would set off for the woods together with our knobby sticks, to bury the birds as they fell from the sky, we were not many.)

They tell me that my transgressions—if merely phenomenological— are punishable by a public scouring, and so I live each day thankful for what I have, although what I have—apart from my threadbare aspirations—is only the sack. If given a chance, I will request another, not because I like it, but because the one I have—if it conceals my apertures as the Powers would have it—leaves my knees and legs bare. If and when my request is gratified (one must remain hopeful), I will ask for my socks back or, preferably, a new pair. I like to imagine the socks are brought to me in a white cardboard box, and that they are wrapped in white tissue paper stamped with the manufacturer's name: Mothwing. Each night before sleep (such as it is) the box appears as if by enchantment, and I whisper: Here you are! Praise destiny! I open the box very slowly, and I take my time with the paper too. Sometimes I fall asleep even before I see the socks!

*

The first pair of socks I received were yellow—a transgressive color, so like the sun, so like the yolk of an egg. If it came to be known that

I owned a pair of yellow socks, the color of an evil star, of the yolk of an egg—the tangible proof of procreation—it would all be over.

The yellow socks warmed my feet, and that first night I slept until a thin ribbon of light made its way into the closet, awakening me. Looking down at my feet at once, I saw that the socks were gone—a good thing, as had the Vector appeared, he would have seen them at once, and then . . .

But this did not happen. The socks are programmed to dissolve at the break of light; a mere whisper is enough to stimulate their dissolution. (I do not know if in the long run the process will adversely affect my feet.) Between you and me, things would be so much better all around if I could keep the socks *and* be provided with a second sack.

*

I can never tell when the Vector will show up, for he moves about cloaked in his Ginza and treading air. His aversion to the sun is so great he wears two Ginzas, one on his body (such as it is) and one on his head. This makes for an impressive entry. Always he asks that I remove my sack so that he may look upon my scars—each one corresponding to an evil deed. The first time this occurred I pointed out that the scars had been inflicted arbitrarily by the Plotinus on that fateful morning when I left the house (such as it was) with the knobby stick. Until then I had not a scab to my name. Now when the Vector pops in, I attempt to flatter him and then, once primed, use what is left of my wits to suggest that like the cold white moon, my scars provide a key to a vast cosmical system that, once unraveled, will reveal that, like Corytys' painted pet turtle, my body provides a map that leads directly to the Throne of Memory. I am, I tell him, like the berry bush that, long ago in the depths of winter, provided sweetness to the birds searching sustenance in blizzards. As gullible as a cracker pigeon, the Vector, his eyes swelling with tears, falls to his knees when I speak like this. I bid him rise.

*

I awoke from a place in my mind thinking how very odd it is that as I regress and shrink into myself (what is left of it), beyond my closet there are corridors, there are other closets, tens of thousands, perhaps, a vast surgical theater (or so it is rumored) patrolled by the Plotinus, whose other assigned tasks are to assure my breakfast and that the Vector's attentions are timely and scrutable. Should the Vector bring a sack to an incarcerate, say, he would have to secure it somehow beneath his Ginza in such a way as to fudge the pokeabout.

But! Be this as it may, I have been thinking in my mind (such as it is) that beyond all this misery, my own and that of the multitude of others, each and every one an incarcerate too, exists the vast world (or what remains of it) and its moon—a moon as pocked as I am yet, unlike me, swarming with activity on both its dark and luminous faces. And in my mind's thinking it has come to me that although it is shameful without end to be thus reduced, I once (and not so long ago, either) was the one Beauty acknowledged in the world with a look, yes: she looked upon me and smiled.

*

At times, my ear straining beneath the vent, I witness conversations taking place on the other side, on a street or a balcony, perhaps, or a porch—considering my daily dose of sunlight. In the recent past I heard a woman or a child ask for mercy only to be told in no uncertain terms that there is no mercy to be had in this universe—a thing I pondered and will continue to ponder. My conclusion (such as it is thus far) is that if it is so, that there is no mercy in this universe, there may be mercy elsewhere. For it is rumored that the number of universes is infinite, that each is a portal to the next. It occurs to me as I knuckle the grid that if true, well then, perhaps they inform one another in ways both nefarious and beneficial. (Such conjectures got me through the day's interminable dusk and much of the night.)

And what if each thing both inanimate and animate is a portal to the next thing and so to all things?

*

Today (such as it is) I tidied up the closet by sweeping the floor clear of dust with my feet. This afforded exercise and a certain satisfaction; it was a pleasure to see the dust piled up in one corner looking very like a small hillock. I squatted squinting and imagined that I was looking at a distant mountain at dusk and that it had snowed. I imagined that the Vector dropped by with the second sack, that the Plotinus had allowed him to enter, that the sack covered my legs and knees, that the Vector had given me a rope to tie the sack in place, and, what's

87

more, a pair of socks, that these socks were yellow, as yellow as the yolk of the maligned egg, the egg that is considered horrible, that is unsound. In doing this, the Vector had broken all the rules. He had risked his own coherence and contiguousness.

The Vector whispered that the Plotinus was only able to see out of one eye, so that the pokeabout had been compromised and he had passed through without a hitch! I hid the socks beneath the precious mound of dust that, as the sun declined in the sky beyond the air vent, mysteriously glowed, giving off a soft, golden light.

If I had a twig, I said, a small twig sporting maybe a leaf or two, well then, a moment's dreaming and it would contain all the splendors, the raptures, and the mysteries of the world. Like Adam's, I continued, my isolation is my innocence.

I happen to have a twig hidden within the folds of my Ginza, the Vector murmured, as he burrowed into a pocket so deep I assumed it contained any number of things, and, indeed, as if conjured by magic, out came the laurel twig, three bright green leaves clinging to its summit. The closet would soon be submerged in darkness, but before this happened, we got to see the tree proudly rooted at the summit of the snowy mound. I cannot express the gratitude I felt for the Vector then, nor the extent of my happiness.

We were now submerged in darkness; the Vector had neglected his watch. Now that it is night, I said to him, just knowing the tree and its hill is there, I shall pass the hours in peace. Bowing, the Vector backed out into the hallway and vanished.

Soon after the Vector's departure, the Plotinus came clanging down the hallway, its lights flashing and siren nozzle screeching. It raged into my closet, kicked the snowy mound, and, stomping on the twig, reduced it to pieces. Once he had rolled on, with morning faraway, there was nothing to do but sit on my knees still as a stone and consider the positive aspects of exile and of my diminished circumstances.

*

This morning (such as it was), my breakfast was a hard roll, very like a rock; despite my youth I feared it was a tooth smasher, and, indeed, it remained intact even after being hurled at the cruel walls with force. At some point I got to my knees, set it down on the tiled floor, and considered the very real possibility that the object before me was not a breakfast roll but a rock. I decided that this could be used to my advantage as it offered the possibility of a systematic inquiry into brute matter. I had—if some time ago—studied Theophrastus (in eighth grade, such as it was, with Botword) and so know that stones are divided into two main classes: stones and earths. I also considered a third possibility, that the thing before me *had been* a breakfast roll and was now a fossil. Therefore, I began my inquiry by putting the thing to my nose and inhaling. I smelled nothing but my own smell and this provided no comfort. For this I decided to be grateful. Had the thing offered an atom of the dairy, the oven, or the kitchen, surely my heart (such as it is) would have broken. Yet, risking this, not long after, I sniffed at it again, thoughtfully, taking my time—so that, inevitably, I began to brood on the distant past, when each home had its hearth, its pantry, and a kitchen that—if only on special occasions (and this before Clampdown)—smelled of butter and yeast. And I recalled the poached eggs of antiquity, that subversion, that obscenity, the egg swelling from within its muffin, incubating beneath its blanket of cream sauce. The sacred egg that would one day grow wings, rise to the skies, and sing (as, believe it or not, was once the case, for, yes, in antiquity the skies were schooled with birds).

*

Theophrastus insisted that all stones *are formed from some pure and homogeneous matter.* When I look at the thing I ascertain that it *is not pure.* And I cannot know if it is homogeneous without breaking it. Theophrastus goes on to say that this homogeneous nature is *the result of a conflux or percolation.* (The same could be said of a breakfast roll.) All I have to abrade my rock's shell and in this way continue my investigations is the nails of my fingers and toes. (I refuse to compromise what is left of my teeth.)

*

Sometime later I heard the Plotinus on its way back (and this could not have been more fortunate) with a jar of water capped with a cork. As soon as the Plotinus had moved on, I dropped my rock into the water jar. What happened next was momentous. The rock dissolved and in this way provided sustenance of a kind—even if I still had no clue as to its true nature.

Having breakfasted (as best I could), I considered the day's gifts— the rock that had proved to be a breakfast roll of a kind; the water (and so a broth that would now sustain me for a time); the silent breath of sunlight leaking from the vent; the vent's percussive capacities; the fact of a floor that, if cold and hard, was dry; the extraordinary luck that the shithole had a cover of sorts and that this cover was carefully considered by its manufacturer—a thing all too rare. Then I sat on my knees and considered the possibility that the sun was greeting me as best it could considering its limited access.

Then, when the sun's breath vanished and the night claimed the closet, I, grateful for the magic water, remained on my knees and, bending over, continued where the vanished rock left off. Theophrastus wrote: *Some stones can be melted and others cannot; some can be burnt and others cannot . . . and some like the Smaragdos can make the color of water the same as their own.* In other words, my rock was named Smaragdos.

*

All was quiet and I was quiet; I remained on my knees forever and a day—or so it seemed—as still as a body can be, doubled over just as a rock that has been tested by fire folds upon itself; just as the brain forming within its bone is the child of enfoldment. At some point I got to my feet and, knuckling the air vent, *was stung by a hornet.* At that very moment, the Vector—and his name is Furanus— appeared; Furanus, a corruption of the name Furmastic (the tyrant of the myth of Cordplaster, who bore witness to the birth of the moon). For a time we squatted together in silence. If the floor is cold, it is also filthy.

Master. The Vector startled me with this greeting. I have brought you yet another gift. Poking about the depths of his Ginza, he eventually nabbed a small glass jar and, with ceremonious attitude, handed it over. Inside was a piece of fresh honeycomb, the color of the sun itself. As the keeping of bees is punishable by death, I looked into his eyes inquiringly.

I live, Furanus told me, far from men in a valley where there remains a vast stand of lime trees. When he said this, I could see the valley and its trees, and for a brief moment I thought I could smell the lime trees in blossom, could hear the gentle buzzing of the bees. Furanus handed over a spoon. As there was no way I could hide the jar from the Plotinus, I had no choice but to eat the comb at once. After a spoonful of that honey, wax falling apart between my teeth, I wept, awakened from the dry well in which I had been living to be deposited in a sunlit valley. I could not stop weeping, although I feared that at any moment the Plotinus would appear and Furanus and I would be torn to pieces. When I caught my breath, I said: You have provided the last pleasure I will ever know, for by the time the sun breathes into my air vent, I will have turned to stone. Deep into the well of my ear, the Vector muttered: Inevitably.

*

This evening rain fell in a purple light giving way to hail and, later, a heavy fog of dust. Our sons are endangered by betrayals, the Vector had said to me once before departing. What am I saying? Even before they are born!

*

With little to occupy my thoughts, I am a keen observer of the self's decline. (As is said: The floaters dissolve, revealing the beloved's face, the mole on her cheek.)

*

There is a hum within my head as within a hive bereft of its queen. An angry hum. The companion of my solitude, it provides a white noise of a kind; it is like a broom. My anger is rooted in my losses. The loss of my knobby stick, the path that led to the woods (such as they were), the loss of those diminutive graves we cared for. (Sometimes a bird would fall alone; other times an entire flock would rain down from the sky. Nonetheless the Beauty and I would give each one its own place to rest, each resting place marked by a stone.)

*

Sometimes I think that had I a honey drop I could suck on, I would be happy, would need nothing else. A rock needs nothing, yet a little sweetness is not a bad thing. One lives, after all, for pleasure. Pleasure happens, the Beauty once told me, laughing. Gently nibbling on the open palm of my hand.

*

Today the sun was of such force it tore into the vent and collided with the back wall, where it settled for not a negligible time. I could tell by its magnitude that the sun was facing my way, that its back was not turned on me as the Plotinus had insisted the day of my arrest. It was and is always my conviction that the sun and moon do not turn away from us but look upon us with benevolence. That light, as it is intended, benefits those who dwell upon a planet made of rock and fire. It is known that our moon and sun are by nature wanderers, yet choose to stay near us as they know we need the light to withstand the terrible rigors of loneliness. It does not matter that the moon is fickle, first scowling and then it beams. Unlike the sun, which recedes only to return. (I am telling you nothing new.) The moon shrinks only to swell. (It is thought with seawater.) This swelling of the moon allows me to swell; as it wanes, so do I wane. When the sun rises, so do I rise. When the day is as dark as ashes, so am I dark.

I await somewhat breathlessly news from Mars, should this news reach the public. My question is: will the sun and moon turn to face those who look up from the Martian soil, or will they keep their backs turned? I will question the Vector when he reappears. I will ask him to keep up with the rumors as they surface. There is never a paucity of rumors! I was taught that the planets hang like fruit from a tree, that the motion they make is caused by a wind generated by the gods in conflict and in conversation. This verity is outdone, however, by troublesome rumors. Just prior to my arrest it was whispered in the streets that those who went to the "Martian Lamp" were in no way impeded by a branch or a string.

I was taught that some lamps burn oil and others fuel themselves. I would like to know if the Mars Lamp is made of fire or clay or a luminous dust. I am well aware asking such questions is unwise. If I could, I would ask Gazali. If there were still astronomers, I would ask them. But the Vector is the only one I have and he has, after all, proved a sympathetic witness to my sorry state; he appears to approve my mission to become a fully integrated saturate of self. To become a thing that knows nothing beyond *what it is*. (The Vector appears to think of me as one who has a sacred mission, who knows more than I know. I know nothing.)

*

Sometime later in the day, knuckling the vent, once again I was stung, stung to the quick on my thumb so that the swelling compromises this telling—yet I persist. For if thus far the conversation is one-sided, still it is ripe with possibility, its outcome unknown.

The question of the day is: have I been horneted (as it were) by the same hornet or not? These digressions—the knuckling, the horneting—disrupt my intentional project: to fossilize in place. For the pain in my thumb has awakened me to the fact that my body is the vessel of my mind and so myself.

*

Restless in the night, I recalled a poem my mother recited before she put me to sleep:

> *Do you not see how the fish*
> *Swallow the burning stars*
> *So that we may get on with*
> *Our evening?*
> *So that we may get on with*
> *Our dreaming?*

*

Today (such as it was) in a pool of light the size of a thumbnail, I found a saffron-complexioned hornet on the floor barely moving. Although it was surely she who had stung me twice, still I was entranced by the sight of a living thing on the floor beside me and in need of my attentions. I searched the floor centimeter by centimeter to see if by chance a crumb of sweet wax had fallen there and, sure enough, within a moment, I found a crumb big enough to excite a hornet's interest. Very slowly and making what I hoped was a reassuring murmuration, a cross between a droning or buzzing and a purring, I managed to approach her and to position this crumb before her face, a face with eyes of such intensity I felt their fire burn into mine. Slowly, and with unexpected grace, she approached the crumb and, with a paw, gave it a gentle knock so that it rolled closer. A trace of honey sparkled in what remained of the day's light.

I noticed that her body was striped with amber, and that her eyes were the color of blue apothecary bottle glass. A cobalt blue threaded with gold. Her face is elegant. She has what was once called a *frimousse*—meaning an irresistible, somewhat feline look: good cheekbones and a delicate, nicely proportioned chin. My beloved's face was like this; she too had a *frimousse*, and I could not help but find myself deeply taken with this tiny creature that is—as I am still—sentient. I could tell that this was so by the way her eyes met mine, the way she prodded the wax with her little paw, the way she tilted her head this way and that, the way she gazed at the crumb only to then gaze upon me, then gaze back at the crumb once again. In this way the day passed into night. Its arrival was sudden, as if a lid had come crashing down upon us. As carefully as I could, I rolled away from her so as not to frighten her, and, afraid that I might unwittingly harm her in my sleep, remained awake and vigilant throughout the night.

*

Morning came in this way: something like a tear of light appeared just beneath the air vent; the vent itself was not visible; the tear descended farther and then became a smudge; over the minutes the smudge solidified, gathered a certain muscle and heft, and all at once became a bright octagon. At this moment in time, the sun swarmed the vent, providing one bright rectangle, bright enough to illuminate the sleeping hornet, who lay comfortably extended, her ambers, ebony, and gold marvelous to see. Her eyes were closed, and the crumb? The crumb was gone. Instant by instant, as safely as I could, I walked to the pitcher and dipped my finger in the water. Returning to her with a wet finger, I let a drop or two fall a centimeter or so from her face. Her eyes opened then, and when she gazed into mine, every nerve in my body awakened to a delicious stinging, banishing each and every thought I had had and might have had about intentional fossilization. Then she stood up.

The movement she made was somewhere between that of a cat and a camel. That is to say, her bottom rose first and as it ascended so did she stretch out her front quarters, her little arms and paws reaching out before her. I noticed how slender her legs are (she has six!), they could not be trimmer, and her paws! They could not be more delicate.

Theophrastus said: *Some stones are rare and small, such as the Smaragdos.* It came to me that as my hornet was (surely) rare and as she was small, I should name her Smaragdos, so I did.

Smaragdos! I murmured. The day has begun, and it is ours! The Vector will come, and when he does, I will request more honeycomb, as I see you have polished off the crumb as I intended. Smaragdos then bowed her head and, closing her eyes as if in expectation of delight, stuck out her tongue, a tongue as delicate as a silk thread, and lapped up the little pool of water.

*

At some point or other during the morning, and after she had breakfasted, Smaragdos took off through the air vent and I continued with my account of things (such as they are). The Plotinus neglected to bring me breakfast, and so when the Vector showed up, I was nearly delirious with gratitude. For one thing he had brought two breakfast rolls tucked away in his Ginza and studded with raisins. And! As I had dreamed, another little jar of honeycomb appeared an instant after. This morning I breakfasted like a king. I secreted the second roll within my uppermost sack, where it would provide not only tomorrow's meal, but a little warmth. (It had just come from the baker's!) I was uncertain if I could risk sharing with the Vector my good news about having a companion named Smaragdos; I also feared that to speak of her out loud might compromise my luck and she might never return. I said nothing, but, thinking of her all the while, was careful to drop a good-sized crumb of wax to the floor, for despite my fears, I was optimistic, certain she would be back, that the stinging I had felt when our eyes met, she had felt too.

*

Are you, I asked the Vector, familiar with the words of Theophrastus?

It is not safe to speak of Theophrastus, the Vector whispered, but . . . the Plotinus is currently under repair (or so I have been told), having collided with a second Plotinus in the corridor. Both are under repair, he added, his whispering grating on my ear like sandpaper.

I have been thinking about Theophrastus myself, he added, for yesterday a house was burned down along with its library and an exemplary collection of pottery. As the fire was immensely hot, the pottery exploded, creating a terrific ruckus in the neighborhood. When later I heard what had happened, I recalled what Theophrastus said about the many stones that break and fly into pieces as if they are fighting against being burnt—like pottery, for example.

It has puzzled me, I said to the Vector, that Theophrastus would speak of pottery but a moment after speaking of true stones such as the Smaragdos! As I said this my heart leapt, for never had I expected

95

to have such a conversation with anyone locked away as I was in my closet! And it leapt—need I say it—because I had found a way to say her name *out loud*—not to myself but to the Vector, another person entirely. (Or so I presume.)

*

After the Vector left, things became stranger. In some ways they became better because I could no longer hear the dreadful racket the Plotinus made when it raged through the corridors, up and down, back and forth. But I did hear a commotion somewhere far away in the streets, and at the same time, the pleading on the porch (or balcony?) beside me worsened. There was also a fair amount of smoke coming through my air vent—a thing I should have the right to complain about. And I feared for my beloved Smaragdos, for I knew the smoke would offend her as well. I also heard explosions and supposed more pottery was losing its battle with fire.

This digression reminds me that just when I had the chance to ask the Vector as to the nature of what lay on the other side of the wall, I forgot.

*

All day (such as it is) I wait planted in one spot so that I may scrutinize the air vent. Again and again my thoughts return to that moment of moments when my beloved, her tongue a thread of silk, appears as if on fire and of a sudden—as does a falling star. When she does appear (it must happen!), a sky studded with dead planets will once again be hung with mirrors.

I have resolved that when she reappears, I will greet her with my eyes and direct my gaze (and so her own) to the crumb and its pond. I will look on in a fever as she paws the crumb and tongues the water.

*

It comes to me, after a day on my feet, that truth is *not* found in consequences (i.e., my restless waiting), but, in this current moment at least—is the *cause* of consequences (my restless waiting). The truth is the moment Smaragdos's tongue prods the crumb. (This gesture is ambiguous.)

*

My beloved's eyes are like candles of camphor.

*

Smaragdos is not a hornet as much as she is a fairy.

*

My night was mired in perplexity. My second sack had vanished—an impossibility as none but the Vector and nothing but the Plotinus— now too compromised to travel—could enter my closet. Not only that! My second breakfast roll, the one that had given me such unaccustomed warmth, had vanished as well. I am certain I had not eaten it. Vividly, I recall my decision to keep it for the morning. There was nothing to do but search the closet's every corner (all four of them) in the dark, taking care not to disturb the previous crumbs until the roll revealed itself; it did not. Nor did the yellow socks, which mattered to me as much, exist anywhere within reach. I spent the night on my knees, a mad hope in my heart, and then, when the sun came up (a thing I am unable to actually witness), I stared into each and every corner, only to once again find nothing. The crumb too remained unscrutable, but at least I knew it was there; my eyesight, never very good, has, or so it seems, been further compromised by my unrelenting seclusion. (I have lost all notion of time, such as it is.)

*

Today I returned to my position beneath the air vent as is my custom, to continue my coded rapping. After all, this activity has precipitated my quickening, the assurance that despite evidence to the contrary, *life is happening!* I know I risked a sting; I longed for that sting. Smaragdos's sting rings my bell; its vibrations—so like the fluids emanating from the sun and moon—assure that the moments proceed rather than sink into one another.

*

Living under diminished circumstances (to put it mildly) means that one is apt to make mistakes of judgment. Today I did just that. I spoke to the Vector about Smaragdos, her beauty and the stings she had inflicted. Told him that her stings had precipitated a quickening, the assurance that life continues to happen. I told him that Smaragdos's sting is like the ringing of a bell, that its vibration (how it rocked my entire being!) is akin to the fluids emanating from the sun and moon; her sting assures a feeling of instantaneity—a feeling I have not felt for many months or longer; years, perhaps. Her sting's reverberations flood a body with light; they illumine the heart and mind. I told him of her fairy ways, how I looked on with admiration as she prodded the crumb with a grace the likes of which I had never seen.

All I desire, I said to the Vector, is to witness such beauty each day—even if at a certain distance. (It is true that all I have ever desired of the world is beauty, yet I have been mightily punished for this desire.)

Until that moment, the Vector had looked upon me with something like awe, even affection. But now he appeared to rise above me like a hydraulic lift, to take on height and heft. His visage veered rufulus and his mood erupted.

To love an animal, he scolded, is as hateful as loving a member of one's own sex. It is abhorrent in the eyes of the Archons, the heart of the Hierophant, the mind of the Vectory, the souls of the planets, the ears of the Mantis. When the Mantis hears of such madness, his ears bleed. For it is said:

> *The one who lusts for the hornet*
> *buggers the beardless youth.*

But! I began . . . The Vector turned away, his face frozen to the opposite wall. But! Don't you see? I attempted, addressing the back of his Ginza. This was too much for the Vector, who had already vanished as if in a puff of smoke and never to return.

*

The Vector gone, there was no hope for breakfast, let alone conversation. The Vector be damned, I thought, the Mantis be damned. I returned to my position beneath the vent, and with my knuckles continued my narration with something like a vengeance, thinking of the possible pleasures ahead as well as the risks. Such considerations were abruptly canceled by a harrowing sting, followed by the sudden encounter face-to-face with a hornet at least three times the size of Smaragdos who had come to settle accounts. In no time he had toured my closet, polished off the honeyed crumb, and, his wings ferociously buzzing, helicoptered in place an inch from my nose, all the while threatening me with his eyes.

*

I spent the night famished and scolding myself. For a time I would scold myself, and then I would imagine the things I would order if there had been a way to order takeout. Before I knew it, I was wandering Fred's Grocery, that church of absolute and authentic good, its unfailing magnitude, its everlasting qualities extending in all directions simultaneously and never depleted, never knowing exhaustion.

When morning came, my misery was unrelenting still, for I knew the day ahead offered nothing but solitude unrelenting. I would not see Smaragdos again, I would not see the Vector, I doubted I would see the Plotinus ever again. It was rumored he was in bad shape and, in the words of the Vector, replaceable parts were nonexistent. But then, sometime early in the afternoon, a novel Plotinus appeared silently on rubber wheels to hand me an object I had never actually seen (but had heard about somewhere or other) called The Frozen Taco. It *was* terribly cold and at first I thought it was an ice-cream sandwich. When I bit into a frozen pickle I was disabused. The taco came with a small envelope of hot sauce that had expired in a previous century. This I rubbed on my swollen thumb. And then the unexpected happened.

It was already dark when somewhere deep in the bowels of the facility a light appeared. This light was bearing down on me. Indeed, within moments, the novel Plotinus, wearing a headlamp, appeared before me rattling his keys. Before I knew what was happening, a new Vector—or Vectoress, rather—stood before me. Despite the fact that it was hard to see anything clearly, I could see that she was beautiful, her eyebrows unusually splendid and her nostrils as delicate as those of an insect. The moment we were alone, she pulled a box of halvah out from under her Ginza. Her name was Jane.

I know, she said, of the trouble you caused with the Vector, and I have come, and will continue to come, in his stead. His hatred of the animal kingdom and of all things feminine is notorious. As I know a thing or two about his own weaknesses . . . she took a breath and whispered: The Mantis—I have his promise that you will not be prosecuted. She then poked around beneath her Ginza and handed me a cold, fizzy drink. Seeing my excitement (I believe I was panting), she popped it open before handing it over. I had not had fresh water for days, so you can well imagine how much this meant to me. It was something from the brand Past Time called Tumerzip. It tasted terrific. So terrific something deep in my brain popped open and incandesced.

I am here, the Vectoress continued, as a friend. I have also brought you a supply of honey. It is in an invisibility bottle—I wish I could tell you how I managed *that*! And it comes with its own spoon. Having tasted of the crumb—and yes, the Vector told me everything—Smaragdos will likely return the instant you open the jar.

Having reassured me in this way, she left me, but not without promising to return the following night. (The Vectoress is only allowed mobility at night.) Before her departure, she secreted the empty soda can within her Ginza. As I have no furnishings, I did very much wish I could have held on to it.

As soon as the Vectoress was gone, I cautiously opened the box of halvah. The wrapping was clean, and the halvah, pistachio, somehow fresh and moist. I dug into it with my little spoon, recalling the words of a prophet: Halvah is the most noble of pleasures. I could tell right away that it had come from Fred's. This got me thinking, if sporadically, of Fred's all day.

*

At the time of my arrest, Fred's Grocery was the only one left in the universe. Even then the place was more like a museum than a grocery. For example, it had cans of sardines that had fossilized, and a slice of Egyptian cheese over seven thousand years old.

*

Fred's Grocery was unique in its attempt to create a space in which to contemplate things such as the handsome pyramidal cheeses made from the milk of camels, to cones of sugar. It was a place, perhaps the only place in the known universe quiet enough, its inventory inventive enough, its star-studded ceiling beautiful enough, to provide an atmosphere in which to ponder the nature of things. It was at Fred's, sitting on a barrel of nuts, that I came to understand that an egg puts itself together as thoughtfully as a crystal.

*

How I wish I could look out the vent and see the planets in all their variety and in motion. Then I could appreciate their beauty and at the same time acquire a far clearer sense of time's passage.

*

Some time ago, I attempted to share thoughts such as these with the Vector, who warned me that if I continued such speculating alone in my closet *aloud* I risked being swallowed whole by the quicksand of monody. I replied that although this might well be true, silence was a far greater threat than quicksand. When the Vector heard this, he whispered into my ear, his breath's stink searing what remained of my capacities. He said: According to the law, the persistent monologuist shall lose his head. You must know, he added maliciously, that it is evident to everyone: he already has.

It is easy to lose a head, I replied, when arrested on one's stoop and thrashed to within an inch of one's life for stepping out holding a knobby stick. If I practiced silence in solitude, I might as well turn to stone. He reminded me that only recently had I considered this seriously. As Smaragdos had rekindled my fire, I had forgotten about it.

When one is a monologuist, I continued, one cannot help but monologize, and so, despite these warnings, I went on to say that as all things both inert and not are inevitably in contemplation, one day each and every one will awaken aware within its form, knowing it is the idealization of an idea! Then and then only will all things come together in a point of blinding light, ignite, explode, and scatter. Once this scattering comes to a standstill, all things will start over again.

There cannot be a scattering in the mind of the Mantis! the Vector shrieked, stamping his feet and causing the fire alarm to go off and the sprinkler system overhead to send a violent shower of water down upon us. The Vector fled my closet drenched, as I, tearing the sack from my body, used it like a loofah to rub myself down in a deluge that lasted a good twenty minutes. The night proved cold and damp, but in the morning I stood beneath the vent and felt the sun worm its way through to settle on my cranium, my neck, and shoulders. In this way I spent the day (such as it was). I could not stop shivering, but I was spotless. My mood soaring, it came to me that the world

101

(as I imagined it) had come together, or, at the very least, was coming together, or would, perhaps with luck, come together, and that if it did not, at the very least I was renewed (if hungry and needing a night's sleep). By tomorrow, I thought, I will be as prepared as a man can be to greet his beloved in the light (such as it will be), should she return, surfing the rays of the morning sun.

*

But now! This morning (such as it is) I realize that the shower I took yesterday was *before* yesterday, before any number of yesterdays, but not *too many* as, after all, Smaragdos had come into my life only recently. (Of this I am certain.) I wondered aloud what it was I could do, alone as I was, standing in a dark and damp place wearing a sack, longing for my beloved with nothing at hand with which to enchant her. I was like a bowerbird abandoned on a glacier. But then I recalled a magazine article I read in my youth, an old article but wise, that lay on our street in the rain as if it had been intended for me. The article was titled: Celestial Man and the Power of Positive Thinking.

The gist of the article was: the world is tricked out with snares and dubious distractions. Sooner or later it is inevitable that one will fall on bad times. But if you can muster the necessary pluck and spunk, the ambition and the imagination, if you have the proficience, the competence and preparedness, the qualifiedness and credentials, then the universe will open its arms for you and you will proceed with vigor in safety, a lucky star forever orbiting your head top.

I recall being excited by this discovery, excited by its message of hope, but I was also struck by the words: head top; perhaps the article had been translated from another language, yet I could not help but continue reading. Turning the page over, I saw that the article continued on its backside, ending with an advertisement for a pill named Proficience. (Later, when I spoke to the Beauty about it, she said: My dearest, you fool, do you not understand we are made helpless so that fortunes may be made on pills? Use your head top, my love, she added, mussing my hair with her little hand.) I should add that the article continued in this way: The gods will direct you to Luck's portal; you will ignore the son of Chaos, who guards its gates; you will acknowledge but bypass the angels of the interior Heavens, and take the stairs (or maybe a ladder, who knows; perhaps they pass out wings)—all the way to the . . . (the rest was unclear, having been submerged in mud).

*

Recalling all these things, I stood alone tied to a wheel of inescapable questions: What had become of the sack the Vector had brought me, the socks? What had become of the honey the Vectoress had given me in an invisible jar? I could not escape the wheel although I did everything I could to follow the instructions Gazali had given me so very long ago (or so it seems) on how to imagine my mind as a bird. You may choose a gull or a raven, he said, a falcon, a parrot, or a flamingo. The point is not the bird but to fly unrestrained by Space or Time. Beauty informs the vast universe with a grace and with intention, he said; worlds are in harmonious conversations with one another; the stars are ecstatic realms, each one a well-trimmed lamp, giving off a steady light, quivering in the vastness of everlasting possibility.

And then it happened. Or, rather, the Vectoress happened. I mean to say that, her beauty ablaze, her eyebrows the shadow side of the crescent moon, she appeared of a sudden. I had not heard her coming, no Plotinus lit the way, nor had I realized how dark it was. I had spent the entire day on my feet, in my one sack, upbraiding myself, thinking out loud: I qualify! Do I qualify? What if I do not qualify?

The Vectoress stood before me, her beauty blazing, as if she were herself a moon, a sun, an entire galaxy. Opening her arms, her Ginza unfurling like the wings of a butterfly, she embraced me and, holding me close to her heart, as Beauty had in another life, said: Rest assured, you qualify. It is the world that does not qualify.

*

After the Vectoress departed, I lay on my back and attempted to sleep. She had brought no gifts, but so great was my joy in seeing her, I was not aware of this until after she was gone. I thought that if my mind were a raven, I would sleep and I would dream. And I did.

A/part: Notes on Solitude
Kyoko Mori

UNLIKE MOST JAPANESE COUPLES of their generation, my parents married for love in 1954 over the objections of their families, but three years later when I was born, my father, Hiroshi, was having an affair with a woman who worked as a bar hostess. She was the first (and the last) of many girlfriends he had, serially and consecutively. An engineer for the manufacturing conglomerate Kawasaki Steel, Hiroshi worked till late, went out drinking with his coworkers, visited his girlfriends, and returned home long past my bedtime. My mother, Takako, waited up for him, but I don't recall my parents ever holding hands, hugging, or laughing together. My friends' parents, who'd had arranged marriages, at least sat together for dinner on weekends and went on family vacations in the summers, but Hiroshi and Takako were seldom in the same room, in my memory. My father might as well have inhabited a separate galaxy. But they had one thing in common: their inability to be happy alone.

Until I was ten and my parents were thirty-nine, we lived in a newly built apartment complex in a seaside neighborhood in Kobe that the company rented to employees who were saving money to buy their own houses. Japanese people in the 1960s did not take out mortgages, so only the men being groomed to join the upper management could hope to save enough funds. The fathers in our building, which had twenty apartments on four floors, were reputed to be "*shigoto no oni*"—monsters of work—ambitious men who seldom had time for anything but work, but mine was the busiest. Although other fathers also went drinking at the end of the day and some of them, no doubt, had girlfriends as well, Hiroshi spent his weekends playing rugby with his former college teammates, and he didn't accompany my mother, brother, and me on our summer trips to beach or mountain resorts or to my mother's parents' house in the country.

None of the mothers in our building worked outside the home. Every afternoon when I returned from school, a dozen of them were sitting at our kitchen table, laughing and chatting. Each woman had brought her knitting, sewing, or embroidery so the table was covered with yarn, thread, and sewing notions, along with the cups of tea and plates of cookies my mother had baked. I would drop off my books and go outside to join the gang of kids playing hide-and-seek, kick the can, or some war game we made up. Soon the mothers would be returning to their own kitchens to prepare dinner.

Men spent time with men, women with women, and children with children—until we children came home. My friends and I never wondered if our mothers were bored eating dinner night after night with only us for company, or if they felt burdened when we brought our friends over and they had to serve us snacks and entertain us. I cannot remember when I became aware that our fathers traveled all over the country on business and had several sets of friends as well as illicit girlfriends, we children had neighborhood friends and school friends and were allowed to play unsupervised away from our building or visit school friends who lived in different neighborhoods from ours, while our mothers did not leave home except to shop for groceries at a nearby supermarket and attend PTA meetings at our school, and they had only one another—their immediate neighbors—to befriend.

If I didn't notice, it's because my mother was happy back then. Our apartment was where the women gathered to drink tea and do their crafts, or to try the baking recipes my mother had found in magazines. Takako was the oldest of six children, and in the summers when her family congregated at my grandparents' house in the country, my uncles and aunts clustered around her to listen to her stories and ask for her advice. Friends and family alike said Takako could light up a room by just walking in. Even my friends vied for her attention and told me over and over, "Your mother is so pretty," "She is so kind and funny," "I love coming to your house." None of them would have recognized the woman who sat alone in her new home, unable to move from the dark and cold kitchen to a sunnier room upstairs.

Our family was the first to buy a house of our own, in a quiet neighborhood on a hill that was famous for its "million-dollar view" of the city below. From the rooms upstairs, we could see Osaka Bay in the distance and at night, the glittering neon lights of the business and entertainment districts. In the back of the house, separated by a brook, was a large park with an arboretum. In the summer with our windows open, we could hear bush warblers—Japanese nightingales—trilling their songs among the branches. But my mother hated

105

that house. The pine trees in the backyard cast shadows on the kitchen, she said, making it cold, dark, and gloomy.

I now returned from school to find her sitting alone, and there was nothing on the table unless it was an empty or cold cup of tea. Takako couldn't get herself interested in knitting, sewing, embroidery, baking, or any other hobby that used to give her pleasure. She didn't visit homes in the neighborhood to try and get to know the other women. The apartment building was just a few miles from where we now lived, but neither she nor her friends knew how to drive. Besides, women from "good families" didn't go cruising around town to amuse themselves alone or in a group. Takako couldn't even stroll through the park behind our house unless my brother and I were with her because a woman out in public by herself caused suspicion. She had only been able to spend long afternoons with her friends because none of them had to leave the building to sit in her kitchen. They were all staying home as expected.

Having purchased a residence in an exclusive neighborhood and installed us there, my father stopped coming home almost entirely. He claimed to be traveling for business every week, and even when he was supposed to be working in town, he called from some noisy bar past midnight to say he was leaving on a trip after all. As I sat in the kitchen to keep her company, my mother cried and said that she was a complete failure as a wife; she would have nothing to live for once my brother and I grew up and left. It was no use reminding her that my brother, who was sleeping upstairs, had just started first grade and I too was still in elementary school. Two years later, when Takako killed herself, leaving a note to say that she was nothing but a burden to everyone, I was not surprised. Being alone every afternoon—and imagining endless years of being even more alone—had killed her.

I didn't have an occasion to observe my father with his friends, but my aunt—his sister—always said he was the life of the party wherever he went. He played rugby with his old friends until a year before his death at sixty-six from cancer. At his funeral, which I missed but heard about from my aunt, his work friends and rugby friends talked about how they had looked up to him—such a generous, smart, and kind man—and, throughout the service, young women who had worked as his secretaries and receptionists dabbed their eyes with their handkerchiefs. His longtime girlfriend, the bar hostess, who had not been allowed to attend the funeral, called my aunt the next day to reveal that Hiroshi had telephoned her whenever my stepmother—

the girlfriend he married a few months after my mother's death—stepped out of his hospital room. Unlike my mother, my father never had to be alone with no one to talk to.

My parents were both charismatic extroverts, and I was the opposite. I looked forward to the rainy days when I could play alone in my room. There was so much to occupy myself with: piles of books, some from the library, others my own; various notebooks in which I wrote adventure stories and fairy tales and illustrated them with colored pencils; several sets of paper dolls—families from around the world, kings and queens, famous artists and musicians—which I dressed and then mixed up deliberately so I could imagine what had brought the unlikely characters together. I was also obsessed with origami: I folded tiny paper cranes that I sorted by color and size and kept in a dozen decorative boxes. I was always surprised and disappointed when the day was over and it was time for dinner.

I wasn't awkward or shy with my peers—I just preferred my own company. The best month I spent in elementary school was during my third grade when school was closed to prevent the spread of chicken pox. The only child in the entire neighborhood who didn't get sick, I rode my bike wherever I wanted, walked on a deserted beach collecting seashells, and pretended I was creating a city in an abandoned construction site by digging holes and stacking rocks into towers. I still remember the thrill of having the whole neighborhood to myself. Since every other child in the building, including my brother, was sick, I was allowed to be out all day so long as I followed the simple rules for staying safe: don't talk to strangers, don't accept food from them or get into their cars, and don't be late for dinner.

Two years later, crying every night in our new house, my mother made me promise that I would not be like her. "You are smart and strong," she said over and over. "You can't end up like me." She didn't elaborate, but I understood what she meant. She didn't want me to throw my life away by marrying a man like my father. I had to take care of myself and not depend on anyone. Neither of us realized at the time how unnecessary this advice was. She was right when she imagined her future without me. If she had lived, I would still have moved away to pursue my own life, something a Japanese woman from "a good family" could accomplish only by leaving the country to spare her family from gossip. Long before my mother became miserable enough to die, I was happier alone than with anyone, even her.

*

I used to claim that I needed to be alone to write, but the truth is the opposite. I became a writer to justify all the hours I wanted to spend by myself behind a closed door.

In the 1980s in a small town in Wisconsin, I wrote my first novel in the makeshift office that the former owner of the house had built in the basement: a room with a cement floor and a bare bulb hanging from the ceiling. I started every writing session by going over what I had finished the day before. I reread each sentence, then crossed out, rephrased, added, and moved the words around. Tinkering with the pages put me into a dream state in which I could imagine stepping off the ledge of a tall building and being able to continue walking straight ahead, which is what writing, rather than revising, felt like. Only in this dream state could I go on to the next, unwritten part, and proceed to form new words.

Every morning after my run, I descended the steps to the study that resembled an interrogation room to work on a possibly doomed project, because I was drawn to the intensely private concentration that writing required. Just like on those rainy childhood afternoons with my paper dolls and origami cranes, I was making, arranging, and sorting through what I could keep, mesmerized by the order and pattern of what I managed to accumulate. I was more attached to my novel in progress than I had been to my toys, and yet the pleasure of being alone for hours to daydream and have something to show for it: that was exactly the same.

I was married during those years. Because I had heeded my mother's advice, my husband was nothing like my father, who cheated on my mother and still expected her to serve him tea and a late-night dinner if he chose to come home. My spouse accepted that I didn't talk to him or anyone in the morning before I sat down to write (I believed there were only so many words my brain could produce every day and I couldn't afford to squander them on idle talk, at least not until I'd done my quota of writing for the day). He tiptoed around the house and only played instrumental music on the stereo so the words floating around the living room would not interfere with those in my head, one story below. We were both teachers, though, and my time off from the college where I taught coincided with his from his elementary school. So, eight years into our marriage, I rented a small apartment to write in, a few miles away from our house. Five years later, I moved there to live.

That was more than twenty years ago, and I haven't lived with another human being since. As I told him, I didn't leave because he'd failed to be considerate. He was the only person I could have been married to for thirteen years. But sooner or later I had to accept: I can't be my true self unless I'm alone; I can't think with another person breathing and thinking his own thoughts in the space where I am trying to do the same.

My solitude, however, is not pure or simple. All my adult life, I've lived with cats who—contrary to the common stereotype—followed me around and plastered themselves to me. Dorian, my first cat, watched over my writing in the basement office, commuted with me to the apartment I rented to write in, and of course moved there with me when I got divorced. My eighteen years with Dorian is the longest time I've gotten to spend alone together with anyone: *alone, together*—that's how I think of the relationship between my cats and me. It is neither solitude nor companionship. It's more of a merging, an expansion of the self into another being. If Dorian, or his current successors, Miles and Jackson, could speak, I'm sure they would agree that the flow of energy or spirit between us is constant and mutual: I am them and they are me. They are the part of me who watches from a nearby perch while I go deep into my mind to retrieve the words I need to put on the page. I am the part of them who goes out into the world to earn our living. We are one another's lifeline.

My cats are not substitutes for a partner, children, family, or friends. Our relationship is fundamentally different. Every human relationship requires a negotiation of the constantly shifting boundary between individuals, or between the individual and the group: we go back and forth, getting closer, merging, separating, establishing some distance, then starting all over again. This ebb and flow is the challenge and the reward of marriage, family, friendship, mentorship, perhaps even patriotism or loyalty to an institution. Whether we're married or single, with or without families, we define ourselves through our interactions—positive, negative, intimate, distant, at times even hostile—with others around us: we know who we are because we are like them but we are not them.

My cats don't offer or demand the same exploration of solidarity and autonomy, and it's not because they (supposedly) don't impose many restrictions on my life. Dorian, a Siamese cat who was extremely possessive, terrorized all my friends by biting them. Miles, another Siamese, paces in circles around me as if he's trying to corral me; he too is a one-person cat though he is quietly disdainful rather than violent or aggressive toward other humans. Jackson, an easygoing Burmese, clambers onto my lap and presses his head against my hand until I start petting him. Their demand for my attention breaks the endless loops of thoughts, impressions, reverie—or idle chatter—circulating through my mind. With them around, I'm not trapped inside my head, but because I don't perceive them as *other*, whatever they want (and sometimes, it's a long play session that interrupts the paragraph I've been trying to write) doesn't put me in the defensive mode that the intrusion of other humans almost always does. I pay attention to the cats and resume whatever I was doing. My cats draw me out and then return me, whole, to myself. Being with them is the same and not the same as being alone: they complicate and expand my solitude.

Alone at home all day, my mother felt trapped and diminished. After several hours away from home, surrounded even by my closest friends, I feel my entire being contracting into a pebble, soon to become a speck of dust. "I need to get out of here," I think (or sometimes even say). That's what my mother must have thought too, in her cold and dark kitchen. She was longing for the sense of freedom and wholeness she once enjoyed among her friends, just as I long for the sense of freedom and wholeness I can only experience at home, alone together with my cats. I never wanted children because I was certain that being with young children all day long—not having a moment to myself—would make me feel depleted and worn down. Takako worried that she would become further diminished when my brother and I left home. In our opposite ways, we wanted and want the same thing: to be our true complete selves.

My mother was suffering from isolation: she was cut off and disconnected from the outside world she needed to draw sustenance from. Although Webster's defines solitude as "the quality or state of being alone or remote from society" and lists "isolation" as its synonym, the two are not the same. *Isolation* results from an action—its verb form, *isolate*—that forcibly separated the person from the whole he or she belonged to. Alone, my mother felt broken, like a tree cut down and removed from the forest's canopy. For me, by contrast, being alone is the natural state. Surrounded by too many people for too long, I feel fragmented, disconnected. Without solitude, I become isolated from the private world that sustains me.

Home is the most important place for my solitude, but unlike my mother, I am free to come and go. In Washington, DC, where I live now, I begin each morning with a run through Rock Creek Park and through various neighborhoods where I observe the weather, the seasons, the ceaseless human activity, trees and flowers, birds and other wildlife, and the national buildings and monuments with their complex, often troubling history. Far from being "remote," I'm immersed in both human society and the natural world, whether I'm running or, later in the day, looking out the window at the mourning doves, chickadees, finches, sparrows, and cardinals pecking at the sunflower seeds in the feeder I installed on the window ledge to amuse the cats. Immersed and yet choosing, mostly, to be separate.

In my late twenties, still married, I found myself needing two kinds of solitude. Spending hours alone with my writing continued to satisfy my craving for quiet concentration, but the work required an active, complicated kind of solitude. I had to pay attention to every word I pulled out of my mind and put on the page, yet I also had to be in a dream state that allowed me to believe I could make something—a story or an essay—that didn't exist until I wrote it. Being alone at my desk was at once exhilarating and exhausting. To complement the hours I spent there, I needed a less fraught kind of solitude, an interlude during which I was simply an observer or amateur practitioner. Running—once I stopped competing, as I did in high school—was a source of this simpler solitude, but that only gave me an hour or two every day. So I took up a host of other solo activities such as cycling, bird-watching, museum visits.

For a while I was able to balance time for my writing, time for other solitary activities, and time with my husband. But I couldn't manage solitude, marriage, *and* community while also trying to write and teach. I had a handful of close friends from graduate school and a few I had met since, but I struggled to make time for them. I volunteered at the nature center and the homeless shelter in town, only to stop after a couple of years when I felt overwhelmed.

"One is the loneliest number that you'll ever do," claimed a popular song in my youth. For me, two was the worst number. I was more isolated, perhaps even lonely, during my marriage than in the years I lived alone before and after. Like my mother, I was cut off from community. Even though my spouse was not a demanding person, being married meant my default mode was company, so every chance I got, I tried to be alone. When Dorian and I moved to my studio, the balance

111

was reversed and righted. I no longer had to spend hours walking in the woods with binoculars or driving to faraway cities to see art exhibits: I could be alone with Dorian every second I was home. With solitude as my default mode, I had a chance to spend time with friends and volunteer in the community when I wanted to.

I have never believed in the notion of the better half—the myth that humans were originally created with four arms, four legs, and two heads and that Zeus split us in two and condemned us to spend our lives in search of the missing half. I actually feel incomplete without my cats, but our union is a free-form, shape-shifting mystery, not a precise fitting together of half with half. When we were married, I thought of my husband as one of the people I could turn to for help if needed, but not as *the* person who was responsible for my happiness and welfare. The idea of having "a special someone" to take care of me always and forever struck me as oppressive and absurd. Even my mother could not do that for me, or I for her, and if we had managed to, then our relationship would have been as stultifying, or deadly, as her isolation in the house she hated. We would have stunted and suffocated each other in the shadow of those pine trees.

What could have turned her isolation into solitude and kept her alive was not a daughter or a husband but a community. My mother didn't have the opportunities to work outside the home or to participate in volunteer activities or political action. Her parents lived a day's journey away and her siblings had their own families. Without the friends who gathered in her kitchen every afternoon, she had just my brother and me: we were her only emissaries to and from the outside world. No wonder she imagined her future as endless years of isolation. I don't believe each of us needs one devoted companion, a soul mate, whether it's a husband, wife, mother, father, or child. But we absolutely need friends, colleagues, neighbors, a group of like-minded people. Solitude only makes sense when we're connected to the world around us: we can't be apart unless we can be a part of.

I chose a single life and a community over marriage. My ex-husband is now one of the old friends I stay in touch with. He's visited me in Boston and in Washington, DC, the two cities I've lived in since leaving Wisconsin. And, like my mother when she was happy, I make my home in an apartment building and have a couple (though not a dozen) neighbors who are my close friends. I too would have found the house on the hill gloomy and depressing in spite of its million-dollar view. I prefer to be in the midst of society, where I can carve out a small space to be alone and quiet.

I have no desire to live like a hermit on vast acres of land or spend a night in a tent pitched in a wilderness, but in the last five years I lived in Wisconsin, I drove out to the countryside by myself every August to watch the Perseids meteor showers. Just a few miles out of town, farmhouses were spaced far apart and no one drove there after midnight. I would pull over on the side of the road next to a hay-field, climb on top of the car's roof, and lie down. Meteors streaked across the sky every few minutes, some directly overhead, others in the periphery of my vision. There was no traffic on the roads, no planes in the sky. All I could hear was crickets, katydids, cicadas, and, once in a while, dogs barking in the distance. I didn't believe in God or the afterlife, and the traditional concept of heaven—an eternity spent with multitudes of people who managed to hold on to the same creed through life's vicissitudes—was more horrifying than any vision of hell or the possibility of complete annihilation. But alone in the dark under the shooting stars that were actually particles of dust, I could imagine what death was like and not be afraid: just the essence of me going on in the universe, released from who I was. Death, I hoped, would be the ultimate solitude of being apart and yet a part of.

But I could only have these consoling thoughts about the universe and my mortality for about an hour before the sky began to look like a bottomless well I could drown in. Too much nature, for too long, was just as overwhelming as too much company for too long. The universe was so large and I was so small. This thought, though hardly new to me or to anyone, threatened to suffocate me and grind me down to nothing. So I would climb down from the top of the car, get behind the wheel, and head back to town. Even though I regretted leaving behind the stars that continued to fall, I knew I had to go.

Dorian was always at the door when I got home. He would flop down on the floor and wait for me to pick him up. With him in my arms, and my face buried in his fur, my mind expanded like a shriveled balloon receiving air. As we sat together on the couch, I could remember the dark country road as a place where I felt connected to the universe, to its endless space and time. Dorian was the part of me that stayed home and stayed safe: the keeper of my finite being. He secured me to myself so I could be alone.

That's what Miles and Jackson are doing for me now, mid-August

113

of this year of the coronavirus, as we shelter together from the global pandemic. The point of solitude is not to disappear from the world but to claim a small territory around the self, to say: I'm here, separate from everything that surrounds me, but a part of it. I no longer drive out to the countryside to watch the Perseids, but I know we are hurtling, once again, through a cosmic dust storm.

Eel in the Tree
David Ryan

BACK IN TOWN HE IS mostly alone in the shotgun house, but keeps to the upper floor, watching water rising receding listening to television news faces give status of levees while power is on again. Here for now, really, just wondering when will he really leave? There's this man from across the street, a name he always forgets, comes out on his porch. He watches him from one of the small pale windows where below on the floor jagged glass like scattered teeth, vandals, failed looters; glass in his hand, tumbler, more of Susan's brandy. The still air outside a pressure, a kind of boom boom but gently like mad breath. Like fear if it could breathe. Below those gutters foam bubbling over, but at least the rains have let up, he thinks—*you think*, and realize you have been dissociating again.

You've been moving between he and you. The sky all morning (it's afternoon) has been a kind of green nimbus shimmering gray, darker than expected, unusually quiet, veined in occasional specular lightning, a migraine knifing at some livid meat. All accustomed sounds gone—you would think this might make it easier to just sit and nod off on the sofa, or in the bedroom to lie down and drift into some kind of sleep, but that does not seem possible (in dream night before long black shapes streaked Sargasso Sea). Something has been neutralized in the surrounding space; the sky parts its wings, gives off slow air. Neighbor sitting across the street in his covered porch, stone still. (You recalled him there once on the porch a year or two ago with a kid you thought was slow maybe, the slow kid had a little toy dog that had a leash the kid could pull around, the kid was hugging the plastic dog in his arms, moving from side to side.) Then this neighbor rises and goes back inside his wet shack. You've never been in there, in his place (where he collects things: guns, busts of elk on the walls, a jackalope novelty on a stand on a desk, a trash can full of cleft hooves, freezer full of snouts and leg meat, wax candy wrappers wadded on the floor, little coils of copper wire so pretty in the glancing light, Catholic statues of Catholics, a hoard of live cats, Barbie dolls, and these hardened souls that hang suspended through the motes of dust and rays of light from the sun leaking in through the window, hard like candy souls that talk back at him with little mouths in these pockets of air, who snap aggressively as he tries to clear his goddamn thoughts, as he tries to clear the bubbles popping off his private rages of solitude, the *how goddamn you*, as he tries to *motherfucker* his finger pointing accusatorily at the *motherfuckers* on the wall, what you imagine are just these sad trapped cats everywhere bearing the souls of the Catholics, talking down to him, he imagines—you do, I mean). You stare at that porch imagining him in his house, the street glistening dark green and purple clouds welded as if forever now to the wrong sun.

And then a peripheral flick in the sky draws your eye up to that same neighbor's roof and up there you see that roof as you hadn't before. Your neighbor is on it now, above now pulling a rocking chair onto a landing there. He is wearing his hunting jacket, the red-plaid wool odd in the temperature (though perhaps it is a little cooler than usual).

A gold nerve breaks from the sky, just a sharp moment of it, and the neighbor looks up too. He looks up and grins and you look up and then it passes but they (you) both remain staring at the sky, which now seems suddenly to darken into something thicker.

You, staring out this broken window at your neighbor. Your solitude wanders between some Dasein of desire and time and then something between that's scrabbling at both, either, but can't take hold. You're scrabbling between this other house where you need to be, and this current space you can't leave. The other house, in the country, is small but has a grassy lot and a small garden, now killed off by the salt water that has entered the table, the wells; it isn't a city shotgun, a shack like this one. You trade certain conveniences (for instance, the proximity of the river, which is easy to long for). Here, now, down below, manhole covers spume and roil, bubbling up sewage an egg-white foam clings and recedes a threat threading around the bodies, the little pieces of skin and breath fishing the water. The city, now a network of tributaries. Two days ago there were no streets, really. Like Venice or certain places he had seen in Indonesia (seen on the television). None of the graves have lasted, they've burst up, the basin a lung breathing in and breathing out, a lung with a congenital disorder, pleuritic. (The curb gutters pause to listen. This thought. They wait congenially until you finish, then roil.)

Susan comes by and they have lunch. You have lunch. The roads

David Ryan

are fine for now, at least east, she says. I love you, she says, and he
loves her too (and it feels weird to say it at all, because it is so obvious, but it is important to say it, isn't it, isn't it now?). And he tells
her about the neighbor, you tell her about the man across the street
right there on the roof (and she says, I don't see him? but then she
does). He tells her about the story that man on the roof once told him
a year or two ago: about the other neighbor who had moved out, or
had they found him in his attic? (Death, a sackcloth and ashes.) The
eel in the tree story. Had you told Susan this? The eel and one of his
big fat magnolias, or that elm. A nice lunch, this is nice, Susan says;
God what I'd do for just some consistency, just some of the peace we
had once, she says, and they talk into the night and she has brought
that case of brandy he likes. She is talking about moving even farther
inland: a small apartment twenty minutes from the country house.
She has brought the brandy but also she brought the lunch—takeout
from an Italian that is still open, doing great business these days—an
eggplant parmesan (it's not anything he would think to eat or buy at
a store but this is good, a little salty, and you see the eggplants now
as if they are whole, as if they are taking up all the space of the aluminum tray, then growing out of it; Susan has peeled the shiny cardboard off and you see a magnolia uprooted flowing cascading along
the dirty water loosed on the street, but no, in this aluminum food
tray). She has lost weight but you don't say this. It's a little salty, you
say instead. It's good, you say, and she says: They're doing quite the
business these days. I can imagine, you say.

Here's to the future, she says, and closes her eyes again and laughs,
kind of—a habit-laugh, a muscle memory (in his mind, her silent
heaving laughs; she keeps doing it, just a kind of heaving ha ha ha ha
ha infinitely soundless, even as conversation resumes; she's talking
but also she's doubled, laughter writhing).

What are you looking at, she says. And you say: He's on his roof
again. Neighbor sitting, calm, waiting for something in the pressure
of the air. He is as close to God as he'll ever get, you think. Maybe,
you think, it's why he's up there.

What a strange man, she says and for a second you think she
means you. Or she does. Outside, thin tails of smoke rise black in
columns like snakes, like Susan's eyeliner when she reclines (Susan
lying on the chaise now—lipstick on her teeth, her entire face up
close to the sky—it is so easy to tire these days, she says: is it the air
quality?). Two helicopters cleave the mist. Hanging from one, some
kind of airlift dangling like live bait in a wire bin from a flimsy ladder;

117

David Ryan

on the ground below a stray dog is lapping at something in an over-turned shopping cart, the torn hole in a bag of trash, something unmistakably like a prosthetic leg sticking out.

And now Susan's mouth closes over the window, erases it, the helicopters, the dog below, and a collection of feelings presses from her words, gather there with her warm breath—she is not here (as you try to clear her teeth away like Chinese dragon smoke, as you try to clear the memory of her mouth now, as she exhales her menthols like a religious language emerging from the smoke, as you try to trap the clarity of her as if holding that smoke in your one hand, pointing the brandy tumbler in the other like a censer, brandy spilling out images of her face in different aspects of emotion strung in glass beads, hanging there in thin air).

It is getting darker, early, today. No, Susan is not here. She has left, hasn't she? Was she here? Yes, but not today, no. You are still hungry, or are hungry again. This was days ago. Gone back to the little house in the country and the silence. Where he—*you*—will join her soon. The helicopters are gone. It is getting darker too early, daylight wrapped inside sky a giant garbage bag around the godhead (how would you describe the water when it had risen? You, often so at such a loss to its particular nature; this water, it flowed in all declivities where common water might, though, no, more like an infusion of gum arabic, to paraphrase Poe, to say, not colorless of a singular color but flowing purple under the purple and green sky, like the hues and shimmer of silk. And in your mind all traces of the passage of a knife pressed into this water were instantly obliterated, the knife pressing into that water, but a separation effected, like a cut between veins, some bloodless passage, water parting, holding like tissue, like meat. You should have described this to Susan why didn't you; her dog, with beautiful eyes and black lips, and a good disposition, whose name you cannot recall, a human name, it sleeps and you can see the whites of its eyes curl up just a little, its legs twitching, chasing at black fish slapping in water), like razor cutting a single celluloid film frame from the one preceding—two nearly identical moments, severed now into their discretion. You, one way; him, another.

Her dog, at little house, in country. And now: outside your window. Across the street. The man on his roof takes his hunting jacket off. He carefully folds it up into a little parcel then sets it down on the shingles. Behind him the sky is this house full of cruel objects spinning in clouds, clouds capillaried, that gas burst in glowing coals from the ruptured factories, furniture upholstery like cilia tastefully

118

done in that French Quarter gallery, the ironic chaise a long black tongue (the other day you watched that bloated pig floating when the levee was higher, before this temporary recession, and the pig turned so innocently, twirling a kind of iridescent gray in the artificial rip in the artificial daylight, and there was a rainbow from the oil spilled around the creature, and this somehow recalled his experimental days long before, there was a needle under a flame, and there wasn't any rubbing alcohol just cheap vodka they dipped it in, and you decided to snort the heroin instead, as he sometimes would, just to kill off some of the late-night edge of the mescaline or the Hells Angels' amphetamine that was often damp still and yellow when they peeled it off the waxed paper and cookie trays in the back of that Sydney club) and your neighbor (how soon is now) he stands swaying and from his swaying it is clear that he is quite drunk now (but so are you; no, perhaps he is having a stroke? Are you? No you are drunk, have been for days now on the brandy Susan left). And your neighbor urinates off the roof and it is less a relieving, you can see, than a simple mimetic gesture of something from his past, spliced into this moment. And suddenly you feel a warmth in your body passing from inside you to the outside. An eminence, a rising of your own waters, crossing some threshold. The water outside on the streets is holding its breath, roiling and swelling anxiety in the gutters.

Just leaves his fly open. This neighbor once told you the story of that eel in the tree. Couple of hurricanes ago. He was pointing at neighbor Jimmy's house right over there. He said: We don't like each other (you knew this even then). Lot of bad blood. I think it started as he burned out a gas blower I lent him, refused to pay for it. So began my bad liking. But then this one day he comes out of his house. He is standing under one of his trees, that one there, the elm. I'm out on my porch sitting in my rocker assessing damage in my mind. I'm sitting there, I watch it like a movie. He sees me. And we don't say, Hi, which is acknowledging what is by then normal. And then he's standing under that tree when something black and long drops, just drops, from the branches above onto him. It's kind of thick and heavy and it has its own motion. I'm thinking it's a snake. And Jimmy does probably too. He's screaming now wrestling it off him, and then it drops to the ground and begins to sort of have a long black seizure there on his feet. It's an eel, turns out. It was carried by the storm winds, or maybe an owl dropped it. And he looks over at me after his fit. He accuses me of *throwing it at him*. You ever hear something like that? No, you say, said. You say it now, you're alone in your room watching your neighbor's mouth moving across the street, you're putting his story in it from a while ago.

No, you say. You hear something building in the distance and you want to close the window but there is no longer any glass in the pane. Just its broken teeth at your feet. Until this very moment you have not noticed your neighbor's rifle. It's up there now, on the roof, maybe a shotgun. (You recall grappa in that port town, some anonymous German city from which the overnight ferry would take you to Sweden. The last time the air had felt like this. Something about Hemingway and grappa, that it was free at the table and if you were poor you could come in and order bread and drink the grappa for free from the table and this somehow made it taste better to you in Germany waiting for the night ferry to take you to Sweden.) It is a long gun, your neighbor's gun; for moose or elk. There is no more crime for his gun really. I mean, the looters have all drowned is the joke (a kind of silent laughter that continues and you see Susan laughing again, but as if still laughing, like that silent fit hadn't ever stopped—some half-seen double of her there laughing even after her body left). The gun had been lying there flat on the roof all along while the neighbor sat there in his hunting jacket, which is still folded neatly on the roof. He takes a Styrofoam box out of a plastic bag, opens it. He lifts some barbecue up, ribs, pulled pork, it's hard to say. He shoves some food in his mouth, wipes his fingers on his pants.

The neighbor turns and sees you watching him. He sets the Styrofoam box down, and now he lifts the rifle, points the rifle up to the gods. Boom, boom. This is your cue.

Your cue, yes. It is time to leave. Thin dark lips open up on his face. He sets the rifle down flat on the roof again by the rocker. He turns back at you, raises his arm straight out.

A peacock screams, a lament, a plaint. It fans its tail feathers and a hundred eyes stare back at your brain. You've been moving between he and you. All accustomed sound gone.

And your neighbor cocks his finger. Arm extended, pointed. Cocks it like a gun. And then he pulls some trigger in you.

Four Poems
John Yau

UNTITLED (HOTEL)

The blue moon is not quivering, I am

Of heavenly flowers planted, fall, and stick

Sins or since, what does time matter

Now that I have so little left in which to dream

Tangled as I am, I do not want to leave

inflamed quagmire illuminating my brief stay

So much of it spent dreaming of you

I have, in my own eyes, become laughable

To think my thinking matters a whit in this wind

Living in a hotel room only I have a key to

Not even the owners know that I am here

Dwelling on the outskirts of town

I am not a stranger to my own thoughts

There is no footage to save, no photographs

Certainly not the clump of dust I am to become

John Yau

A CASE OF MISTAKEN IDENTITY

I told the uniformed kangaroos they had the wrong man and they agreed and let me go. This kind of thing happens to me often—being mistaken for someone else. The kangaroos—who are notoriously nearsighted— were not sure if they had apprehended the right man (a petty criminal), a poor hapless soul (possibly a dishwasher) or, in my case, a white-haired poet known to walk around the city at night, in search of the perfect pairing of cupcakes and congee.

I told them who I was and what I did and they believed me because they had never heard such a story before. I wondered what story I would tell the next officers I met. It is best to keep changing your tune when you are in a different circumstance.

By the time I climbed the five flights to my apartment I was another person, a decorated infantryman who had come back to the street he grew up on and was shunned by his family and neighbors because the glories of war no longer had the meanings they once broadcast.

After a few months, I moved away and once again changed my name. I lived in a state ending with "x" and learned to do things with my hands that I did not think were possible. I also learned to fly and went to parties. I stood in the corner and made mental notes, starting with "emesis" and ending with "sniverlard." I began telling everyone how I rated his or her sense of humor on a scale of one to ten. Being a strict grader, I made fewer and fewer friends.

In the meantime, I was run over by a car, a freckled boy on a tricycle, and a pilot who wondered why I was lying in the middle of the runway. I raised dachshunds but did not feed them kitchen scraps, as one future biographer will later claim. Joined to an outmoded battery, I began sparking in the middle of the night until the neighbors decided I should move to another part of town—where this kind of behavior was tolerated and even embraced—and I did. This is why I told the police officers they had the wrong man. They were looking for a man who tried to rob an ATM, not a man who thought he should have been born in a deeper fog.

John Yau

VARIATION ON A LINE BY DUO DUO

I love the house on fire
inviting us to lie down

Inviting us to become
its tightly fitting roof

As if the moon is a python
waiting to uncoil

As if our blushing cheeks
did not offer brazen proof

I love the house on fire
inviting us to lie down

Umber summer falling
slowly to its knees

Inviting us to lie down
in its scarlet tracks

Inviting us to embrace
the already blazing sky

LATEST WEATHER REPORT

We join the bughouse battalion of the Last Salvation Army, climb aboard
the purring trucks and head for the valley where the fires still rage.
Death rides beside us in an air-conditioned limousine, a big green grin
sewn crudely to his otherwise flawless face.

The next morning

we stop in a mall to obtain extra rounds of supplies. We are headed for
the hollow space on the map from which we are said to have emerged,
complete and in ruins. The parking lot is full of empty ambulances and

John Yau

crawling with examples of suburban loneliness. We back away from anyone who shows something resembling a face, knowing it is the residue of plastic surgery.

In the rubble lots we passed, children were busy pulling handfuls of stuffing from armchairs and depositing them in color-coded plastic buckets. Their motto: no waste shall go to waste. This is the economy we have adjusted to, living on what the rich have used and found disagreeable.

We buy only the designated essentials: wizened apples marked by star-like bruises and other signs of holiness, domestic animals that have been injected with preservatives at the moment of their genital illumination, fishbowls full of earthworms, blank dresses and shirts, window sills to climb over.

Those who fail the daily quiz are relieved of their maps.

Other than hand signals, most communication takes place at night when we can send ants across each other's skin, their six legs tapping out messages. We were taking turns recounting the plots of android versus zombie movies shortly before dawn stopped and didn't cross the horizon. We got up and began driving.

The mall is a memory fading in a mirror, a relic whose function is no longer apparent.

Death's grin continues spreading across his face.

New reports are being received all the time.

The sun can't be found, but we remain convinced that it hasn't gone far.

Three Poems
Gillian Conoley

IN THE NEXT NEXT WORLD

Day one of the garden I start to get the ground a little wet

before replanting the hacienda creeper

Along earth's curve,

the violet-orange sky means it's a save the air day

The she wolves sprawl on the yard

done dusting the tree trunks with their hides

—go snake go snake a child yells as she roller-skates—

A noon stillness, oxygen or the lack thereof

lacerates on a cellular level

the chemical taste beneath one's beloved's eyes

echoic, piquant, scrubbing out the refrigerator until there is nothing

the human propensity to discover and rediscover what was discovered

Gillian Conoley

wet market wayward went the boat

Above my sapien sluggery flew a blue jay all alone

It's growing our own food that makes us revolutionary

the human propensity to discover and rediscover

what was discovered

but how we brace for news and get on with the day is a whole art

the heart breaks and then it mends but you have to thirst for it

as you do for love's work boots

A steep and rocky trail and at its top a muscular arm

one singular limb that has come for you

not to push you but to pull you up and over

as in to haul—

tendons taut tiny strands of fibrils

fingers spread, it is up there on the mountaintop

you may not elide

you may not go home alone

[you try not to go home alone]

even if you think no one's left but sphere

there is someone [an interlocked

one who waits instead of you]

the acid reflux of your ancestors

a nexus to the morning

a newscast in the evening

the vomiting, you could just hate it, encrypt it

or opiate it, tithe, or kitchen scrap it

WHAT WAS IN THE BLOOD

It was when faced with plague the body donned a robe

and drew blood from another.

Blood left in a container to settle for at least an hour

so its four layers could be seen—dark clot—black bile to hold the scarlet

under a milky buttercup film—

phlegm—and last, as if candlelit, the yellow bile—

127

Rather than return to the immediate data for what was there *to know*

the body got caught in its living shadow, in

the observed/recorded/theorized/forgotten

and hidden, was this what the plague craved most—to take us back to counting?

To the body that wobbles on the pavement

with a slight bend of the head,

shadowless, blindfolded, veiled,

drinking strong the sky—

the body

a not known

that projects, and transmits itself, drops its robe,

leaves one for another,

shimmers, and moves on—

GROWING THE BEING

Where has not ground   craved human shape

         taken blade into pitch

Moving the pleasure   around prodding   my fingers in dirt

     I will be called back   I will look for a camera   see who's watching

Gillian Conoley

I will be in court in asylum

With contour   where sky catches the vocables

            a part of speech still in my mouth

I will denude to the warmer parts

      where my feet were first planted

in concrete   When the acacia rustles   the brief bicyclist

      is crowned   in gold

Once day became plexiglass

vision mask

            Once day became kill

            waste was more than piss

            breath a fissured form of drift

alongside sorcerers, accessors

   drawing our next graphic of disease

            what to do with all the egg whites in the spirit boat

once we've pulled the yolks for glaze

I think to contradict is dutiful

I think after memory, before history,

in a third space

frolics a long-dead warrior queen

If in dying I fall in love with my stupidity

I dream some more of that love

if in the annihilation of all thought

a living heath is yet to come

Four Poems
Charles Bernstein

HEAVEN LAKE

—For Yi Feng

The reflection precedes the image
Floating mid-air
Between up and under
Or taking the measure of the sky
Braided coyly with macaroons
That dot the cloudy firmament
Like the last train to Bayonne
Lurches toward Bedlahem
Where the stains are invisible
To everyone but me

THE AUNT OF MY UNCLE
IS THE COUSIN OF MY NEPHEW

Restive foreshadowing delays
Mourners' piercing pulse
Even as is likely slotted for
Done heartening deplore
Quick messenger in place
Along soldier bars or calming
Grave, the more the more
Intends when scrape embroiders
Fleece-like airs where terraced
Front aborts their frame.

Charles Bernstein

BEFORE THE PROMISE

—For the 2020 class Phi Beta Kappa
of Eta Ohio Wesleyan University

I drew a blank on a torn door
Drew another, then no more
Got stung, pedaled frowns
Knew things was bust
(No way outta town)

Sometimes it done it its way
Then again, harder to say—
What's looking up
Decides to knock you down

Before the promise of tomorrow
Tomorrow came

Morning on this pole
Midnight at the other
Slipping, slapping, sliding
On a cockamamie roll

Yesterday's dreams dissolve
Into today's goodbyes
I set out on a camel's hump
Came back with just the eyes

Before the promise of tomorrow
Tomorrow came

A farther distance that we go
Within each moment spent
Then ever's sent by Heaven
Or scaled by human ken

Before the promise of tomorrow
Tomorrow came

We twist, we turn
Undo ourselves in tripled throws

My goodness, how the time has passed!—
Let's get our stuff and beat a path

To what we never knew
Nor will, nor who, nor say

Before the promise of tomorrow
Tomorrow came

BEELINE

Bee in my bonnet
Stings all night long
Bee in bonnet
All night long
No sooner morning comes
Begin to holler and ball

One time I'm in the hen coop
Next at a loading dock
Afraid I'll tumble down the stairs
Then that I may not

Bee in bonnet
Stings night and day
Dozen flights of angels
Not one who knows the way

I'm game if you are
See you on other side
God says he's hiding
Hope to meet her 'fore I die

Bee in my bonnet
Stings me all night long
Dozen flights of angels
Not one'll take me home

No Good Word
Yxta Maya Murray

I GOT INTO THE BUSINESS because I was good with tools. When I was about fifteen, I was keen to get a motorcycle. A Kawasaki. My father had one, as he was a CHP officer for Los Angeles. That made me want one too. I dreamed of blazing down the highway on my own bike. But my father said that before I could get one, I had to learn how to fix it. So I'd fix his. I learned how to take it apart and put it back together again. We'd work on it together. After I figured out my way around the machine, he said I needed to make my own money to buy one, because he wasn't going to shell out. I went to work for the Simi Valley Kawasaki dealership. They gave me automotive mechanic training, and I learned on the job.

At sixteen, I bought my KZ900 and it became my signature. Leather jacket, the whole thing. I had lots of girlfriends and raised plenty of hell until I met Terry. My wife. She's a hairdresser. She actually didn't care about the motorcycle, she just liked me, she said. Also, once we got together, she told me to get a better job. With more benefits. This was 1990. I wanted to go to the police academy, but I had heard from some guys at the dealership that Atomics International was looking for men. Technical stuff. It wasn't really clear what you would be doing. But they paid and they were ready to hire ASAP. I rode my bike up to Santa Susana and applied.

"I'll take whatever you got as long as I can work with my hands," I told the foreman. We sat in his office as I filled out the paperwork. He was a nice man, a Black gentleman, name of Henry Robertson. He was short but strong. Built solid. With a big neck, and big hands.

"No problem if you haven't done work in nuclear yet," Henry said, nodding as he read my application. "We'll teach you up here."

"Learning on the job's fine with me," I said. "I've done that before."

Henry looked impressed. "And you'll be working with your hands, all right."

"Who'll be training me?" I asked.

Henry gave me a smile, with lots of teeth. "You're looking at him."

I felt excited. Seemed like he'd be a decent boss. My boss at Kawasaki was a yeller. But I got a positive feeling about Henry right off.

"Sounds good," I said.

Henry brought me to the Hot Lab in Building 20, in Area IV. Hot Lab's where the scientists handled nuclear materials remotely. Like, if they wanted to check on the reactors' nuclear rods, to see if they were busted, they'd look at them with robots in the Hot Lab. Or if they wanted to process isotopes, that'd be done there too. Robots they used were the Waldos. They were master-slave manipulators. Named after a machine or a character in a book by Robert Heinlein. I didn't read the book, but Henry told me about it. He said our skills were high-tech and future oriented. And they were, except that we also just did a lot of cleaning. The Waldo had a master arm, which we used in the operations cell, and it controlled the slave arm, which worked with the radioactive materials in the hot cell. The machine was like those little carnival claws in the grab-a-toy game we used to play in the arcades. But big. Anyhow, the operations cell and the hot cell were separated by thick concrete, so that the scientists didn't get exposed while they were handling nuclear materials. It was safety first, Henry said, back then. Thing was, though, we were called in to do more dangerous decontamination work because there was radioactivity everywhere. Had been for thirty years. Atomics International was spending ten million dollars on the cleanup, the first big one they did. I got hazard pay. It was a high salary for somebody like me, and my wife was happy.

My job was taking apart the manipulators and sanitizing them. Repairing them if possible. The Waldos were going to be either disposed of as radioactive waste or fixed and reused or sold to another nuclear facility. We used TCE. Tons of TCE. Trichloroethylene. It's a halocarbon, a solvent. It'd been used to clean machinery since the 1920s and wasn't flagged as a cancer causer until 1999, nine years after I started using it at AI.

I enjoyed my work. It was like a Star Wars version of fixing hogs. And Henry was a fine manager. Really, he was a teacher. He showed me how to disarticulate the encoders and motors, the gripper jaws, all that. He cared a lot about the people who worked under him. He was patient.

"You're doing a great job," he'd say whenever I struggled with the Waldos' working arms, which were delicate. Far more complicated than anything on a motorcycle. "Don't rush," he'd go on, as I wrangled the joints. "Nobody get hurt, that's rule number one."

Henry didn't like it if he saw us walking onto the floor wearing only our red-lines. That's what we called our jumpsuits. "Go get your respirator, for cripes' sake," he'd say. We had all kinds of gear. First, we had these white coveralls, protective suits, which had red trim at the neck and the cuffs. Why we called them red-lines. We had gloves, which were duct-taped on. We had duct-taped booties. Film badges. Dosimeters. Henry was worried about the red-lines not giving us enough of a shield against the radiation. We'd put them on and clean up the Waldos and get hot and sweaty, and after the day was done the clothes would get put into barrels and washed off-site. But after a certain point, if you waved your red-lines at a Geiger counter, they would go off. That's why Henry wanted to make sure we wore everything—our respirator, our booties, our gloves. Except, I was twenty years old. Sort of dumb. Sometimes I'd suit up without the breather because it made me feel like I was choking. Henry wouldn't hear of it. "Get back there and put on your damn mask," he'd say, muffled because he was already wearing one himself. So I'd run back to the cabinet and do what he told me.

We decontaminated the Waldos with the TCE by either dunking parts into buckets filled with the stuff, or slopping them with a rag that was soaked through with it. Come around six, we'd pour the TCE into barrels and that would get carted away, like our red-lines and gloves. I don't know exactly where they dumped it. I heard the chemicals got thrown in the ocean, and Henry said he'd seen some workmen pouring them into the dirt of the buffer zone of the lab site. That was nothing to do with him, though. If the TCE disposal had been his job, he would have done it tip-top.

"Dumb-asses going to get us killed," he grumbled, about the guys polluting the place. He said it to me in private, once, over lunch. We'd started to eat together regularly. We talked about bikes and cars a lot, because Henry was into all of that too. He talked some about science fiction, the Heinlein stuff, the Waldo story. We became friendly, even though he was about thirty years older than I was. He was a dude. He'd tell dirty jokes and make fun of one of the lady supervisors at Santa Susana, but then he'd bring me muffins baked by his wife, Helen, and talk about her so respectfully. Once I brought him some *Ćwikła*—this horseradish spread—as a joke, because I thought he wouldn't like it, and would maybe poke fun at me like my wife did. But he was fine with it.

"Not bad," he said, spreading it on his sandwich. "Wiśniewski, you're Polish, right?"

"Granddad was from Kraków," I said.

"You get on with your grandpap?" he asked.

"Long time ago, when I was little," I said. "He was cool."

Henry took a bite of his sandwich. "How so?"

I shrugged.

"Right," Henry said. "It's all just family. That loving. Can't really come up with a word for it."

I watched him eat the sandwich and felt comfortable with him. I liked telling him about my grandfather. Dziadek and my mom hadn't got along, and Terry sometimes made jokes about me being part "Polack," you know. But Henry, he was interested.

"Pretty much," I agreed, about how there's no good word for describing how you love somebody.

So, like I say, I enjoyed my time there. And I didn't feel scared working in Area IV for the first year, because Henry had things so in control. There were a couple of mistakes, though. One guy not wearing a respirator breathed in too much TCE and went crazy, because it makes you euphoric. Another guy cut himself with a gasket and had to be rushed to the hospital. Other slipups. In Area II there was an explosion, I heard, and a tech got burned bad. And another man in Area III got his hand crushed by a crane. But the worst accident happened to Henry himself.

I was in there with him early on a Monday. We were at the lab before anybody else that morning, tearing apart Waldos. Our film badges were already black, because the Waldos were covered in radioactivity. Henry was dismantling one of them with old-school tools, pliers. "These are the easiest to work with, they do the best job," he said. "The simplest ways are usually the best." To show me, he started disarticulating the slave arm so that its bolts stuck out, and they were sharp. After the demonstration, he waved a hand around, saying, "'Slave arm's a nasty way of putting it, don't you think? Ugly, you ask me." He passed his hand over the bolts and they caught on his glove and tore it, all the way up to his elbow. He stopped talking and looked down at his exposed skin, immediately understanding what had happened. I did the same. Both of us ran to the showers without saying a word.

We had showers in the back room. Silkwood showers is what we joked they were, though it wasn't funny. Henry ripped off his ventilator and his red-lines and his gloves, but he did it in such a rush that

137

he lost his balance and fell on the floor, on the tiles. I worried that I could contaminate him and so I hauled out with his clothes, straight into the disposal closet. I stripped off my protective gear and dumped our stuff in there. When I ran back into the shower stall I saw he was struggling to get up. The fall'd been bad. Blood came down his leg. I held him up and turned on the water. I scrubbed him with soap.

"Get it off me," he was yelling. He had his arm twined around my neck, so as to keep steady.

"You're OK, you're all right," I kept saying. Some of the guys started to wander in and after that it was a panic. They got us towels and bandages. A tech named Craig, one of our crew, helped me carry Henry to the locker room. I dried off Henry's cut and wrapped his shin while Henry sat hunched over and shook his head.

"Don't tell my wife," he kept saying. "She'll take it bad."

Let me admit it, I felt like crying, seeing him like that. Worrying about Helen when he should worry about himself. But my father had taught me to keep my lip stiff.

"No problem, Henry," I said.

Things went back to normal after that. Henry saw the doctor without telling his wife, and the doctor said that people get exposed to lots of toxic stuff all the time and live through it OK. Cheered up, Henry returned to work. This was '90. Not too many accidents. Another guy did get burned in Area II on account of a gasoline fire, but that didn't have anything to do with us.

Then came 1991. I can't say that was the greatest year here in Simi Valley.

There'd been the police brutality case, the Rodney King. Rodney King got arrested, or whatever you want to call it, in March of '91. And that same year, they held the trial against the four officers in the Simi Valley courthouse. Stacey Koon, Laurence Powell, Timothy Wind, and Theodore Briseno. And all that time, it seemed, we'd been watching the tape of Rodney King getting beat, and you'd think that Henry and me would have talked about it. He did bring it up, smacking his teeth and saying, "Can you believe?" But I changed the subject, knowing it was better we didn't get into the details. Like I said, my dad was CHP. I'd grown up knowing what police officers dealt with on the job, and how they believed they had to protect themselves. After a couple other tries, Henry could see that we weren't on the same page, but he was cool about it and we didn't really speak of it again. We just kept talking about pliers versus robots, or Helen's muffins, or Robert Heinlein, or the time I'd saved him, or office politics, or whatever.

Myself, I felt like the whole Rodney King thing had been blown out of proportion. I was glad that the prosecutor had moved the case to Simi Valley, because that's where the cops were. Lots of LAPD live here because of real estate not being insanely expensive and the politics. Our people support police officers, as I did. I knew about the danger of the life, the sacrifice. My father had come home many times real pale, real quiet, because some drunk guy with a gun in his glove compartment reached for his weapon when Dad pulled him over. He had to subdue big, unpredictable men sometimes. He'd told me the stories. About wrangling their arms around their backs while they bucked like horses and my father would think he'd never see me or my mom again. He lived with that fear. And he didn't trust—he thought that certain people—he had some particular ideas, I'll say. That's how I grew up, with that perspective, you see. So, if Rodney King—I heard he had resisted arrest. It was said there was a part of the tape that showed that, him resisting. I don't know, man. You believe what you believe.

There was the trial. It was a weird time. I could tell that Henry was tense about something, and I guessed it was that. As the weeks wore on he got a little sullen. One day, at lunch, Craig said he didn't think the trial was going to "come out good." But Henry shook his head. "If they don't convict, there'll be a fire around here," he said. "Because it's all on tape." Craig was worried that there was going to be a hung jury or an acquittal but Henry said he had to have faith that the trial would come out the way that he wanted it to. As for me, I hoped that the police officers would be exonerated. I wanted those men to be freed, all right. And I was as sure about my thoughts on the matter as I am right now that in the day there's the sunshine and at night there's stars.

Ever since the indictments, my dad had talked more and more about how if there was a guilty verdict then he and Mom were going to move to Nevada or Texas, some place more in line with their way of thinking. "Nobody respects the police these days," he said one night over drinks, and he started crying. "That's what hurts, that disrespect." After that, I got filled with anger about the Rodney King case. Because it was, like, hurting my father. Terry didn't care one way or the other. But I started talking about it every night at dinner, like Dad did. I thought that this new political correctness had gone too far, and California was getting overtaken, and that Mexicans and Black people hated white people now.

"Whites will rule the world until the trumpet sounds, baby," Terry

139

said, laughing at me in her breezy way, and drinking her glass of red wine, like to calm me down.

The verdict came out on April 29. I still remember the date. A Wednesday. Craig, my friend at Santa Susana, he had a transistor that he listened to sometimes on breaks, and he told me what the jury had decided. He'd heard a report that there was a disturbance at the courthouse, on Alamo Street. Like a crowd coming together. I didn't see Henry at work that afternoon. I don't know where he was. But when I clocked off, I changed into my regular gear and went over to check out what was going on.

An ugly mob stood outside of the East County Courthouse. Some people had signs, pro and con. People were arguing with each other about the rightness of the verdicts. I stood on the side of the people who thought the acquittals were good. A woman on the other side started singing, "We shall overcome," and it made me mad. I thought about my dad crying and saying, "the disrespect, the disrespect." I loved my pop. So when another woman yelled at our side of the crowd that we were "racist pigs," I let her have it. Not physically, of course. I yelled back at her. I said, "You have no idea what you are talking about. The men in blue deserve your gratitude." Everybody started booing me, and I yelled some more. I said some not-great things. And at some point, during the fuss, I looked around, and saw Henry at the edge of the group with the civil rights people. He was looking at me with a grim and watchful expression on his face.

"Hey," I said. "Hey, Henry."

But he didn't say hey back. He turned and walked away.

After that, it wasn't the same for me at work. Henry and I never talked about it, but when I invited him for lunch, he said no. "Busy," he told me, not meeting my eye. I knew what was up. I guess I hadn't realized what an important relationship that was to me, but now that he was cutting me off, because we had a difference of opinion, it made me sad, at first. I kept following him around, trying to make jokes that he didn't laugh at. And, finally, I got angry. After that, I quit.

I went into the force, like Dad. I was twenty-seven at this point. Terry wasn't wild about my decision, because she was terrified about

140

me getting shot, plus not having as good a salary. But the benefits were all right. I made detective. Did commercial crimes. I was in the Burglary Auto Theft section.

Terry came around to me being in the police. She settled into things, and we had two kids. Cheryl and Nina.

I thought about Henry a lot after I left. I wouldn't say I shifted over to his world philosophy after I joined the department. If anything, I believed more in the other direction, because that's what the job is, that belief system, about bad guys and good guys. In my opinion.

Three years passed. I was in touch, off and on, with some of the men from Santa Susana. Mostly Craig, the one with the transistor. He lived about four blocks away from me in the Valley, so it was easy. I saw him when I gardened and he'd walk his dog by my house. In '96, we went out for drinks at Berrigan's. I think he liked hanging out at the cop bar; it made him feel tough. But that night, he had a couple beers and didn't ask me for any war stories. He seemed nervy and embarrassed.

"What?" I said.

"Henry's in the hospital," he said. "First Methodist."

I looked at him.

"He's got leukemia," Craig said.

I nodded, because there were other guys who'd got it, from where we worked. We heard stories here and there about people getting blood and bladder cancer, other things. But Henry wasn't other guys. I started to feel like I'd been shot in the stomach. I didn't say anything, but it was like something was tearing at me. It surprised me, the intensity of it. I pressed my fists into my eyes, and Craig got uncomfortable.

"I'm sure he'll be OK," he said, patting me on the arm.

I told Terry about it. It didn't phase her. "That's sad, but he's not a nice man," she said. "He blew you off, just because of something to do with people neither of you ever met."

That didn't help me much. I felt strange. Sort of shaky on the inside. I didn't know how I could help him. And Henry probably wouldn't want to be bothered by me. I mean, people who are sick, they don't want to be bothered, right? Give him his privacy, I thought. This went on for about four months. I busied myself with investigating my cases and helping take care of the kids. But Henry stayed inside of me. I kept thinking about how I'd stripped him and washed him that time he'd fallen in the shower, and we were so scared. How I had saved his life. But what's that thing the Chinese or somebody says? Once you save somebody's life then you're responsible for them for good?

I went to the hospital. I knew some orderlies and security there from my days on the beat. I asked around, but Henry had been discharged at the same time Craig told me about him being sick. I couldn't get any other information on him.

I had his number, still. His landline. It was on an old directory I'd kept from Santa Susana. I called it and Helen picked up.

"Hey," I said. "I'm an old friend of Henry's, and I'm calling to see how everybody is. I heard about the bad news."

"What?" she asked. She sounded tired, and harried, like she was doing a hundred things at the same time. "You're a who?"

"Friend of Henry's," I said. "From AI, the lab."

"Place killed him," she said.

"Oh," I said, holding my hand to my face. "Is Henry dead?"

"No," she said. She started sobbing. "I shouldn't have said that. He's here. He's alive."

"Can I get you anything?"

There was silence on the line for a while. Then she said, "I could use some groceries. I don't have the time to make the trip."

"Tell me what you need," I said. She gave me a list, and their address, because I'd never been to his house. I ran to the store and got the food and drinks and within an hour and a half, I was at their door.

Helen let me in. She was thin. But not a natural thin. She looked whittled, like she'd been worn down. I've seen that in some of the cases I've handled, with women who are dealing with too much. In policing, you'll see that kind of look where a lady's got a troubled kid doing drugs, or a drunk husband, something like that. But she was just beat from taking care of him.

She stood in the kitchen and watched me like a sleepwalker while I put all the groceries away.

"What else can I do?" I asked.

She closed her eyes. "I need to take a nap. It'll only be fifteen minutes."

"OK," I said.

She walked down the hall and went into a spare room and closed the door. I was still in the kitchen by myself with no idea what I was doing there.

I washed the dishes in the sink. Went into the dining room and smoothed the tablecloth. I wandered into the living room and tidied up the magazines and books that had been spread out on the coffee table. After that, I tiptoed to the bathroom, and used it. When I came out, I heard Henry calling for Helen in a soft voice.

I went into his room.

I'm not going to say exactly how it was for him, because that's his business. But I hadn't understood what it meant to pass away. The physical process of it. He was awake, though. His mental outlook was fine. It was the physical that was the problem. I stood in the doorway and he peered up at me and started, like he was scared of what he saw. He didn't recognize me. Maybe he thought I was an intruder.

"Henry," I said.

"Oh," he said, and then relaxed back down on his pillow.

I came over to his bed. His eyes shone up at me. He looked at me the old way, like when he'd eaten my Ćwikła or taught me how to dismantle the slave arms.

"Hi," I said.

"Hi," he said.

"I'm sorry," I said. I hadn't realized it until right then, how fucking sorry I was.

He knew exactly what I was talking about. "Yeah," he said, after a long while. "I didn't like what you did."

"I'm sorry," I said again.

"Where's Helen?" he asked. "I need a bath."

"She's taking a nap."

"Good for her," he said, and shivered. That's when I saw how much he was sweating. Sweat poured down his head and throat, soaking his shirt.

"Are you hot?" I asked.

He said no. "It's the medicine."

His home care setup was complicated and involved a lot of tubes and parts. He could not get out of bed. Little comforts had been scattered here and there. On a nearby table, there was a bowl of water and some clean towels.

"I could pitch in," I said.

"Like that last time," he said, then started laughing and coughing.

143

"Looks like it didn't do any good," I said.

"Probably would've been dead within the year if you hadn't," he said.

I went over to the bowl and dipped one of the cloths in the water. I walked back to the bed and started wiping his face. Henry closed his eyes. I wiped his throat, and his right shoulder. I freshened his arms. His legs. His feet.

When I was done, he laid back, staring at the ceiling.

"Henry, I'm a fuckup," I said.

He shook his head.

"Do you forgive me?" I asked.

He was quiet again, for like five minutes.

"I'd like to be alone," he finally said, his voice hoarse. "I can't help you out."

"I'll help *you* out," I said.

"No, Greg," he told me. He wouldn't look at me.

I walked back out to the living room. I tidied the magazines again. I put away the remote control and dusted the coffee table with my sleeve. But the way I felt was, I suddenly didn't even know who I was. Like I was all blanked out. I can't explain it. It was the same as what Henry had said before, that there's no words for loving somebody in your family. Whatever I was feeling then, there's no word for it, except that it broke me down.

Helen took my calls every once in a while after that, and gave me updates. He died about six months later. She let me go to the funeral. I think she knew all about me, and who I was, and what Henry heard me say at the courthouse.

My feelings about Henry got worse when he died. I could never relax. It was like I'd been poisoned. Like I hated myself. After a while, I got angry at him again, like I had been all those years ago, when I'd quit because he wouldn't have lunch with me after he'd seen me protesting. I kept thinking, why me? What'd I do? I went over there and bathed you, and that wasn't the first time. Why couldn't you be nice? Why couldn't you help me out?

My wife was like, "This has got to stop." But what was happening was, I was changing on the inside, and she couldn't really understand it.

*

About a year after he passed, I had a case involving this car-theft ring, out of Burbank. A chop-shop crew. It was about six African American gentlemen who were suspected of working with a larger syndicate that was spread throughout the city. They were alleged to specialize in Chevrolet Camaros. It was high-tech theft. They reprogrammed Camaros' ECMs—engine control modules—with their laptops, and that confused the cars into thinking they didn't need a specific key. Actually, I don't know if it was six guys; that's what our CI said. Our confidential informant. One morning, in '98, winter, we got a no-knock warrant at a condo where half the crew was supposed to live. The CI said they had guns, and so I got a squad of seven men, and we went in armed to the hilt at five in the morning.

There was only one guy living there, about fifty years old. Black man. And we couldn't find guns or even tech anywhere. We had the wrong address. As soon as we raided the house, the occupant started screaming and resisting. He jumped out of bed and slapped at the officers, who reverted to their training and subdued him to the ground. They used more force than was necessary, though it probably wasn't illegal, because police brutality's a high standard and there's a lot of immunity. What happened was, one officer named Jed Hauser hit the man on his shoulder and his hip with his baton, first when the guy was smacking him and then when he was flat on the ground in his pajamas. Now, this should have been mother's milk to me. I'd seen way worse. This was nonlethal, a takedown, mostly ordinary protocol. Except this time it seemed different. I wasn't thinking about Henry exactly. It was more like I had that feeling again, like I didn't know who I was, like I was all blanked out. I felt like nobody. I ran over to Officer Hauser and I tore the baton away from him and used it to beat him away from the man on the ground. I knocked Jed out and broke his jaw. I also injured the suspect when I swung the baton back and accidentally hit him in the head. The guy got a concussion and needed seven stitches.

It sure wasn't any hero story. It wasn't a Black Lives Matter. If I didn't like the degree of force, I should have exercised my authority as the lead officer and told him to stand down. But instead, I beat the shit out of him and hurt the other guy.

After they fired me from the department, I was charged with aggravated assault and wound up serving eight months in county jail. My wife left me, and I lost custody, and my father carried his grief about me to his grave. So, that wasn't the best. I went back to fixing motorcycles. Which is what I still do now.

145

*

I think I'm talking about myself too much because what I want to talk about is Henry. I mean, Henry's dead. I wish he was alive. I'd have liked to make it up to him. It's taken me a long, long while, but I don't feel blanked out anymore when I think about what happened. You get blank because you know you're in the wrong, but without that wrong, you think, what are you going to hang your hat on? I did feel like nobody at all for a long time, though. I mean, I loved my dad and still do. But then you become friends with somebody, and see what I saw, and, I don't know, it can make you lose your way. And that's not really bad.

It's all because of what happened at Santa Susana. The government put something unnatural there, something wicked, and because they did that to us, I had to save Henry with my own hands. It's not a normal thing to do. It opened something up in me. Opened me up to another person. Because, what was I thinking to say that? "The police deserve your gratitude." And I haven't talked about everything I did in the force. I hurt people.

I can't ever make it right, but it's not about me, it's about Henry, and the kind of person he was. Telling me to put on my mask. Worrying about Helen. Talking to me about my granddad. Telling me about Waldos. That shame eats you. Well, so it goes. You got to let it, and know you deserve it, and try to make sure that, when you get to see them, you don't wreck your children with the lessons that ruined you.

Night Is the Best Counsel
Marc Anthony Richardson

ONE CANNOT LIE TO ONESELF in the snow: there are times, the woman tells the man, who is next to her, trudging toward the river, when what is going on outside in the world is what is going on inside of me; climate change is more evident in the wintertime, she tells him, on this crisp air trek through the snowbound vale of the forest; farmers can no longer count on nature for any reliable means; planting season is earlier now, but in turn more crops are being destroyed by last-minute snowstorms and unforeseen stretches of cold. We see the change. We have always seen it. We just never let it do what it needs to do to us: turn us into men and women and children of change, of action and not reaction. Our reaction is to do nothing. But it is only early January and they, the lovers, and everyone else and every thing still move between a sky so blue and an earth so white that they blind one to other things; ice and snow have covered the landscape for nearly two months now and the lovers and the provincials are growing more and more solitary in the subzero atmosphere, for some days it is just too insane to go outside; but if one must, the nose needs to be muffled; the woodpiles have dents in them and the woodstoves are working overtime, so that now the lovers and the provincials are all eyeing their split logs more carefully and counting more cords and space heaters per square foot to make sure they'll be covered in the cold stretches to come; today, on their way to the river, there are outbursts of animal tracks everywhere, and the lovers following them see them as reviving reminders that not everything slows to solids in winter or sleeps, as spurts of verve, for rabbit and deer and predator trails spread so seemingly inexhaustibly that almost anyone can track their triumphs and defeats, so that on this crisp air trek through the snowbound vale of the forest, the Black and Asian couple—as the provincials have come to know them—encounter something unusual in this wild grid of newly grown evergreens in the form of a puff of snow, for since they didn't see anything at first, they can't say for sure what has vanished—but now they can: a coywolf, a hybrid of the coyote and the wolf, a liminal being that is

147

bounding up a wood-crested hill on the other side of a clearing when it turns to look back so that they're staring at each other for a bit, fixed, the lovers and the descendant of the lupus, the size of a shepherd dog, though the lovers cannot tell this, its black-tipped tail and reddish, grizzled gray coat and face frozen in place, yet they stare, until it turns and ascends swiftly into the wood. The lovers stand in silence, then the man, concerned about a pack, wonders if they should return to the cabin. The woman tells him that coywolves are not known for hunting humans, especially when they're afraid of them and when there's an abundance of white-tailed deer about and being cunning and all-devouring, opportunistic, one can certainly see how they could sustain themselves on anything, from raccoons to rabbits to muskrats, from minks to moles to mice, from flora to fruit to refuse: they have the most plasticity of any other species up here; yet, since the lovers are not wearing their fluorescent orange vests over their double layers of winter wear and coywolves are now hunted throughout the season, they are overly cautious about nearby hunters missing their prey—and there is always that lurking racial concern, if only in the man's mind for the moment. It is getting colder and cloudier as they head back and on the way back fat plenteous snowflakes begin to fall as they follow the still-visible foot traces of their past, for in the vale of the forest it is easy to get lost, everything looks like everything else every which way with wispy fingers of flurries curling and curling come here come here; the crystal skeletons of snow-covered deciduous trees and the shaggy white coats of evergreens are as far as the eye can see, which is why the lovers backpacked provisions—the vests escaping them—yet without the evidence of their movements in the snow, indeed, it would be difficult to navigate the return; in advance of the ascent to the cabin—when they'll be laboring without words and stopping to catch their breath, ungloved and mouthing and breathing on the tight beaks of their fingertips—the woman tells the man of another dream, a recurring one, and though she last experienced it seven or so months ago, it remains as intense—if not even more— as the recent one of her father, for it reminds her of her mother: In the dream of the black wolf, she says, I am frightened of it, not because it harms me but because it *refuses* to harm me; it does not maul me as I lie there on my side in the snow, my spine against the spine of an oak, a colossal sawtooth, with the snowfall covering me like a comforter. It waits. It is waiting for me to die. For even when the pack arrives, having spoored the alpha, they too wait. One is forever foolishly intrepid, though, and starts to inch forward, belly to snow with the snout shoveling it, throwing sly glances at the alpha to test it, until a snarl makes it retract into the pack. I lie there. The dream always ends there. The lovers reach the ascent to start their zigzagging climb toward the cabin, but only when they stop for a rest does the man decode the dream: The alpha is not showing pity but prudence, he says; it will not let the pack become contaminated, it will not let them feed off your desire to die—for they are all one and the lowest of these wolves is you, in this disease state, the omega, and the highest is the alpha: it knows that it has to let this part of itself starve itself to death. Soon, after another rest, they reach the summit, and then come upon the cabin. After the sun has set, after they have settled and had supper, they decide to retire, but by lamp-light, in a bedchamber of the double heart, the woman lies alone in her lover's bed. She touches the closed maroon curtains of his room, tempted by the dark window mirror, but she does not open them. The space heater is humming, and it is getting even warmer when he returns, the lover, having stoked the fire in the furnace, fed it wood. He gets into the bed, sitting up against the headboard, and covers his lower half with the comforter as she spies the papers in his hand, folded in thirds; she fancies him having saved them from the furnace, the pages of one of his missives, but she knows he only retrieved them from his desk in the rec room, for she recognizes her handwriting. Night is the best counsel, she says, so, forever foolish-ly intrepid, she glides a finger over his knuckle and on down to the digit to make him slowly expose it, the missive, to unfold it and to hold it up to her face, for her to inhale herself, for her scent is still there in the mind but her slit hardly knows it, remembers it, it only remembers forgetting it—like a short piece of thread that had been passed through to the other side of a needle's eye—but with the black oblivion outside and the maroon curtains closed, like inverted labia aroused by a rub, after drawing back the curtain of shame, the black oblivion *inside* now opens her inwardly: *Hold me open*, she always opened, for once more he is reading one of her missives, yet aloud and dearly to her. He will be conducting a séance with it. It is a memento, a reminder of a powerful memory of discovery while he was reading it on the row, in a place where he had thought there were no new memories worth remembering, no new feelings worth feeling, it was one of the few missives he was allowed to keep, for since it was written after those interviews—after which he had been humiliated and beaten and then taken into solitary—it had yet to be written, thus confiscated, a missive he had received only after

149

he'd heard he was to be released from the row, from prison, for since she did not want to burden him before she now felt that he needed to know what her memory had in store, in full, for them—though she had written the missive *months* before she sent it to him—for up until then he only knew that her son had been taken by that act of God, and man, but not about that act *during* the act, so that now so that now as her lover is reading this, as the voice of the missive is possessed by another's, or rather *dispossessed* of the body of the missive by another's, not the man's, *open my mouth*, says the voice, *pull back the curtain of shame so that I may give back the name, for I can still smell the reek coming from it, my mouth of sex, that nautical stink that won't sink and be at peace in me and my belly for they—some shadowy they—say that it will take me the same sum of years as my son was to grieve him—five—and it has only been two and a half and so I cannot expect for him to sink and be at peace in me midway and perhaps he never will as he should, as I ought not to be, for I am a sibyl who is her own and only oracle now, a god who is her own and only atheist: I do not believe in myself, my love—so how can I believe in what I have done?* And as the man becomes the woman, metamorphosing into his new form, as this voice that is not *his* voice possesses or rather dispossesses hers from the body of the missive the cabin and the double black oblivions are all meshing and blending and metamorphosing into a sea and snow into salt water and dark into daytime *for there will come a time*, it says, through her lover tonight, *when water will turn into blood* and soon she is smelling the salt water and feeling the scalding summer sun kissing her suntan-lotioned face as the soft, fat frame of her sentient son, at the great brown-green girth of the earth, in the warm equatorial waters of the Atlantic, splashes between the support of her open arms, and then there is another, and another and another and there are several other mothers here at this great brown-green girth of the earth, all gathered together today beyond the broad break of a sandbar, and she is in her midthirties again, over three years ago, and is transatlantically in water as warm as bathwater on a fiery foreign beach on a spotless noonday today under a skin-darkening star, this American, this Asian American, and her son, girdled by a dark indigenous assemblage of West African women, and her guide, a friend of a friend, all glistening under this skin-darkening sun and holding *their* sentient children above the water's hazel surface to show them how to stroke and to float with their fat in the sea salt without any floatation device, for there are none on this nontouristy beach besides the coconuts attached to the fishermen's nets, for this serene broad break in the waves before the sandbar, in the hazel iris of these equatorial waters—their movable pupils being the calm centers of distant storms—is a deceptively perfect place to play today, today she is not *other* here, she is not an Asian of Asia or an Asian of America, for though she is often referred to as *the American* by these women when speaking to one another—merely out of convenience, as a quick clarification of who is being spoken of—she has been *unothered* by these other mothers who are much, much darker than her on this primordial megacontinent in the hot equatorial junction of the dark blue thighs of all mankind all colors and creeds and where the custom is coastal and postcolonial and now allows for these women to partake of this newly unrestricted sector of the sea at this time of day and heat where they are *all* free to laugh and to bare skin and breasts and teeth under a sky and no male eye so blue with a sun so bold that it blinds one to other things, but these *indigenous* women are the mothers of the human others, who are so dark that they are black and so black that they are blue and bright and as shiny as obsidian stones—a darkness that had long since birthed the many permutations of beauty across the globe to maybe one day eclipse the lunar surface itself—yes, obsidian, yet malleable and rhythmical flesh and discourse and diatribe so that this whole world seems much heavier and fuller than her own, elemental and alive and innate, only to have these thoughts parted and dispersed by a colossal cruise ship, anachronistically passing by like a penthouse gliding across the waters, very long and multilayered, the building beneath it immersed—*Look! Look!*—some of the women are yelling in unison, in colonial or Creole or tribal tongue—*The savages are waving! The savages are waving!*—the American's guide, a friend of a friend, among them, and then they are all laughing and waving and shifting their hips without wondering why or if this great white ship is passing by too close, for they know *why*—it's a safari by boat, with their bare wet bosoms in the passengers' binoculars—and *if* has never really bothered them before—for ships rarely passed by in the past and so close and when they did the women were never permitted to be here and when they pass by now the women rarely are—the American's guide, another indigenous woman with a child, a son, has a face that bears the marks of her tribe and diatribes, a friend of a local friend who invited her here today, who speaks the colonial language of the vanquished so the American can understand her, a colonial language unlike the American's colonial language yet one the American has been speaking fluently for years, during her past wanderings across other countries that were once colonized by the same tongue and prior to her matrimony, prior to her pregnancy, despite her family— for she is not normal—but now the American's arms are under the soft, plump torso of her horizontal son as a swell rolls across the sur- face, so that now she is standing on her toes, her chin barely above the surface, her heart in her throat, but her boy is laughing and splashing and treading water without needing any help from her, as the other mothers around him are treading water as well, *holding* their children, these women who are so much like the market women who are always smiling and doting on her boy, calling him Buddha! Buddha! while pinching his cheeks and who is kicking quite well with the water even higher now, dog-paddling in a tight circle, say- ing, *Mama Mama look!* with her treading water as well, though now the water has leveled again, at her chest, and standing again, feet in the sand, she continues to study her son, his strokes easy, no wasted energy, and she remembers the saxophonist from the other night, from the hotel jazz club, the local who was trying to seduce her by offering to give her son swimming lessons in the hotel pool today, while her husband, another Asian American, was answering a critical call on his mobile cellular phone outside where it was less loud, as their son slept fifteen floors above them—where her hus- band is today, in the hotel room, taking a video conference call on his portable computer, at the behest of his boss—for their local friend, their nanny, was watching their son last night, whose own child, her daughter, they'd find sleeping beside their son like a little wife—*For to them*, the voice says, through her lover tonight, *everyone is theirs, and I notice this mostly with yours, but not so much with mine, yet due to an appointment, fortuitously timed, the nanny couldn't come to the beach with her daughter that day*—and as her husband was still away, after she graciously declined the saxophonist's offer, he spoke and spoke about his music without ever taking a breath and so she had to stop him to ask him about his *sustained intensity*, about his *circular breathing*, and he said it was like being in the middle of a pool, like steadying yourself on the slope between the shallow end and the deep end, with your chin barely above the surface and your heart in your throat and while standing on the tips of your toes— that, he said, is sustained intensity, which equals ecstasy—but she is glad to have brought her son here today, to this beach, instead of to a swimming pool, for she is not normal—*Salt is sacred*, says the voice, *the salt of the earth*—and now *Mama Mama look!* for she has been

watching her son kicking and swimming while thinking of the saxophonist, yet only now is she really *seeing* him again, she embraces
and kisses him, and then watches as the guide swims around them
and her feet disappear, as her body goes vertical—for the sea is rapidly
receding—and they, the American and the guide, are both embracing
their sons as the sea sucks them in, their legs, the receding seaweed
catching at their ankles and the seabed sifting through their toes, for
the sea itself seems to be coercing them to devolve or regress and return
to some piscine way of being and breathing by way of this circular
motion, this path of least resistance, for some of the other mothers
are now shouting and rushing for their children, who are several feet
away from them, for a massive wave—born of the cruise ship's colossal wake—surges and overwhelms and pummels them, breaking beyond the sandbar behind them, the massive uprush of the swash now
feeding the massive backwash into the vast and foamy brine by way
of a path of least resistance, the board break of the sandbar—so that
now so that now they're *all* caught in the rip, the mothers and the
children, moving at a velocity much, much faster than any one of them
could ever swim against, than *anyone* could ever swim against, trapped
in this atrocious pipeline of water maybe fifty feet wide and who
knows how long while shooting out to sea at several feet per second
perhaps, so that whoever's at hand is in hand, as these mothers move
farther and farther away from shore, grabbing and gripping hands and
thinking of God thank God or oh God oh God: my child is not my
child; *I remember,* says the voice, *I remember one of the sisters
saying to me, one of the Buddhist nuns later on, that it was a selfless act, yet all I can see is my hand still holding on to that dear
little hand for its dear little life, onto some other woman's son
and not even thinking of mine at the time—and this and this is
what gets to me, that I wasn't even thinking of mine not so much
of mine if only for a moment, but when I am I can do nothing but
allow this rip to take me and the child past the breaking point
and out into its head and I can only hold up his head by having
him on top of me and riding on my back, scanning the sea only to
see some trying to swim against it, the rip, who'll get tired and be
swept away anyway and then my eyes fall upon my guide, whose
own eyes must've fallen on me at the same time, for though she's
far away she is crying and screaming for me—no no not for me—
for her child, she is screaming for her child who is half-limp and
on my chest, yet when he hears her cry carrying across the surface
he starts and struggles and I have to swim fast to catch him again*

after I lose hold of him—but then my heart stops: for my son is farther out; I can still hear her, the cries of that guide carrying across the water her horror, for though she's out of the rip she's out of her mind, yet treading water, she has gotten and is getting smaller as her son and I slip toward my son, and I will never stop hearing her— Bring me my boy! Bring me my boy!—and I will never I will never stop seeing it, the sight of my son dog-paddling—with no wasted energy—for where he is the rip seems to have ceased as he looks and looks straight at me—I know I know he's looking at me, I can feel it as far as he is from me—he wants he wants to get back to me as his own goddamn mother is moving away, swimming side-ways and cursing herself, with one arm wrapped around another child while her other arm is stroking away, swimming parallel to the shore for some shadowy reason—for some shadowy reason they must've told her to do so, for she never knew to do so—for she must swim toward someone and she can't carry them both, so that once she's out of the rip she starts swimming toward the shore, toward the guide who's now swimming toward her too and once she meets her she can scarcely see her for already she is swimming back, childless and alone, but her shoulders are shot and her lungs are shit and she's gasping and thinking and think-ing and gasping you are not going to drown you are not going to drown, but she can't see her son anywhere anymore, and she's not even sure if she's swimming to the right spot, for the life of the rip has stopped, yet she just keeps on toward the head of that dissi-pating stream of foam and dives under and then nothing but noth-ing but a stinging brown murk of aqua and bubbles and seaweed floating about, as her legs cramp and her arms end and her sinuses are shot with salt, the sharp pain at the base of her brain, as her mouth opens and closes and opens to swallow you are not going to drown you are not going to drown you are not going to drown. . . . Now, at night, in the dead of winter, she is lying in her lover's arms. His back is still against the headboard, but her missive is now scat-tered across the floor. She is crying. You can't come in me anymore, she says, you can't come in me anymore. I'm sorry I'm sorry, he says. I won't have another I won't have another. We won't have another we won't have another. And then her eyes rise, for her cheek was against his chest: We won't? We won't? We won't, my love, we won't. . . . The worst thing, she says, after a while, is thinking about what he must've thought when he saw me moving away. That I didn't want him. That I didn't love him. And then her lover says to her, very softly: At that moment, not any other, you had a life in your hands. That's what one of the sisters said to me, she says, one of the Buddhist nuns, and that not saving my son was a selfless act. I thought about that, about them, about becoming one of them. Yet: I would've had to disrobe to love you. I would disrobe to love you. . . . We had to focus on one pant leg at a time, she continued, my husband and I. He stayed with me for six months afterward, when my own family would not, throughout the insane asylums of the recovery resorts, throughout the drinking. I could've lied and said that I didn't see him, our son—but that would've been unbearable—We have the right to be angry, I said to him instead, but it is not our duty. And then later, before he left me, You are not a walking reminder, he said to me, as much as I am a walking reproach—and can't help it. I want so badly to but can't help it: you would do it the same. And then I looked at him, for I couldn't look at him until then, and he looked away: I am a mirror, I said, and men don't like what they see in me. But we continued to have sex for a time, and now he has long since remarried and has his twins, a boy and a girl—which made me relapse when I heard about it: I *wanted* to be alone, you see, but I wanted him to be alone with me. God, what awful conduits we are, you and I: two disconnected cords trying to retain their identities, still believing they are holding some past electricity—and the only reason we are not drinking too much now, my love, is because of the forest; we really don't need to have spirits in the house. Even the coroner, a man obsessed with them, had said it, that death is a myth. I kept coming to see him, that blue-black man in the morgue, with his white crown and his silver flask and his steely gray beard, even though he never sent for my husband or me: I was a zombie, you see, so I knew where I ought to be; we stayed in that country for a week, my husband and I, and I couldn't sleep, I couldn't eat—all those things moving around down there and just nibbling and nibbling away—I was a vitamin-deficient organism existing in the lavishness of a touristy establishment, contemplating flight from the fifteenth floor—yet I *still* don't know why I never did it—feeling the acute caress of a phantom limb in the darkness of a hotel room—that agony we, the affluent, always hypothesize about between martinis—but the body would never be found; three children had died on that day and they only found two, another boy and a girl—and I couldn't even find a comfort in this, in this sick perversity: that somewhere in that dry and loud and dusty city two other women were ripping their wombs out and wrapping them around their heads to carry the ghosts of their dead around like buckets of water from the river; and the only reason why I wasn't among them, the dead, was because of a fisherman who had fished me out, right after I swam back out, the one who saw the wave wipe us out, the voyeur; he retrieved me and revived me as the warm water on my bare breasts, under that skin-darkening sun, evaporated quicker than I could wrap my head around the matter. You are a miracle, the coroner said. Yet I felt and still feel that nature does not and *cannot* absorb this variety of raw and invisible anger, it can only provide a protective covering to numb it—for you will *always* be conscious of the supreme and irrefutable fact that it didn't need to happen. That is the rack. But you could've *never* let that other child go, the coroner said to me, during my last visit, for he was a comfort to me, for he would always say *let me see* whenever he spoke to me—as *you* would say to me. Let me see. As if I were a body without a murderer. Or rather: as if I were a murderer without a body. Maybe we kept each other company, because he was always surrounded by spirits that only spoke in terms of the present, like amnesiacs, who still believed in the delusions of their egos so deeply that—even beyond matter— their minds still moved around: But to be honest, he said, before taking a swig from his flask, I would rather be calm than right.

I Wanted to Tell You about My Meditations on Jupiter
(Not All Celestial Bodies Revolve around the Earth)

Anne Waldman

Grasping at fragments I want to tell you at a distance—*distanced*—
about the Recital, and its amplification. I thought "unicum" in
the varying versions, urgent meditations on Jupiter my remotest
wandering, its chilly motion, ice and patterns, striations seem to
be models of tissue and imprint, solitude, solicitudes. In Persian it
might be a sign of geomancy. What is the sand you imagine trapped
in your echo chamber? A telescope of no small size, a clepsydra of
wondrous watery proportion. The greatest clock of tidal universe.
What can you know? *Recital* as a dispatch as a way signaling a spin.

This is a meditation on Time, made of glass. When the electricity
stops the clocks go off on their own, those not surveilled. Switched
calendars. In the new technology they will place an "OWL" in
your classroom, to keep track of your study, your payments, your
assignments, are you on time? For class? In an alienated classroom,
the talismans of your own mind.

And you feel split in time. You feel your head dizzying as your eyes
land on the handmade machine of words, repeating forms from
Dante's inferno, dancing in a circle of left-hand turns. Tuning up
on the Day of Reckoning as you ascend. I love the syncretic. I want
everything to pile up in solitude. Counting backwards.

The time you thought you were on, then there were paused
interventions. All through your life. Ventricles, I need advantage and
ventilators, I need vehicles as in the lesser and greater vehicles of
Dharma.

The Recital of Hayy ibn Yaqzan was written during his detention
in the fortress of Fardajan. The narrator, or author Ibn Sina, speaks of

157

a time when his soul was at home and could go out to the familiar but find places that lay hidden in his own city. Captivity in a cosmic crypt, a dark pit in which also the pilgrim of "The Recital of Occidental Exile" is stuck in static transit. An inward escape, call it.

Solitude summons Hayy ibn Yaqzan's vision. *"Waiting for the invitation to leave the prison whose jailers know not they are themselves captives."*

What is imprint in a brain? Symbols? Allegories? What can we learn of carceral in a book? A day "in the can" when you want plutonium off your Front Range, when you want to control the narrative of toxins in land, water, the cellular throb and breath of toxins, and you protest all day, all months, all thousands of years. Deformed sheep born at dawn. An eye missing in a dispatch. The gasp is echoing through time, here, in capsule. Study the surfaces of sand in an age that crumbles like sand, count the eyes on potatoes, study a Field Chart of Matres of Mothers, write a book that opens to the sky. Conjure Hermes Trismegistus who witnessed the bringer of good news, the Angel Jibril of six hundred wings, in a dream.

My chambers are like cubicles in the Library, the shelves swaying as in a hallucination. I had to leave that all behind, although I still hold a key to a Research Room, and pray they will let me in again, study scripture, the rise and fall of everything, and the Age of Reason, again.

Not a philosopher, I am reluctant to get loose with poetical intuitions but they are all of the above, what I have admitted here into this cavity. How to be urgent at remote control, shake a dying body awake for an instant, happy recognition. Mysteriously guided to text that fluctuates in the mind, comes and goes. Lost the little pencil for my requests. They arrive as if telepathically.

Fragments, as I've said. On the nature of prediction there is none arising. The crystal mirror is cloudy.

Watching the child on the small screen she is learning K she is writing K the first time. I think of Aya Sofia that elder Library where it is recorded this kind of memory. The first K of Knowledge. Her name is Kora.

158

Anne Waldman

These were the categories of her studying:

WANDERING

ROAMING DAYS OF cold light

MIND NOT CAUGHT YET BY the Death Clouds

Breath of death

Breath of life

IMPELLING DAYS

Mind in the heavens with distant moons.
Enceladus, her oceans hidden under icy crust.
Lift the curtain, you may see the future of water.

CRISIS

JEOPARDY

    Propulsion and Scrying

HAZARDS
RESTLESS BRUTAL PATROLS
CORNER OF A watery eye

KEENING from the Womb

Io, Europa, Ganymede, Callisto, as top moons for the dark time.

ORAL TRADITON TOLD THE FUTURE THAT THIS WAS
ANCESTRAL TRANSMISSION
HOW TO BE ALONE with the Four Rotations.

HOW NOT GO MAD.

I thought her thrill of discovery, child's first instinct, she be in this,
looking up. But we are not awaiting Martian travel. We notice
patterns of solar systems. What is identity in this? Naming? Make a

159

list lifting the supermoons out of a host of seventy—or is it seventy-nine now? The counting of myriad moons. Volcanoes and snowfields of Io, a moon of fire and ice. Colors would show red, orange, yellow, black, white. Smallest of Galileans, Europa encircles with cracks and fissures that would haunt your notebooks. Twenty to 180 million years old, a young face. Ganymede, highly cratered, and "light-grooved terrain" across the face. Callisto probably unchanged since its formation, how could you ever guess? Out of the radar of Jupiter's magnetic field. Beyond Jupiter's radiation belt. Untethered. More to study, each moon a year in your life.

Reflectivity. That's the dispatch here. Perhaps oceans beneath the surface could flourish with life.

A wandering mendicant in my heart and this was wanted to say to you, mendicants coming after. Crying for all the others in plague to know truth of suffering. Could be signaling the end of entire civilizations. You go studying. The plague of Cyprian, the plague that ended serfdom, Great Plague of London, shortest in a year, only one hundred thousand dead. Think with me now on all the friends, all the last rites for those afflicted, AIDS. Like the strike of a large gong. As you say it "AIDS." The Fallen.

Solipsism is my instrument for seeing. We keep thinking about the future. This fluctuating, uncertain magic is apocalyptic by nature, and we are forgetting our rituals, our Jupiter glowing out there right now, sitting here, it's 3:18 in mountain time. Look out my hatch on the sky, an ingenious bubble of shelter. See the comet glide across your "wounded galaxies." Because you have a mind to project that heartbroken song.

Evidently, celestial physics and astronomy define the soul's itinerary, like a comet. If you want to greet it that way, with an angel as a guide, escape right now. Traces are discernible in *The Recital of Hayy ibn Yaqzan*, realizing a kind of transmutation where there is interiorization of the cosmos, emergence, as is said, from the cosmic crypt. The Recital is imploding in on itself. What is the data? An enveloping sphere to save phenomena. A body's motion considered in longitude in latitude. Swiftness and slowness, proximity and distance from the earth, here, us again. We think like that, our earth.

I keep saying "distanced." Us as homocentric, to the center of the earth. Seven spheres, and then there was the eighth enveloped, and the whole was the "Sphere of the Fixed Stars." Would that be absolute? Why would anyone want that? But the Moderns, followers of Ptolemy, added a ninth. A starless sphere, communicating that the astronomer must try to solve the notion of an unmoving earth. What will we continue to know when science leaves us stuttering. Turn off the light? Enter that little cavity, find a corner. Gather up your amulets. A movie theater inside your brain unsafe in 2020, in 2021, 2022, 2023. 2099. How long is your plague? Is it really so dark stuck inside? Or out?

Firsts

Vanessa Chan

THE FIRST TIME YOU LEARN the word *hymen*, you are nine and your mother is screaming it at you. You have just tried out for the school's rhythmic gymnastics team. At school they are the queens, and you have always wanted to be one of them—these girls who flutter their colorful ribbon apparatuses behind them like bright moths, these girls with their perfect posture, butt cheeks raised by the tight, shiny spandex of the leotards they wear to class. At night in front of the mirror, you suck in your stomach and pull your Snoopy pajamas tight around your legs, pretending that you too wear gold and purple spandex. You practice standing *en pointe*. You work on doing the splits and every day you get your legs a couple of inches farther apart. The pelvic muscle under your skin twitches and wriggles as you stretch. You imagine yourself jumping through air, a regal streak. You do not make the team.

Instead, at tryouts, you strain your groin. Your mother, furious, says that gymnastics are only for little girls whose mothers do not care about their virtue. She says that the splits will tear your hymen. She says you must protect your hymen.

When you tell her that your neighbor and best friend Junie's mother does not care, and that Junie, two years older but somehow smaller than you, had, in fact, made the team, she says, Well, we do not make moral examples of Junie and her tart mother, do we?

You ask your mother what "tart" means, and if it has something to do with the fact that Junie's mother wears shiny dresses to Mass, walks down the church pews smelling like flowers and alcohol, and, also, that Junie does not seem to have a father. Your mother ignores you, but later you hear her yelling at your father about *the slut next door*. You wonder if "tart" and "slut" are the same thing. You don't know if she means Junie or her mother.

You also don't know what a hymen looks like but you are determined to find out. Many afternoons you squat in the kitchen, bent over in two, your head touching the floor as you angle your face as close as you can to the lips to try to see up, to find this hymen. Junie

162

rolls her eyes when she catches you doing this; she calls you Inspector Vadget, a joke you do not get at the time. All this bending hurts your neck, and sometimes it smells like armpit down there. You can't see very much. But you like to imagine your hymen as a pane of glass, refracting rainbows as light catches on its surface. You like the idea of a rainbow living in your vagina.

At times you resent Junie, who manages to be both petite and willowy. But most of the time you love her, because being friends with her means being friends with other people too, especially older girls. Junie knows a lot more than you do. For example, she tells everyone that one of the girls in her year, Elaine Deng, who sits with her legs wide open so you can see her dirty white cotton panties, has gonorrhea, though Junie pronounces it *goo-no-rah*, and for the rest of the school year, Elaine has to duck when boys throw paper airplanes at her nipples.

Your mother has told you that Junie comes from a "troubled home." You do not fully understand what that means, but you do recall a time when you were young, before you wanted to do rhythmic gymnastics, before you learned the word hymen, that there used to be a lot more shouting coming from Junie's house. You remember one stormy evening, pressing your nose to the window, the glass cool against your left nostril, watching Junie stare with big, open eyes as a thin man, who had the same eyes as Junie, was led away by a policeman. You also remember Junie's mother grabbing her by the waist to carry her inside the house. Your mother came to the window to grab you as well. You remember that both you and Junie turned back, looked at each other wordlessly, and screamed.

The first time you bleed out of your vagina, it is premature. Christmas Day, the year you turn ten, a day unusually hot even for Malaysia. The women in the family, led by your grandmother, dash around the kitchen preparing lunch after Mass, pies and trifle and quiche, the one time each year when the household uses the oven. They dab their upper lips furtively as the heat from the oven melts off makeup. The men sip warm cognac in the living room, wiping droplets of sweat off their foreheads, but no one reaches for the ice cubes—it is a silent competition to see who is man enough to drink the most cognac in its intended, warm form.

Walls of the little bungalow sweat, the humidity smothering every bit of energy in the house to a halt. Every bit of energy, that is, except your own. Your feet are encased in a pair of very old metal roller skates, the kind that has a flat, cool base for the foot, a raised edge to hold the heel in, and leather straps that you are too lazy to wind around your ankle and tie in place. *Clack-clack*, the wheels go, as they roll over the gaps in the grout on the tiled floor. You press your heel against the metal back and the sharp edge scratches at your ankle; a blister will form there later. The breeze is cool as you whiz around the dining table, arms outstretched, imagining you are the lissome Thye Chee Kiat, the youngest, most beautiful of the rhythmic gymnasts from the gold medal–winning national team at the 1998 Commonwealth Games. You remember weeping when she scored the 9.5 that secured the medal.

Your mother reminds you that you are fat and stocky, unable to catch anything that requires the coordination of hand and eye. She tells you that the games were likely rigged, and that the world will always be rigged against you, a woman-to-be; that you will rarely get to choose what anyone thinks and says of you. You are not yet old enough to know that all Malaysians believe national triumphs to be grounded in corruption, nor are you grown enough to understand the futility of womanhood.

The breeze whistles through your hair and up your skirt as it billows behind you. You ignore your mother yelling at you to stop so the family can say grace. Your grandmother emerges from the kitchen with the turkey, browned, plump, and ready. Everyone wipes sweaty palms on their clothes and links hands around the table. You skate around the grown-ups in their best church outfits, crepe skirts and black pants and white shirts with sweaty patches sticking to backs. You want to shut them out, these adults wobbling around with whiskey breath, who seem to do the same boring things every day over and over, eat, drink, work, sleep—nothing bigger, nothing better.

Bless us for this bounty, O Father, as we thank your son, born of a virgin . . . your grandmother intones.

You feel the skate pull away from under your right foot, clacking over the floor. Your body leans forward, its instinct to propel you into balance. But your body fails you, and you feel yourself falling right on top of the metal skate, the edge cutting through the folds of your most tender parts, cold first, then sharp, then wet.

At first you look around you, and everything is very tidy. It appears you have fallen into a graceful seat, white dress puffing about you, covering any indecency. You are relieved. But then, you feel the warmth pooling around the white tulle of your Christmas dress, and it turns a brilliant red. You see the flaring, horrified eyes of the grown-ups. An aunt seems to have forgotten how to blink. A cousin puts her fist in her mouth. Someone screams, Is she dead? An uncle carries you, dripping like a carcass, to the kitchen table. Your grandmother dabs a wad of paper towels hard against the red gush.

Your mother howls, Is my baby torn up inside?

You wonder what a torn-up hymen looks like. Is it like a bubble blown out of a bubble wand, oddly shaped but still catching the light at the right angle, a wonky rainbow? Or is it simply shattered to pieces, bits of glass floating in a cavernous hole?

The first time you actually bleed, you are eleven. Your mother hands you a maxi pad and says, For you it makes no difference.

When Junie got her first period, her mother mortified her by throwing a celebratory "You're a woman now" party. Junie got to lie down in a comfortable bed with a hot-water bottle pressed to her womb, as other women in her family fluttered around feeding her all her favorite foods.

You do not tell Junie that instead, your mother feeds you various herbal concoctions designed to heal the hymen. She mutters as she mixes the herbs, all shades of brown, in a cavernous pot, next to the wok where she fries fish for dinner, her permed eighties hair coiled in tight ringlets around her scalp. As she boils the herbs, the tiny house smells like burnt forest, stale oil, and fish scales.

Some nights, your mother rolls you on your back, pushes aside your cotton panties, and peers into the vaginal realm with a magnifying glass, her right eye huge and bulbous like a fish.

I can't see anything! your mother yells. Does it grow back?

The first time you hear a boy talk about sex, you are thirteen. It's an older boy at school, sitting at the table behind you at recess, his mouth full of the fishy, oily snack keropok lekor. Junie won't eat keropok lekor; she says it looks like a gray penis. The older boy is yelling so loudly he nearly chokes on his food. He says when he first stuck his dick into a girl, he thought that his dick had fallen off. There was blood everywhere, man! And she was crying!

You realize you don't know how to explain that when the time comes, this won't happen with you. You research fretfully how Victorian women brought vials of pigs' blood into the bedchamber

165

on the wedding night to throw on the sheets when the man was in the throes of pleasure, to provide proof of his conquest. You sneak-read back issues of *Seventeen* magazine that you hide inside your textbooks, looking for articles on how to fake a hymen, but the only articles you see are ones about how to fake an orgasm.

The first time you contemplate letting a boy put his hand up your skirt, you are fourteen. Every girl in school seems to be talking about the possibility. You start worrying that if a boy does this with you, he might be swallowed whole, that the vacuum of your vagina, limitless with no hymen boundary—sucking, angry, empty—will absorb his fingers, one by one, that it will engulf his hand beyond his elbow, till nothing is left but the roundest part of his as-yet-undeveloped bicep, the one he flexes so hard to prove it exists.

Junie, who by this point is letting a different boy put his fingers up her skirt every day except Sunday—Sunday being the day for prayer—says that sometimes boys don't even know where the holes are. Sometimes they put their fingers in the wrong hole, and sometimes they miss the hole entirely and jab you so hard that their nubby fingernails feel like thumbtacks poking into your skin. And sometimes, she says, they do away with poking entirely and just slap your vagina around, and you're supposed to say, *ooh* and *ahh* and their eyes will get big and glassy and they will be pleased.

You remember when you used to think your hymen was a bouncy bubble rainbow, when you didn't feel secretly deformed, when your mother used to look at your body with hope, not with eyes blackened by shame and disgust. You know by now that no one can tell that you are hymenless just by looking at you, but you squeeze your legs tighter together anyway. Junie sees you, laughs, and says, Are you turned on? and you smile weakly because it is better to let her think that is the case. One of the girls asks how many fingers can go up there, and everyone stops as if to imagine a bloom of fingers opening in their vaginas.

The first time you get your heart broken, you are fifteen. One day, Danny Nathan catches you looking at his left dimple and middle-parted nineties boy-band hair. His friends point at you and knock Danny about the shoulders, and he grins shyly. You find this charming, so you agree to walk around the mall with him for your first date. On your second date you sit stiffly, shoulder to shoulder, in a darkened movie theater and find it difficult to focus on the movie because all you want is to touch his thigh. On your third date he grabs your hand, and now his hand sweats on top of your hand as he asks you to be his girlfriend. You date Danny Nathan for two months. During this time, you hide in the school library to make out between shelves of Jane Austen and Sweet Valley High, but soon, Danny begins pushing you onto the floor and tries sliding your legs open with his knees. You ask Junie what to do and she says, *Do* it, and you are shocked by how blasé she is. You don't know how to explain to her that even if the scars have long faded, every time you think about sex, you think you can feel the sharp edge of that old roller skate worming its way inside you, through you.

Instead, you have Junie teach you how to perform hand jobs on a banana. She tells you to focus on the tip, and that disgusts you because that's where the pee comes out. For a while Danny seems grateful enough. But then at school the boys start calling you Prudella, a cross between Prude and Cruella. You ask Danny about this and he denies that he has anything to do with the name; he says it is uncreative. But then you catch Danny mouthing Prudella along with the others. He dumps you just before you dump him, and this seems like the gravest insult of all.

The first time you watch *Cruel Intentions*, it's the day after your breakup with Danny. You are in Junie's bedroom, and you feel guilty because you have told your mother that you are tutoring Junie. Of course this is not logical as Junie is older than you and even if she is a bad student, you do not share classes and are not able to tutor her, but your mother thinks it is a very Christian thing you are doing and applauds your charity.

As you watch the movie, you find you have to cross and uncross your legs because it tingles so badly down there when you watch Ryan Phillippe grope Sarah Michelle Gellar. It feels somewhere between wanting to pee but holding it in and wanting to scratch but letting the itch escalate until you can't not scratch it anymore. You tell Junie and she rolls her sharp, eye-lined eyes at you and says, Don't you dare dirty my bed. She explains that there is a button down there you can press to help with that. You tell her you don't want to touch it at all, but she tells you, No, silly, the button isn't inside, it's outside, and you don't have to worry—and suddenly you feel very Selma Blair to her Sarah Michelle Gellar. She goes on to tell you that it's really about time you got it over with; that honestly, you've made it such a big freaking deal about sex that you are developing a reputation, the bad kind, the kind that will follow you through secondary school, and that the boys will stop trying to touch you, and that this will be the biggest tragedy of all. You do wonder about the balance between Junie's mother's "tart" reputation and whatever rep it is Junie says you have, but you don't say anything; you just nod, mutely. She sighs and says, Do I have to teach you everything, and before you can protest, she says, Fine, I'll show you, obviously I'm experienced, but it might help you to see how boys like it. You don't want to embarrass yourself, after all.

You want to ask Junie how she is experienced and why she knows so much more than you. You remember three years ago, your mother pulling you by the hair to get you into the house when you saw that the man who was led away from Junie's house by the policeman all those years ago had come back. He looked older, balder, thinner. Junie stood on her front step, frozen, saying over and over, "Dad." Your mother called the cops that day, and you have never seen her shake so hard. She said words like "sex abuse" and "predator." Junie's mother came to your front door for the first time ever that evening, and from the kitchen where your mother told you to stay, you saw Junie's mother mouth Thank you, and your mother nod stiffly, before shutting the door in Junie's mother's face. It felt rude, you recall, because when other ladies from church came by, your mother always ushered them inside and offered them tea.

The first time you plan for sex, it's not for you. You steal a condom from the stash your older brother hides under the bathroom sink, you pick a day when your mom is out, you lay out new sheets on your bed, your favorite yellow sheets that are only pilled on the sides so the middle part is smooth and soft.

It's Junie who brings Danny Nathan over after school, and your heart jumps to your stomach because you haven't spoken to Danny since the Prudella incident. He is confused to see you there. He looks quizzically at Junie, then back at you, like, Why is *she* here?

Junie says, Lie down, Danny; no, *stupid*, take your pants off first; and he says, I thought you said you were going to lend me the textbook, and she says, Danny, are you gay, lie down. He says, No, of course I'm not gay and pulls off his school uniform trousers and lies flat on his back on the smooth yellow sheets, but his right leg twitches and he is still looking over at you, unsure. You hand him the condom, and see his erection straining through the Superman boxers he wears, the ones you remember from your library days, the ones he still thinks are cool. Junie's pulling the shoelaces out of her shoes and she yanks Danny's left arm over his head and shouts to you, Give me a hand! Danny starts yelling, Whoa, whoa, this isn't what I signed up for, and tries to leave.

Junie seems possessed and she taunts, Are you gay, Danny, is your little thing not up to the challenge? You sit on Danny's chest, his stubbly chin chafing against your knee, and Junie sits on his ankles so he can't move, as you use Junie's shoelaces to tie his left arm and then his right arm to the bed frame, tight.

You open your mouth to say, Junie, I think maybe this isn't a good idea, but you say it so softly she doesn't hear you, though Danny does, and looks at you in the most piteous way. His eyes remind you of Doodle, the old dog that your mother put down a year ago, minutes before the vet injected him.

Geez, Danny, Junie says. Your thingy's all gone down; you're not scared, are you? And Danny says, No, of course not, but you see him blink rapidly and tug at the shoelaces around his wrists. Junie pulls at Danny's Superman boxers, her eyes ablaze, her eyeliner a little smudged on the bottom. But then she changes her mind and says to you, You do it, you make it hard again. You feel like something is wrong, very wrong, you feel your chest collapse and your breath catch and you worry you're going to have an asthma attack even though you haven't had one of those since you were a kid. But Junie's staring at you, and Danny's staring at you, and you know this is supposed to be a favor Junie's doing for you, and there is no way to explain to Junie that it isn't about the sex. That it is really about how all you ever wanted was to be a rhythmic gymnast, but then you became your mother's heartbreak, and ever since she has looked at you like you are something broken and soiled, and for years you were consumed by dreams of your vagina as a fathomless pit, absorbing boys alive, humiliating you, a parasitic trap you can never get away from because there is no hymen, there is no barrier; there is nothing to stop the badness from coming to the surface.

So, you do it. You take his penis into your hand and muscle memory kicks in for both of you. You tug as hard as you can, the way you remember he likes it, and he groans as he remembers how much he does.

Vanessa Chan

Out of the corner of your eye, you see Junie pulling off her skirt, and then her yellow flower panties that you notice match the bed. You see the dark shadow of her pubic hair under the white school-uniform shirt. Now watch carefully, she says to you and pushes your hand away from Danny's penis, which is now sticking straight up. You resist the urge to smell your hand. She angles herself carefully on top of him, and as she lowers herself onto him he groans, low and sonorous in a way you've never heard him do, but you also hear him say, No, no, and he strains his left wrist against the shoelace so hard you know that it'll leave a mark tomorrow. Junie smirks, See, she says to you. It's honestly not that difficult. She bounces up and down a few times, and you say, Junie, please stop, I think we have to stop.

But then you hear Danny cry out and his face is filled with a fear you've never seen before. His nose is bleeding, a little trickle down to his chin; you don't know if this is from stress or from getting kneed in the face by one of you. His leg, which was twitching before, is now shaking uncontrollably. You feel the yawning chasm of something break through you, want, or shame, you don't know. Orgasm crests through his body, yet his eyes are dead, black, bottomless.

You look away, somewhere, anywhere else. The room is hot, stuffy, and smells like fetid soil; you feel sweat everywhere on you, under your armpits, on your upper lip, behind your knees. Your underwear is drenched, from arousal, from fear, you don't know. You notice the sunlight refracting through the window, leaving shards of light, a broken rainbow on the white ceiling, your hymen, a specter, watching.

Ararat Tiny Houseboats

Cyan James

I ASSURED THE SHORE DWELLERS I would be fine. Really, I would. Kumud cupped my face in her hands to evaluate the hardiness of my resolve. Long working fingers that probed my chin and the hollow beneath my jaw.

"And what will you do out there?" she asked.

Feeling lazy with love, somnolent and strong as a swamp alligator, I allowed my eyes to half close and told her I would think of her. She would get me through. Her careful self-questioning. Her cape of glossy hair. The way she had gone over and over the data that formed the bedrock for our little empire.

"But you've never been truly alone before," she said.

"And now I'll never be alone, now that I've known you."

The foolishness of my one-hour-ago self. Since then I have discovered how the *Noah* rocks like a coracle, like a soap bubble. What is it made of? I am all too conscious. Wooden planks, hardly anything more than the bleached slats extracted from packing crates. What had we been thinking? What does a tree know of how to stay afloat, how can an organism that so carefully adds rings of bark year after year master the art of bobbing on stray currents?

A scientist would comprehend these things about cellulose and wind and water. I am made primarily of water, and assumed this familiarity meant I could understand it. But no, no, it is all still chaos. An octopus has nine brains, and maybe I need eight more myself before I will begin to understand water.

The land has just fallen from sight, the same way a plate of toast slides off a table when the dog decides to drag on the tablecloth. No wonder we used to think the world had hard edges. But the tablecloth is off now, and the world is the table, splintery and hard—I didn't know water could be so hard—and I am the piece of toast, fallen into a sea of fear, fear soaking into every crumb of me.

I fumble around the cabin. "Where is it, Kumud?" Apparently I am already talking out loud to myself, what desperation. That wasn't a habit of mine on land.

171

I am convinced Kumud has left me a surprise. Some love token, a note in her tumbleweed penmanship, attached to a Reese's Peanut Butter Cup package. A cable-knit scarf. Fingerless gloves maybe, or— I can imagine her perusing the antiquarian shop, burnished copper trim and green art nouveau light—an old-fashioned sextant. She could have rolled a hand-drawn map into a tube, she could have drawn the map herself and populated its margins with elaborate, exotic monsters. My core knows it: my Kumud would not have let me bob away without a token of reassurance. I scrabble through ditty bags. Look how quickly I am grasping the mariner's mindset. Already I understand the imperative to hang on to superstitions. I can practically feel the Saint Christopher's medal I packed, laying its small and comforting weight just below the notch where my collarbones meet.

Kumud said there would be fear, and here it is, so that in its own way should feel like a reassurance from her. But I feel no comfort. Adrenaline is crawling all through me; my head rocks, and my legs crumple like Kumud said they would, and if this is what it feels to be adrift, then I am not sure we should be launching our company, Ararat Tiny Houseboats. It does not seem ethically responsible. I wouldn't do this to a dog; I wouldn't even do it to one of those pink-eyed laboratory rats.

They only let me come because I'd never been on a boat before. I would be the ideal tester; I should know how it feels to push off into the waves. And it would be good for me to spend some time alone out in nature. I don't know why I told them that. Look how I have dumped out my bags; look what a mess has filled my living space. Hard to wrestle it all back into place. I think of intestines spilling from a belly. Still I'm searching. Searching, searching. Where *is* it? That little indicator that Kumud loves me, and that because she loves me, I will be safe.

Look around, man, I tell myself. She's in every line of this damn boat. She's on every side of you. We had designed the *Noah* together: four and a half feet of draft, twenty-eight feet stem to stern. A two-burner gas-powered stove and a desalination and filtration system for potable water, solar panels mounted on the cabin, a navigational system. Everything as trim and compact as a VW Vanagon. Shelves that pull out of the staircase. A fold-up triangle of a table, held up by a hook-and-eye fastener.

Cold comfort. On every side of the *Noah* heaves the sea. The sea! I am a waterlogged walnut held in its nutcracker mouth. It has only been four hours since I launched; dusk has not even arrived yet. My brain is thrashing like an eel stuck in the body of a midwestern flat-lander who has never so much as spent an afternoon on a beach.

Notes. Take notes, I remind myself. Track developments. Someone else will also feel this way, no doubt, in a year or in four, bobbing on black waves in one of our houseboats. Breathe. Breathe like one of those millennials terrified of rising water around the world. The water is rising, the water is rising, but we have a watertight business plan, that's what I've been telling myself every evening when anxiety swamps me and I wonder what it is we are trying to do. I had kept reassuring myself, No, you are all right. People will need your boats.

So focus, Mr. Test Case, I tell myself now. Stay alive. What do you feel?

Pilot study voyage, I write at the top of a surveyor's notebook, the kind with faint grids on each pale green-gray page. Impending abandonment, I want to write. Looming inadequacy.

Where is the token from Kumud? Even a little square of hotel chocolate would wring gratitude from me.

It's darkening out. I feel the gleam of being watched. Not by the land, which is already invisible to me, curled back into itself like a gray husky that tucks its tail over its eyes when it goes to sleep. The sea, the sea is watching. I am floating on the heaving, rolling eye of the sea. I am one of those meaningless see-through squiggles that dog-paddles across the wet eye of any living creature. The sea is rolling in its socket, and I am rolling with it too, not always in the same direction.

Nausea.

In the logbook I write, *Adding weight to the keel would contribute to a more grounded feeling*. What do I know. I have no sea legs. I do not know how swells are supposed to feel; I do not know how any of this is supposed to feel.

Kumud sent me a case study a few months ago: men from a certain village in Sri Lanka had gone out as usual, like their fathers and fathers' fathers, in open-air fishing boats, wrestling fish, arranging torn nets, amassing the day's catch. Tearing the heavy guts from tuna. Big metallic-looking things, tilting round eyes, torpedo-tube bodies. Their scales falling through shafts of sunlight in the seawater. Flash-flash with the knives. Like any other day. But the boats sailed back full of catch to a village that no longer existed. A tsunami had been there before them. No more mouths to eat their catch except their own.

So did they eat it, I wondered as I read the case study, or did they drop the dead fish quietly over the sides? They had to get strength from somewhere. They realized that now they could take any job in the world, now that they were unneeded. They'd slipped their moorings of braided love and need and familiarity. They'd become the slaves of grief. Did grief smell like raw tuna dashed with seawater, did it feel like the rolling sea? How did they stand salt water after that?

I drink Earl Grey tea and swallow two saltines and one anchovy. That's enough for now. I notice a lemoning happening in the sky. I should check the flashlights and fastenings; I should double- and triple-check the course setting and make sure the running lights are set out aft and stern before total sundown hits.

I write another header: *How to Survive for the Next 30 Days.* I list *Breathing exercises,* and *Keep the desalinator going,* and *Establish a routine.* A routine leaves fewer cracks to fall through. That's what Kumud and I learned from our prep session with Margot Klein, that fourteen-year-old who was setting the solo round-the-world sailing record until that storm off Chile snapped her mainmast, and from Guneer Chakraborty, that day laborer who escaped pirates holding up a Maersk cargo ship by plummeting overboard in an inflatable orange raft and then surviving fifteen months adrift in the Indian Ocean. Once those two signed up with us as spokespeople, I exclaimed, "See, I prophesied we'd get off to a good start!"

"Prophesy" is an archaic term, but it fits our Noah theme, our Ararat brand, our quaint repurposing of biblical ur-myths to fit these modern times. As a threat, I tell Kumud I am going to grow an enormous beard. I will learn archaic facts about ritual sacrifices and how to please the kind of deity portrayed in the Old Testament.

Margot and Guneer were vital to us. Because, as Kumud said, there was so much we did not know. Kumud's Nepal has the highest mountains in the world, but makes no claim upon any ocean, though all that mountain snowmelt is sluicing straight off into the oceans now. And I grew up in Nebraska, a boy much more familiar with cow-waste lagoons than the coast. The first time I saw open sea, I clawed the sand to stop the surf from dragging me into its endlessness.

In spite of all that, tiny houseboats, I told Kumud, will be selling faster than hot dogs outside an Omaha sports bar on a winning night for the Huskers. No matter that we're in the middle of the waterless Midwest, the Middle West, as it used to be called, without even two good lakes to rub together like nickels in the dry pocket of that land. No, the Midwest was the original frontier, we remind ourselves, where railroad barons cut their teeth and common folk got honed to prairie steel by the wind. Once again the heart of the States will point the way forward for everyone else.

But by no stretch of the imagination could Kumud and I be called experts at wilderness survival. Margot and Guneer, on the other hand, knew dirt-practical things: how to drink urine, or, more precisely, how much of your own urine you could drink before imperiling your kidneys and your sanity. How to treat salt sores. How to catch fish with the bones of other fish, how to persuade an albatross to land so you could seize it.

After her fishing poles washed overboard, Margot had fished from a line unraveled from a canvas bag, braided and tied to a bent hair clip. No more than two mouthfuls of meat on the kind of fish a get-up like that could catch. Think of all the hours spent with the line rotting where it draped over the rail, wrists sore, waiting for a bite. Guneer had become an expert in trapping and funneling water within his raft. Once, he seized a small manta ray from the very sea, jerked it into the raft, and kept it corralled there until it flapped itself to death, after which he dried it and sat under it as if it were a proper umbrella.

Those two had been to places Kumud and I could barely imagine.

Rolling in the *Noah* I tried to get into the right spirit. What if I had to get through three more days. Three more months. What would Margot and Guneer do? Is it possible to teach someone to be creative enough to wrest everyday life from disaster?

Yet there is no disaster yet, I observe to myself. The running lights punch only the tiniest of holes in the dark. Waves sound like the jostling of large animals, the rigging makes the sounds of a small banshee, and these are completely normal conditions. Not even close to a storm.

Margot and Guneer had both said to pay attention to the stars. The only company you might get besides yourself. Fierce, savage, heartless, lovely. The kind of beauty that can be wringing the life out of you, and you will still be thinking about its beauty instead of your mortality.

Before this pilot trip, Kumud had been apologizing almost every morning, during the slow moments when she was still gathering up her confidence, for the idea that has so infected us. "What have I been thinking?" she would ask, staring at herself in the bedroom ceiling. The previous owner had mounted mirrors up there, wide plain-like expanses of sparkle. Needed to entertain himself, probably.

175

Strange, to stare up into our own faces, but the mirrors spread sunlight around the room like marmalade.

"I hate seeing my hair sprawl out like that," she would say. "God, I look like I'm falling into a tar pit." She would mime a slow crawl out of bed, as though she were a floundering dinosaur.

I would tell her, "Everything you have been thinking makes sense. We're tracking, my little Thunder Lizard. The market's going to come around."

All our combined money poured into this venture. We had only eighteen months before we needed to turn a profit. Every second was a termite gnawing at our complacency. Keep it together, I keep reminding myself. You are the cheerful one, the optimistic sunbeam who pulls Kumud's chin up from the tarry depths.

I could never tire of seeing her fingers flicker through photo galleries online. All those marble bathroom-sink basins precise as coconut halves, the slate counters the size of chessboards, those origami beds that fold into the walls. Everything must be precisely arranged; everything must be functional and foldable as a hedgehog.

She connected the dots. She noticed the trendiness of tiny homes, the sweet appeal of compact things. The tininess of modern wallets, how little money anyone can afford to save these days. She noticed the struggle of moving through each and every day. Finally, she noticed how stubborn the water was in New Orleans, in Anchorage, in Florida, and other places, more every day. The water was creeping onto the land while everyone else slept. The water was taking tiny swaths of territory. Nothing anybody wanted at first, but Kumud said the oceans weren't going to be content with that, they weren't going to stop there. The water was going to absolutely terrorize us. We were going to enter into guerrilla warfare with it, despite being made of water ourselves; we were going to cry out for protection against it, but nobody would hear us.

Chart all those observations out and you have a powerful business proposition. It made sense to anyone she explained it to. The fundraising process was actually easy; there was more fuss in picking out the pencil skirt for her presentation than there was in running through the pitch. Limitation, she would insist during these pitches, was the mother of all invention. The tiny space was good. It limited possibilities, it made true creativity blossom. Just watch what we could do with 150 square feet. Plus upper-deck space. What Kumud didn't like was the guilt. Profiting off other people's pain. What was the alternative, I tried to comfort her. Offer floating shelters for free? Leave people to the mercies of FEMA and their moldy trailers? Go drown quietly in the cold, confusing night?

"We'll be fine," I'd tell her. "We have to do what we have to do. You were first with the idea, that's all. We might as well run with it, because other people are going to try it too. We'll make it as afford-able as we can."

When I saw her beside a railroad line running through Kathmandu, I immediately recognized her pragmatic brutality and designer's eye for beauty for what they were: a life raft. Not only had she amputated her own leg above the knee—much more ambitious than simply sev-ering a foot and rubbing dog shit on it to ensure a piteous infection—she had strung up images of her own X-rays in the stall where she worked, which lent an air of medical legitimacy, and which, when glimpsed through Kathmandu's early fogs, were eerie and hauntingly beautiful. She knew how to make you feel something, in other words.

She also relied on multiple income streams. She made chai in a large vat and set mugs of it on her stump, as if she were a slab of fine Carrara marble wiped clean for sophisticated Sicilians to set their little espresso cups on. *Coperto*, that's what the charge to sit down there is called, and Kumud already knew to charge extra for those who wanted to sit on overturned five-gallon plastic buckets to watch her display at length. Her customers worked at paper mills and tan-neries and textile factories and tried to keep their limbs intact while Kumud crushed more cardamom pods into the chai and rubbed her stump with coconut butter.

Now she sources filigree chandeliers and specialty solar panels. Yellow-painted fingernails fast on every keyboard, fast on every sur-face, taketytaketytak. She lines up calls with potential investors around the world. Mauritania had nibbled; Bangladesh was intrigued; Kumud had a list a page long of coastal mayors around the States who said they wanted to take a meeting with us.

Headlines in the papers had been getting worse. More erosion. Sewer system failures. Golf courses in Miami were sliding away; hillside mansions in California were clattering over cliffs. Insurance policies everywhere were going up, and some companies were flat-out refusing to ensure coast dwellers. That got attention. That's where we started with our pitch. Why put up with those prices when you could spend the same amount and actually have a get-away-free plan, parked in your backyard and making you money as a rentable space, if you wanted, until it was time to board, time to feel the earth slide away from beneath you?

More than half of us in the States live within fifty miles of coastal water, that's what Kumud always mentions in her pitches. The water is coming for us now. Why not move out upon it instead?

Now I was disappearing. Somewhere in the gulf, I was inconceivably small. Fumbling at the latches. Weak in the knees and ankle joints. As though I could find a big enough bottle of ocean repellent in one of those cupboards. Did you know that a panic attack can last for hours? I had no idea.

"I am in a retiree's paradise," I reminded myself in the morning, when the sun gilded the waters. "Marlin devotees would pay through the nose for this privilege. An open-water cruise. Blue-sky fishing." Like an alcoholic fixated on one more silky, stinging swig, I tried not to spur the little fifty-horsepower engine toward the harbor. I almost threw the radio, for emergency purposes only, into the depths to prevent all the Maydays rattling in my fingertips from getting out.

"Think of—," I told myself. But think of what? I had no problems with the plains, how they were flat and heavy as a businessman's mahogany coffin. But the water was so horribly restless. It was terrible the same way the muscles under a tiger's skin are terrible. Rippling while he paces and he pants. The hot breath of the sea was all over me. It was besieging me. What if Kumud had been washed away by the time I returned? What if the dock, the ramp, the stretch of beach beyond, and then the twenty-some acres of swamp beyond that were swallowed up within a month? What if I was left the only man afloat?

Under the tiny houseboat's hull the sea teemed. More life-forms had elected to stay there than all those who had crawled out upon the land. I knew their language was luminescence; I knew they spoke in flashes of color and bursts of chemicals. Some marine creatures can remain alone their whole lives. The octopus, for example. And some are schooling fish, which must be in groups of six at the very least or they will lose their sense of what they are and melt into the next predator's mouth.

I am a schooling fish, I know that now.

Every thought was panic, water, aloneness, the motor, the imaginary rum, the invisible gift from Kumud, the compass, the waves. Where I should have been taking readings for my records, I was instead trying to describe loneliness. How it was deep green and blue and how it contained veins of pure cold, and how it seemed to have no boundaries. This sounds ridiculous, I know. To be reduced so quickly. But a part of me considered panic a good thing—if I could feel like this in still waters on a good day, imagine what people would feel in disaster times. How quickly they would be reduced to their very cores. How lucky I must have been not to have felt this loneliness before. How did people cope with it? I did not know, not at all, not after hearing from Margot and Guneer at their consulting sessions, and not from anything I could dredge up from my imagination.

Eventually came soft bumps and taps against the hull. I heard them while I was three-quarters asleep. This was my message from Kumud, my subconscious said. This was a glass bottle stuffed with love messages and instructions on how to sail through the loneliness. I swam upward from the sleep, still alone.

The thumping turned out to be a Jarritos soda bottle. The vanguard of a great Sargasso Sea of garbage. Plastic bags and six-pack rings. Bottle caps in candy colors. The junk-food wrappers that stuff the stomachs of the seagulls. All the effluvia of being human, which should have nauseated me. Here were all the times someone could have tipped their trash into the garbage bin and didn't. Styrofoam pellets. Flattened juice packs flashing silver in the sun. Straws. Plastic lids. Fragments of toys. The clamshell packets that hold apples and bundles of lettuce. Styrofoam take-out containers.

With the net I caught everything I could. I lined up the bits I caught on the railing. Examined them in all their pitiful glory. I wove plastic bags together. Double ply, triple ply. I fashioned a huge plastic-bag net that billowed behind so I could collect everything possible. All those human moments. The picnics, the beachside spreads, the containers for salads eaten hastily at desks. Bottle caps that would last longer than bodies. Condoms that would survive so much longer than what they covered, containers enshrined far beyond their contents. We lived in the Age of Uncontained Containment.

I know I'm sounding mad, but the loneliness had at least lifted.

I made a museum of those human moments. That sounds intentional, but as I was raking in garbage, I felt nothing even close to volition. I just wanted all those indications of humanity as close to me as I could get. Kumud, forgive me, but I crammed your precise and elegant little space with as much garbage as would fit. I left myself only the smallest of places to step. I blocked the lovely little portholes so I would not have to look at the sea.

People don't stop to think about it, but there is so much humanity to be found in our trash. It looks so clean and sterile, the plastic, and at its core is made of life. Little chains of petrochemical vitality. The floating plastic wrap that once covered a slab of macaroni and cheese was once part of a dinosaur's thigh. Or a leaf larger than a Land Rover. It's liberated from the earth now, and in its newly incarnated form it floats over the entire world. Garbage involves the preservation of every temporary toy and every passing moment. It's the mundane ephemeral made tangible.

I made up stories for the bits of plastic. The margarine tubs, the shower caps, the cups for bubble tea. It could be that I was the trash, a container wrapped around a void. A human fast-food wrapper. I thought I'd had more in there. I had felt so solid. On land, at least, when I was sourcing wood and other building materials. Proofing contracts. Inking agreements and starting things. Renting storage space for the materials we were gathering up, starting to think about buying land for a dock so we could tie up models of the houseboats we'd soon be producing. But I hadn't imagined it would feel like this.

I hadn't known how to imagine escaping in a tiny houseboat from land become uninhabitable. That's why we'd hired Guneer and Margot as consultants. Guneer had been late, Margot early, but both of them had stared at the glass on our conference-room table, replying to our questions with only the tersest of answers, pinching the skin on their elbows, whirling around inside their own minds.

"Do you remember the salt sores or the stars more?" Margot asked. That started them. Talking and talking. As though the rest of us were not there.

We transcribed their conversation and read it over later. We circled the charged words, like "burn" and "lonely." We searched for the themes that would help our buyers as much as possible. We created categories: "Hopeless," "Dirty," and "Boring."

"Did you notice," Kumud said later, while she chopped scallions for our ramen, "how they just sat there afterward staring at each other?"

Two of the only people in the world forced to attempt survival under conditions of horrible uncertainty. I remembered how Margot touched her water glass. Not like someone afraid, but rather like one who had to remind herself of all the steps to drinking. Look at glass. Put hand out. Close fingers around glass. Pucker lips. Lift glass. Tilt glass into mouth you have opened. Swallow. It made me think that living is a set of actions you have to carry out like a recipe, and that it might be possible to forget certain ingredients.

The main thing, we realized, is that even a person prostrate on a life raft, on the eight inches of rubber and air that separates them from a vast ocean, does not want to change. The brain will keep scrabbling to make the raft seem like a regular home. The brain will play stupid childhood songs—"Walking on Sunshine" for Margot, for example—and will start placing hope-inducing illusions on the horizon. Making things up, in other words, when reality doesn't measure up. Guneer saw flocks of swans in rainbow colors.

I remember how Kumud stayed up late with that transcript. She was trying to imagine what could combat hopelessness. What, in the two hundred some square feet one of our tiny houseboats affords, could inspire hope for someone watching waves lapping over her former house, and, if things were quite bad, the grave of her grandmother or her child? Kumud's shoulders rose slowly toward her chin.

"Did you properly hear them back there, really hear them? They said the uncertainty was worse than the discomfort or the dehydration or any of that, even the loneliness. So how do we plan for uncertainty?" she asked.

I didn't know. I could have consulted people who had lived through earthquakes and divorces and political coups and bad haircuts. I could have held séances and sat beside graves hoping to hear how those who have already perished dealt with their own uncertainties.

When stressed, Kumud clenches her shoulders, but as for myself, I am a runner and a pusher who makes himself fly through everything as if nothing is wrong. This is my way of convincing myself that my momentum alone will carry me through any problem. Nobody else knows what they are doing either. Just go faster.

So we worked hard for weeks on the tangible things. Blueprints. Boat finishings. Reading journal articles about astronauts and biosphere dwellers, people trapped in small spaces. But the research could be off, Kumud pointed out, because all those people had a consent form, a protocol, and a known end date. So I watched apocalypse movies, read science fiction, shut myself inside a float chamber to put a toe in the void.

It didn't work. None of it seemed real to me—not the impending disaster, not the money to be made, not even the possibility, really, of a future. It was a fog.

Out at sea it's a different fog.

Maybe I'm sentimental, maybe the sea had rubbed me raw, but I was treasuring my little museum of human moments, even though it reeked. I too was starting to stink. I've heard fear has its own smell, and maybe that was making things worse, but the fear had seemed to stabilize into kind of bedrock with me moving around on top of it.

181

The fear was firmer, less like a waterbed, and I felt I could start to trust it. I had been able to eat a proper sandwich. I had made a few legitimate logbook entries. I had organized my museum a few different times until I was content with it. The garbage touched me somehow. All of human striving, and this was what was going to remain of us. Wrappers and remnants. Give it enough time and I suppose it would all go back to the petrochemicals from which it came. It seemed poetic at the moment.

After a few more days I thought, I'm getting the hang of this. Having stopped searching for messages from Kumud, I just imagined the messages I would like to receive. I had thrown up over the side a few times, and marveled at the clean, scraped-out feeling of hunger after vomiting. I started to realize, with amazement, how resilient we humans are. A tsunami or wrecked house can boot us into a new place in life, but give us a few days, a few weeks, and somehow we will have settled. Still flying, like those oceangoing birds who only have to find the right currents to stay aloft for months. Years.

This was good. I was learning. Everything I would tell potential investors and buyers from here on out would have the ring of authenticity.

Margot and Guneer had mentioned the chattering that happens inside the brain. At different speeds, and sometimes only nonsense words, but they both said they felt as though they would go crazy not from dehydration and heaving waves and sun exposure, but from the restlessness going on inside their skulls. Shut up, brain. But it wouldn't. It paced around in there, growling nonsense to itself, losing the plot and picking at stray threads, magnifying past slights and dwelling on minor grudges and just getting bitter and nonsensical all around.

Maybe that's happening to me now, I told myself. A cluttered noise was traveling over the water. It sounded like yelling. And club music? Surely I was nowhere near Ibiza. But I was hearing it in my mind. An audio hallucination, that's all it is, I told myself. The hallucination behaved according to the physics of real sound. It got noisier as I seemed to get closer.

And then, a dirty white boat sprang up on the horizon. I'd been looking at the curves and planes of the sea for so long, the boat seemed immediate and full of edges, full of corners. I was startled. I hadn't invited that boat to appear—how could it be that it was just there?

Of course I know I cannot claim the sea. But this is what humans do. We get used to a situation and lay claim to it. We get territorial. I had not realized that an uninterrupted horizon had become necessary for my sense of safety, of endless blue space between me and anything else—but I suppose it had.

They must have had a good sound system. Strains of a Cardiacs song were reaching me. I could hear yelling, bellowing, some raucous, glass-breaking noises.

I assured myself this kind of thing would happen to people in our houseboats. They'd have to face others eventually. Maybe we needed to think about elements of defensive design? It's normal to feel this kind of fear, I told myself. It's only that you don't know those people yet.

They pulled up even with me, though their boat was much larger. An old yacht? Rust bloomed around the waterline, and they themselves were flaking with salt blisters, yelling something I couldn't catch given that their music was so loud. I counted twelve of them in view, wearing the kinds of clothes I had only seen so far in photographs of Burning Man, as though they thought the sea would also be a desert.

"Come for dinner." That's what they were yelling. We had gotten so close, a wave might throw us into each other; I was so nervous I hung out the little rubber bumper meant to protect my boat from docks.

"Look at me now, Kumud," I thought. About to make new friends, or about to become merely another pirate victim. I just kept learning things about the sea. About size and inevitability. All that water and nowhere to get away, not unless I scuttled myself; no, I was at their complete mercy because everything I had was right there, spread in front of them. Nothing but my thin little words, nothing but hope they wouldn't be interested in anything I owned.

"Do you want to see my museum?" I yelled back. Louder than I thought possible. I was proud; I also sensed that if I advertised what I had, they might lose interest, go away, and leave me alone.

But this encounter had its own momentum. They were tossing lines, letting down a ladder, reaching for me with dirty hands, and I thought, "Well, this is happening," even as it was indeed happening. I was climbing; I swung upward through back slaps and welcomes, then I stood on their deck, gazing down over the rail. The *Noah* looked so small. How had they even seen me in the first place? I was afraid for our little boat. One moment and the lines could snap. The boat could roll and drift away. The sea could swallow it.

But Kumud would want me to do this. For curiosity, if nothing else. She wouldn't have said, "Consider what might happen" or "Maybe *you're* the dinner." No, she said we always had to think the best of others. At least give them a chance.

Their lower deck was a mess of coiled lines; the upper deck bristled with antennae. The planks felt soft and scraped, and the top coat of varnish on the rails had peeled. The vessel smelled like a hostel. A line of socks waved in the breeze like semaphore flags.

When I'm nervous, things come out of my mouth without first asking permission.

"Is this some kind of alternative living community you've got here?"

They laughed. A guy wearing a yellow bandana said they were just pirates. A pause. More laughter.

"Radio pirates!" he said. He told me to call him Igor, and said they were running a pirate radio station, "Playing what people need to hear."

"Who's listening?"

He said I'd be surprised. Did I want dinner?

"We'll take care of her," he said about my boat. I caught him nodding at another guy. Doug. Guneer and Margot had said nothing about times like this. When you had to deal with other awkward, hulking people. When you had been longing for human contact for weeks or thought you were, and then *boom*, there they were, strong as their perspiration, wanting who knows what.

"Keep them talking," I thought.

"How long have you been out here?" I asked.

"Three years!" they claimed. Igor was guiding me down a narrow set of metal stairs.

"Where are you going?"

"Nowhere! What about you?"

I tried to tell him about the business plan, the little boats we thought could save people, the rising sea.

"Though you probably know a lot more about it than I do," I told Igor.

His teeth were as white as bottle caps. He wanted to know what kind of museum I was running, and immediately I felt so embarrassed. I realized how I smelled, how I should have been keeping better log-books, how I'd let my mind just float. Lack of discipline.

"It's only junk," I said. "I was so lonely I just picked up everything that floated past."

He was listening, really listening. Careful eyes surrounded by the wrinkles one gets from squinting against the sun.

"Would you call yourselves nihilists? Anarchists?" I ventured. Trying to channel Kumud.

"We're just waiting, man. Saying what comes to mind. Waiting to see what happens. Trying to celebrate what *is*, you know?" He grinned.

"Here's the radio station," he said. A bunch of gear soldered together. Band stickers, notebooks scrawled with short speeches, a handwritten note above the mic: *"I know not all that may be coming, but be it what it will, I'll go to it laughing."* The guy behind the controls reached his hand over his shoulder for me to shake.

"You like Hanggai?" he asked. "You like Merleau-Ponty? You want to say something to everybody out there?"

Igor waved me toward the mic.

"Go ahead, say anything you like."

The green on-air light glowed and pulsed; the underlying static of the open line felt thick and soft as velvet. They wanted me to say something, me? What did I know?

All I knew at this point was that I wouldn't know how I felt until I actually felt it. There was no anticipating any of it. Which doesn't make sense when you're trying to build a business based on anticipation and sage expectations, but that's what I would have to try to explain. Your mind and heart just wandered around out there, doing random things and coming up with strange after-the-fact explanations. Who knew what you might need? A mount for a harpoon gun or a record player playing Blanco White or a set of empty cupboards where you could store the plastic human waste that could keep you company. I didn't even feel disappointed by realizing there was no way we could anticipate our clients' needs.

"We're here," I said into the mic. The men were waiting to see if I would say anything else. I could smell a fish stew cooking, a spicy Caribbean smell. I thought my boat was probably fine. "We're all here," I whispered, suddenly hoarse.

Margot had accepted our bottled water. She had opened a bag of salted peanuts and lined the nuts up on our conference-room table. I remember wondering if she'd developed a special sense for the sea. If she felt bereft when she could neither hear nor feel it. Something that had almost killed but in the end had not. In cases like that, do you feel a special bond, a tie, an affinity?

The sea had let her walk away, had not asked for her seawater blood back, had let her walk around like her own ambulatory saline bag stranded on the land. And maybe that felt like a betrayal somehow.

Kumud had sworn there were different kinds of people. Typologies was the word she used. The ones who dug in and isolated themselves in the face of existential threats and the ones who gathered close and turned up the music. The hermits and the hedonists.

"I guess we'll find out which one you are," she had said to me before I set out in our little, bright boat on the big, bobbing sea.

Milk

Clare Beams

THE DOWAGER, WHEN SHE WAS the queen, never spoke to me. When it was her son I suckled, she nested in her distant golden rooms, and she kept her eyes from mine when for public occasion she held the babe in her stiff arms. Her interest in him only grew as he did, and by then I had faded into the background to nurse young dukelings for a time.

But now the old lady has time for conversation. It's her son the king who's busy now, and to a lesser extent his young wife—a girl so gray and thin it's hard to believe she produced this strapping new grandson-princeling for the realm. Though the strappingness is thanks in no small part to me.

"He's moving eastward again," the old lady says on Thursday morning, coming into the room as the princeling polishes off my first side.

Of course I know who she means; being the king means being the only *he* that matters. So, more locally, does being a son.

"Why?" I say.

The old lady's eye lingers on my breast before I tuck it away. I am as old as she is, both of our faces changing now in different ways, mine pursing, hers thickening—but my breast is younger than young. It has been full of milk for the thirty years since I came to live in the palace, for all the thirty years of babies' mouths it has filled, and so its skin has had no slack for wrinkling and is as soft and pliable as my cheek at twenty. There is hunger in the way the old lady's gaze hangs on it. She knows herself to be looking at the secret of eternal youth, which somehow I have kept here, right here, inside the front of my own dress—if partial, if requiring the constant sublimation of the self, whose thirsts and hungers and backaches are always secondary to the suck, suck, suck, suck. To do this work so long is quite unusual.

"Why? What do you mean?" she says. "Because he can."

Her son the king is a charmer, a carouser, and deadly with a war. He makes the other kings love him so he can kill them unawares.

I pull my other breast from my dress and guide the springy nipple to the princeling's mouth. The lazy chub, he hasn't even opened his eyes, just makes that little mieu and there, he has it, what he wants. His little fingers petting my skin. My fingers petting his, and all the smooth, soft back of him.

While I nursed him yesterday afternoon, looking absently at the ceiling, I thought *Purple.* I can't say why—I just felt all of a sudden full up with the color. *Purple, purple, purple,* picturing the skin of a plump grape in high summer, and the spurt of deepest-dark blood from the vein of a chicken midslaughter, and the ribbon that hemmed my marriage underclothes. *Purple purple purple purple* gathering in my breasts, welling up and then rushing toward him through all the rootlike treelike fingerlike branches of me, a feeling somewhere between beginning to sweat and the bursting of skin. *Purple* from me and into his mouth *purple.*

Once he opened his eyes and I sat him on the floor to play, he reached for a painted ball behind his toy dog.

"Purple," he said, clear as day. You would have no reason to believe me, but nonetheless it is true that he didn't blunt the *r* as is usual for babies. All the children I have nursed have talked early. Done other things early too.

Now the princeling sucks, hard, bites. "Ack, little shark," I say. His eyes flick open, then find mine, and he smiles around the nipple, mouth full of his prize.

The old lady is watching him. "Isn't he," she says fondly.

I pat at his back again, where I seem to feel the flesh thickening up. And that's what will always save me, unnerved as the old lady may be by the eternal youth I bear on my chest, irritated as she may be by my questioning habit. I am the best anyone has ever seen at this. I am the loaves and fishes of women. Out of water, out of air, out of a not unusual quantity of food, out of these two smallish breasts, I make and remake a miracle, as many times a day as a princeling or dukeling could want. Milk, milk, so much milk I almost drown them, I choke them with the life of it, I fill them so full they can't think of dying.

Not a one of them has. A perfect record. There's not another wet nurse on record with a record like mine.

Still I would be wise not to let my questioning get the best of me.

"Little shark," the old lady says, and rests her hand on his head before she pulls out her sewing. She likes to sew with me, these days.

*

188

How strange that it is this life and only this that we all occupy. Each of the luckinesses and accidents that have befallen me has created a haunting beside it, a shadow life of other unrealized possibilities. The shadow life, for instance, in which I would have had other babes who were really mine, beyond just my Robert (because after all there was no untoward thing in the getting of him, no trouble in the birthing, and my husband did have a grin that could have caught my eye for years and years), and been by now a busy grandmother in an out-of-the-way town.

In my real, present life, my husband died before I could do my duty by him many more times, leaving only Robert and me. I remember looking at my own only babe on the day of his father's death, as he played on the floor. Again and again he put into and out of a tin cup a little wooden rabbit his father had carved for me when we were courting—shaking the cup each time, laughing, at the hiddenness or at the pattering, who knew. I noted the healthy curves of his cheeks and thought very calmly that we would both starve now unless I could think of something. We would slip off the surface of life just as my husband had, pain in the ear one day and gone the next.

I was twenty-one years old then, and Robert two.

Two nights later I heard howling in the lane. The neighbor woman, whose grown daughter had been the wet nurse of the wee kingling—and didn't we all know it, with how much the woman talked—had had a letter. Catarrhs, it seemed, could reach even within palaces.

It was not merciful to rise in the morning and present myself and Robert at the palace gates, and, when the guards were not inclined to let us through, unwrap my bursting breasts for them to see. Knots of milk pushed at the skin—I'd kept it there that morning though Robert cried—in a way that mixed up looking and touching. I was making a deliberate choice to read my own opportunity in others' misfortune. But I was not then in a merciful frame of mind, and I knew there would be a hungry babe awakening in his expanse of rooms, and that all the many richnesses around him would not be what he needed. The woman who could give him that, whose breast he suckled next, would take a life for herself even as she gave one.

It happened as I planned. I just hadn't understood then what it would mean for me to give what I gave as I took. I wish even now that I understood that better.

*

A letter from my Robert arrives in the evening, carried to me in the rooms I've held these thirty years. I of course sleep on a couch in the nursery, but in between feedings I am permitted to retire to this space I have made warm and vivid, soft and neat, everything I touch a comfort. Robert too once lived in these rooms, to which this paper version of him now comes.

He writes that they are well, or that he and Willy are well, Anna only middling, as is to be expected. They are thinking it will be a girl this time because of the different intensity of her sickness and the strangeness of her cravings (lemons, dirt). He finds his baking tedious in this hot weather but persists, as he does. They hope I am well. They send their love. They wish me to know that Willy has recovered fully from the congestion I'd inquired about so anxiously.

When first I saw Willy's scrawny length, it was all I could do not to seize him and put him straight to my breast. But I understood that this would not be well received—suspicious Anna watching me murderously from the corner. Nor would it have been allowed. I am the exclusive property of whichever royal boyling's mouth I fill at the moment; then I was taking only two hours away from the infant viceroy. A condition of my employment thirty years ago when I came to nurse the baby king had been the weaning of my Robert. He had cried and reached for me and I had given him cups of cow's milk instead, bits of bread cut in the shapes of animals. A rabbit, a duck, a cat. He cried and bit off their heads. It is a fact that he is the babe I have nursed for the least amount of time, and the one who has amounted to least.

Of course Robert was not born a duke or a prince. Still, even given their positional advantages, my princelings and dukelings are an unusual tribe. By the time they wean at four they are bright-eyed and canny, preternaturally aware of what the people around them think and feel. They speak like smooth-voiced little men. As adults, they triumph. These traits seem more pronounced in each successive nursling, as if whatever current flows from me into those mouths were coursing faster with time, nature itself having made a decision about where the future lies.

Words, for instance—particular, individual words—that is new.

I have wondered if these gifts I give are really only the natural abilities of an adult bestowed on a child, who then may combine them with those time gives to him and become richer than he should be by rights, and then use the richness to steal for himself still more. I have wondered too why this giving should be a thing that only I seem able to do, when nothing else about me is unusual. The sensation is something like I imagine slowly bleeding to death might feel. A seeping diminishment, an emptying marked by a weakness in the arms and a clumsiness with words, a dimming of colors, a lessening of my certainties in deciphering expressions and tones. This last worries me most. In those expressions and tones I have read at times the truths that have separated me, and Robert, from death.

By now, though, we must be safe. People talk about the difference between other men and the men I have grown—just whispered rumors, but they are enough to ensure that my milk will feed only princelings and dukelings and that a contest plays out when one nears weaning for the prize of being my next. The coming babes' fathers, with their round, sick wives hovering behind, exchange land, money, titles.

My poor Robert got only the least of it. Only good milk, enough to grow him fat and strong but not enough to give him any particular gifts. So he lives in Meddlemeare and bakes his bread.

I stretch out my fingers and imagine touching for a moment the curve of his pink baby cheek. I kept it full. That is something.

My gaze falls now on the heavy cloth of the curtain at my window. Purple, it is purple, but the word swims for a moment away, slides from my grasp before at last I catch it, before I can think *purple* and name what I see. The fear of this evasion feels large enough to swallow me.

I get out my paper. *My dear Robert,* I write, *thank you for your letter. I am relieved to hear that all is well. Tell Anna to chew ginger root for the cravings and the sickness. And please oh please do wrap Willy's throat.*

The next morning the old lady comes again to the princeling's rooms. "We are going to France," she announces. "A visiting mission. He'll bring his son."

During such missions, my boy babies are wondrous assets. They embody the continuation of the line, richly swaddled and wrapped and even more impressively cosseted in rosy flesh. There is a risk in travel, but my milk takes the risk's teeth.

"And me," I say.

"Purple," the princeling says, pointing to the old lady's jeweled brooch, where amethyst speckles the petals of a metal flower like ancient hardened drops of blood.

"Oh," the old lady says, her eyebrows shooting up as if the word has pricked her. "Clever boy." She looks at me. "That's quite early, isn't it?

"His father was early too."

"Not this early."

I don't see how she'd know, distant as she was from the kingling at that time, but in fact she is right.

She raises her eyes from the babe to mine. "Of course you must come too."

In my rooms, directing the packing, I wonder if there might be some way of frightening the king out of his plans. I might tell him of a band of marauders or a skilled assassin likely to intercept us on the road. Some rampant local plague waiting to fell us. But his reflexes are quick, and neither he nor his son is much susceptible to plagues, and they are the only ones whose prospective deaths would terrify him.

Some dire political consequence then. Some repercussion that would follow close on the heels of his butchering of this French king, swamp him in disaster, and undo all that he has worked for.

Except in my mind I can see the smile with which he would greet the announcement of such a threat—that smile I will know until I die, though I do not see the king often these days, because I have felt it beneath my fingers and felt those lips pull everything I have out of me. He would only smile. For has he worked? And can he be undone?

Purple, purple, purple.

In a harsh voice, I tell a servant to pack my blue silk.

My thoughts I work to soften. One king may visit another. A visit of state is not always a prelude to murder and seizing, and then who am I to say what a king should do, how he should direct the work of his hands? Even if I suspect I am the one who made those hands so adept at all their doings.

A visit of state is all this is, and I am only an attendant. I speak no French. I won't understand a thing unless I work to, and why should I? I have only to keep the young princeling fat and happy and living. What can be wrong in keeping a baby alive?

On the road, our king is irritable. He is an uneasily folded weapon: he finds it hard to suffer stillness. His ankles spring beneath him as he sits on his cushion. They are fine and shapely and they spring well. He pats the hand of the queen, who looks grayer than usual, as if the road does not agree with her—perhaps she is pregnant again—and argues with coach drivers about routes. He looks straight through me while I hold his son, though his son he certainly sees. "Is he warm?" he asks me.

"Plenty warm."

He nods and smiles that easy smile my fingers know. I watch him twist at a bit of his auburn beard, his thinking tic. When he went to visit the Polish king, I hear they played backgammon for hours, and though I was not there I know he would have twisted his fingers in his beard just like this before the difficult moves. He left after the signing of the treaty he had gone there to propose. Three months later the Polish king, having let his guard down—his actual guards drunk and dozing—was murdered in his bed. Our king whistled as he clomped down the hall the following morning and had a large parcel of the Polish king's land by Christmas.

We drive; we break up the driving. We stay at inns we have commandeered. We take a boat, then drive more and stay at more inns. Through it all the princeling sucks me dry. I find I do not want to eat much—the jouncing on the road, the swaying on the sea—but still I fill up and up. I lie awake in strange beds, listening to the princeling breathe so sweetly and sometimes, in his sleep, practice his new words. "Sun" and "road," "horse" and "neigh" and "night," "soon," "toy." All so perfectly clear, and each one I know I have given him. I have tried to stop but the words keep coming to me, then going to him, as I nurse. And so when a horse whinnies now I think *whinny* before I think *neigh*.

Sometimes it is possible to give a thing and still have it yourself, and this is a miracle. But it is, I know, an unpredictable miracle.

I watch the ceiling, these nights of our trip, and think about why these other kings would keep inviting our king to be their guest. Perhaps he is becoming such a force that they feel they have no choice—he is a new kind of weather, and they must make their peace with him, their preparations. They think they'll get out ahead in this way, despite the record of those who've thought the same. Perhaps that is another condition of being a king: one never thinks the precedents apply.

During the days the old lady bounces her knees in the coach while she sews. I catch her looking at me occasionally in a way that holds a question. I cannot guess what answer she wants.

*

At last we arrive in France. It looks disappointingly like our country. I wonder if this occurs to our king; why should he bother taking something so much like what he already has? Released at last from his traveling place on my lap in the carriage, the princeling toddles across the ordinary grass of France, surrounded by guards, toward the palace. He walks better in France than he did at home. I wonder what this place will be called when the princeling is the king of it, and what else he will be in the process of claiming.

The French king, younger than ours, does not seem younger. A bleeding disease runs in his line, and though thus far it has not been proven to inhabit his veins, he moves like a man afraid of opening them. His wife is plump and sturdy but his sons—he has two—are thin as he is, and they too wear fabric that seems thick as armor. The French king and ours stride the hall toward one another to perform all the steps of their ceremonial greeting. I watch the French king measuring the fearlessness of our king's gait. I see him looking at our solid princeling, who is just now in his mother's arms for the picture the placement will make, though she looks like a narrow-stalked plant bearing fruit beyond its capacity. Her smile is pained.

As soon as we are out of sight the queen passes me the princeling and sighs in relief. I put him down to walk—he is a burden for me too, hefty thing, for my arms are not eternally young, and the travel has been hard on my hips. He looks up and smiles. No matter what else happens, I think I will always love that smile. There is a sweetness to this princeling that is all his, a simple life-giving warmth that reminds me of soil in summer. Perhaps he will keep that along with his new acquisitions.

The old lady follows us when we turn for our room at the top of the stairs. "I want to see where they're putting him."

Does she know of some danger here I haven't scented? She smiles. "No reason to worry. I only want to see."

And the room is fine. The princeling runs to the bed, squawks, and pulls on the coverlet. Turns back, looks at my face, returns to hug my knee. "Sad?" he says, this boy just nine months old.

"Not sad," I tell him. "No, not sad."

"Well then," the old lady says, and leaves us to change for the evening.

Next comes a feast of the sort given when everyone involved would rather be feasting on one another. The tables are laden with sticky sugared buns, candied apples, cheeses and breads, but mostly plates and plates of meat. Pheasant, venison, duck, boar, rich browned carcasses arrayed in a line as if they have marched here to their deaths, through them to our nourishment. The air is thick and warm and salty, almost tasteable. My mouth waters.

The two kings are seated at the head of the room, at a table that faces everyone else, their queens flanking them and their children farther out in the wings, where we, their nursemaids, attend. The French nursemaid is only barely done being a child herself. The French children squirm on her lap.

The princeling stirs a little on mine. "Be still," I say to him. "Show them how good you are."

"Good," he says, and waits, very still, for his plate of meat, which is soon brought to him, which I cut into small pieces lest he choke, though I know he will not choke; he has good strong teeth and he uses them well.

The French king stands. The room quiets, and he raises his glass.

"To new friendships!" he says reedily.

I lift my own glass. My hand looks like the hand of an old woman I do not know; the veins stand out, the bones.

"To new friendships," the room intones in a collective French-accented voice.

He sits again. Our king says something to him in French, which the French king greets with a pleasant smile. "Thank you," he says. They go on talking, our king speaking French, the French king speaking our language, so that I understand half the conversation. Except slowly there is more and more I can understand, because slowly our king reverts to his own tongue.

"A hard world," our king says, "isn't it?"

"Yes, I pray very often," the French king tells him.

Our king shrugs. "That's all we can do."

I watch them playact regret and uncertainty, these divine instruments, slouching gracefully in their chairs. Their queens touch their arms and smile.

The meat in my mouth sends its salt juices down my throat. I am used to only some toast and cream at night; I can feel my breasts already bursting with this surplus. The princeling leans his head back against them and I wince, and he looks up at me.

The French princelings are now back behind the table, one marching and the other, our princeling's age, crawling, with the flustered nursemaid in pursuit. I take pity on her and push our chair back, say

195

to my own princeling, "Would you like to play?"

Set down, he gambols toward the other boys.

The nursemaid smiles at me for turning her boys' inability to behave into a general playtime. My princeling reaches out to touch the French princeling's cheek, mystified, probably, at the wanness there.

"Gentle," I say.

"Gentle," he repeats.

The French nursemaid gasps. She looks at me. "Speak?" she says.

"He speaks, yes."

She squints, and I watch her struggle for words. Finally she points to my chest. "How?" she says.

"How?"

"How do it?"

I would tell her, if I had the words to name this current that passes through me, mine and not-mine. All I know is that I gather my whole life in, and then I let it all down. It is made of the sound of my father's voice singing in the kitchens in the morning when I was a girl, the feel of my dying husband's hot, dry palm in mine. Of the cleaving pangs of birthing Robert, of cold winter sunlight on my skin, of the nip of underripe cherries on my tongue, of every question I haven't been able to answer, every longing, every fulfillment of a longing, every truth and lie and love and aggravation, the taste of tea, the smell of new cloth, the look of my husband's face across a room and Robert's in sleep as a child.

It is too much to say to any person, in any language. "I don't know," I say.

The French nursemaid seems to understand that the problem is not one of translation. She smiles and looks away, disappointed—she would like to guarantee her place as I have. She doesn't know that living it over and then giving it away, again and again, brings the exhaustion of uncountable lifetimes. She doesn't know the fear at my core. That pit there I have opened by emptying myself of so much, over and over, the way I am full of missing.

Inside my dress I strain and strain.

After the young princeling has sucked me dry—dryer than dry, so empty I am a husk, even my breasts hanging temporarily like sacs that will never be full again—I cannot sleep. I drum my fingers, knots and twigs, atop my loose-skinned belly. In his crib beside my bed the princeling puffs his gentle, peaceful breaths. I imagine all the bright shapes that pass beneath his eyelids. I wonder whether he knows yet that every last thing he sees in his life will eventually belong to him, whether that changes the seeing. His breath is milky and sweet. I love and loathe its smell.

Softly, I rise from the bed and leave the room. I am not meant to leave while the princeling sleeps. He is to be attended at every moment, so that death will always know it may not stop here. But it feels as if staying here will kill me.

In the hall I breathe deeply. Inside me already the miracle begins again, this air I take into myself fueling the milk milk milk that I will let out. Making something of almost nothing.

What does that mean I am?

Voices, down the hall.

The two kings turn the corner. I stand very still. They pause, embrace clappingly—"Good night!" "Good night!"—and part, the French king turning away and going back down the hall without ever having seen me, to sleep in peace, for how many more nights?

The king comes in my direction.

I smile while my head buzzes: *I came out for a drink of water, the prince seemed to want a blanket, three blankets, six, he is fast asleep and I wanted to fetch him anything and everything he might ever need before he even notes his needing.*

But the king only returns my smile as he strides past in an absent way that means he doesn't see me at all. He is only indirectly in charge of the rules that shape my life. He knows in theory that the prince ought not to be alone, but he trusts that others have ensured this state and does not trouble himself about the details of it, or of much else. No danger has ever really touched him, not even as a baby, not since the day I arrived in his rooms and put him to my breast. I remember he drank desperately only for the first moments. Then his gulps slowed, and his face became unsurprised and satisfied while I watched dust motes float in a sunbeam that fell on his gleaming nursery floor.

Now he keeps on down the hall. His broad back is turned so blithely to the empty expanse of hallway where any danger might lurk for another man.

"Your majesty!" I call.

He stops and turns back, bemused: I am meant to be only the stone from which milk springs, and I have spoken. As if he has no reason to know I am human; as if he and I had not spent hours and hours with skin pressed to skin. As if I had not cradled his entire ripe little

197

Clare Beams

head in my palm, held the whole space in which he now dreams and plans in such brilliant, bloody color.

"Are you enjoying your visit?" I ask him.

"Enjoyment is not really what I expect of these visits," he says, the liar. "But I'm furthering the interests of our great country."

"The king is as you thought he would be?"

"I never think before I meet them," he tells me. "When I meet them their faces tell me everything, and I don't have to think. I just see."

I see.

"This king," I say, "he seems like a good man." I'm trying to call my own king back to his baby self—to push deep enough to touch some place of real feeling in him still. "You should be—"

There is a word I want, but it won't quite come to me. It is as if I have put my hand into darkened water and am skimming the word's teasing, slippery edges. I try and try to close on it but it slips, slips.

And so I dangle here having begun to tell a king what he should do.

Watching me, he twists his beard.

Fear hums between my shoulder blades. I have forgotten myself for a moment, how little I mean; I have leaned on a relevance that only I feel. This king is no longer a baby, does not remember being a baby, and why should he feel beholden to the forces that kept him alive then? He is alive. He lives as memoryless as he chooses. If he wants he can throw me from a window. He can cut me down where I stand, or snap his fingers and call a guard to shut me in a French dungeon. If he desires it, I will disappear, and no one will ever speak my name again. He can take away that word too.

He watches me and I can tell that he sees all of my thoughts clearly; his gaze holds no safety, no mercy. "What? I should be *what*, nurse?" he says.

I close on a word I can find. "Kind. Kind, with him."

"Gentle?" the king says.

Even in this way, I am relieved to have the word back. "Yes, gentle."

"Of course." He looks toward the door to the room where his son sleeps, and I begin to take heart, for his son has relevance, and don't I have relevance there still? His son, dreaming perhaps of *purple, sad. Gentle.*

"He is well?" he asks.

No need to say who. For the king, the princeling is the only *he.*

"Always," I say. "Just as you were."

"And am still, dear nurse," he says, and reaches out to touch my

198

shoulder. His skin, my skin; a thin piece of cloth between him and the first territory he took from. I turn for the nursery door, step inside.

Overnight the princeling is ravenous. He usually nurses once or twice during the night; this night it is still deepest dark at the window when he wakes for the fourth time. His fingers stroke at me with sweetness and ownership. Perhaps soon he will be able to see with those fingers, hear with them, and after that, who can say? By morning I will be the oldest of women, and I will have nothing left inside me at all.

The fifth time he stirs and cries, at first just a small noise, then angrier, then angrier, I lie still and wait to see what happens if I do nothing. I love this baby fiercely, as I always love them, but I think I will try out not giving him what he wants this time.

The door opens. The old lady stands there. "Nurse! What are you doing?"

I raise myself on an elbow.

"The prince is crying," she says.

Her hair is tufted up at the back of her head, and her face looks defenseless. For a moment I almost mistake her for someone I might explain things to. *I'm afraid of what I might be feeding.*

Then she closes in on the bed. She pulls me up by the arm, and I see her again for the hawk her life has made of her. "The prince," she says, "is crying."

This is the truth.

It is simple, so simple, to sit up and reach for the baby, who reaches for me.

Our departure day comes a fortnight later. Concords are signed, with flourishes on both sides. No one writes his name so large and curling as a king.

"Write," the baby says, watching his father sign and laugh and thump the French king on the back, and reaches out his plump little hand as if expecting someone might put the pen in it. Terror rising in my throat at the idea that he might take that pen and fashion letters, I fill his palm with my own finger, and he tips his face up to mine— those liquid eyes I love. What do I read there?

We process to our carriage. The king and the queen climb inside, and then the old lady. I am coming around the back of the coach, the prince on my hip. In a moment I will put my foot on the step and he and I will be inside too, and they will close the doors behind me and we will drive away into the future.

For now, though, I am behind the coach, out of the line of sight of anyone inside.

I take just one step out of line, one step closer to the French king than he is expecting, just enough so that he draws back and looks at me, his pleasant farewell face slipping.

"Watch," I whisper.

"*Quoi?*" he says.

But I have said all I can say, more than I can say. I have only this word to give. I try again to give it. *"Watch."*

Watch everything that comes toward you out of this future we will drive into now. All of it will be coming from us, and none of it will be what you want. We are driving away with all that you want, and we will build walls behind us to keep you from it, because winning means taking, and we are always learning new ways to win. I look deep in his eyes so that he might see.

The princeling giggles. "Now bye-bye!" he says.

The French queen gasps, takes the king's arm. He puts his hand over hers.

I turn and leave them that way, skin touching skin. I climb into the carriage and the doors close behind me with a neat snap, and I smile at my king and my queen, and they smile at me. I settle myself, my princeling on my lap. My life, my life, at least I can give it to someone. Beneath us the wheels turn, grind.

Yonder Shines the Big Red Moon over the Devil's Lost Playground
Brandon Hobson

ON A SUNDAY NIGHT in our last days at the boarding school, the dogs escaped out of the courtyard by chewing apart the bottom of the fence's rotted wood and then crawling underneath it, and at sunrise on Monday morning when the alarm rang throughout all the buildings, the school awoke to the news that Little Bird had disappeared too. Only then were we allowed to go and search deep into the woods without our uniform coats, as some in our dorm had wanted, or without using butcher knives to cut through the thick brush and twigs, as the sergeants had proposed, because all we really needed was each other. The administrative staff and teachers and sergeants, who weren't concerned with finding the dogs, claimed they would call the police and began searching in the more open areas down the hill from the school grounds, but they sent us, for whatever reason, into the dark woods. We weren't afraid of finding animals or snakes or even murderers, not after all the physical labor and punishments we had endured over the past year. Going into the woods was like entering the thin, cool atmosphere of a land we had only heard about in stories read aloud to us, because the air was calm with a brooding tranquility, and the silence held a sensitivity that gave us an immediate sense of repose. We were silent too, not even clearing our throats or gasping as we trudged slowly through the wet leaves into the slanted streams of morning sunlight. All across the twisting paths that curved around trees, where the worms and insects crawled in the dirt that held the tracks of deer and rodents, we heard the sound of footsteps from ancient spirits running away from us, and though we never caught a glimpse of them, we did manage to see a vulture ahead of us pecking at the ground, eating something, and as we moved closer it lifted its head and looked at us as if saying, *Not another step*, which frightened Esther, Little Bird's sister, and she began crying right there and told us she was worried it was her brother's body the vulture was eating; however, Santi Lone Wolf told us the vulture was in fact eating a small dead animal. Nonetheless, we turned and headed down a different path.

Little Bird had run away once before. The first time the staff found him had been at the beginning of the winter, when frost covered the grass and icicles hung from tree branches after a recent ice storm, and still he walked away without even trying to hide as if he knew he was predestined to be caught and punished, which was inevitable in that dull, sleepy town. When they brought him back he told them that he simply needed to go for a walk to clear the bad thoughts from his head and adjust to the new thinking of the everyday people, that's what he told them, that his mind was an enervating dissolution of vulnerability prime for brainwashing. We were always a little uncertain as to whether Little Bird was brilliant or just a smidge eccentric, possibly even borderline crazy, but we admired his courage. In his earlier punishments, for instance, he had avoided so many food restrictions, so many beatings and deprivations, that it seemed horrific for him to prefer the long confinement of the Columbus House basement. Yet, as the days passed and the rest of us continued chopping wood and pulling weeds and loading piles of dirt in wheelbarrows, even the most impervious among us waited until we were back in the dorm at night to share our predictions, such as that Little Bird would emerge from confinement unable to even speak, that his mind would become so deranged from the isolation that he would no longer be able to recognize us, and that he would die down there from having a seizure. It was only minutes after he was set free from the basement and we saw the look on his face that we knew he was fine, that he had in fact preferred the confinement because he was able to find the books he had hidden behind a pile of wooden shelves when he was supposed to be sweeping and cleaning in there some time before. Confinement became a spiritual awakening for him as well because he grew closer, he told us, to understanding the Great Spirit, which he sought for comfort, whispering *Wado* repeatedly, and soon he was listening to the distant laments of ancestral voices that encouraged him to be strong in faith and not project his anger on to the everyday men whose foolish words and actions were cruel, and also to speak very little and listen closely, which was why it was so difficult to get him to talk about those nights of punishment and solitude. Even the most incredulous of us listened to him describe the visions of fleeting stars that were enchanting enough to make the most beautiful people on this earth swoon. Previously, during the extra free time on certain Christian holidays or on weekends, Little Bird would shut himself in his room and read and write as much as he could, telling us later he actually missed that about our public schools back home,

202

reading and writing stories, so certainly he devoured as many books as he could, reading them late into the night with the flashlight under the blanket, knowing he would be tired and work so hard the next day that his muscles would ache, yet he still stayed up late sketching faces and bodies, reading his classic books of literature, and writing stories and poems in his journal. No one paid much attention to his journal until Esther told us he was writing about his own death in the future, and that he had, at the age of seven, predicted the exact date and manner of death of their paternal grandfather, who died on Valentine's Day in his sleep, facedown with his left arm under his head as a pillow, three years after Little Bird's documented prediction, along with several other predictions listing the specific dates of world events that included bombings, mass shootings in the US, and a horrific flood that killed over ten thousand people and wiped out an entire town—all proof, Esther told us, that Little Bird held the crucial and compulsory predictions for what was to come for the boarding school, for the evil everyday men who made our lives misery, and for all of us. Yet, when we asked Little Bird about these predictions, he had only written a story, and all events that passed were merely coincidental, that's what he told us, but those of us who knew him best understood he wasn't being entirely truthful, and it always seemed he displayed strange behavior after the lights were out in the dorm; some would see him with his ear placed to a window in the hall as if he were listening for something outside, others would say he levitated in his sleep, but nobody was ever completely certain who was lying and who was telling the truth despite how much we trusted each other and everything we had been through together, all the daily work and harsh punishment we had endured. What we did know was that he sketched the faces of spirits and other haunting images such as images from the Native myths we'd heard as children, stories of snakes and wolves, trickster coyotes, and giant leeches crawling out of a bubbling stream to eat children and leave their bones piled everywhere until the vultures arrived.

The path we took in the woods twisted around trees until we got lost, and for three hours we continued searching for Little Bird and calling his name, listening for anything we could, and despite all the frustrations we pushed on until, strangely, we noticed ahead the floating blue and white feathers that rose and slowly formed into the shape of a boy we recognized was the image of Little Bird. The woods were surely filled with the ancient spirits speaking to us, so looking back now it wouldn't be too surprising to see such a strange

203

formation occurring, and we thought of our ancestors who roamed the land to give us messages and the elders who told us to look for them everywhere. *Listen*, we heard the air whisper. *What do you hear? What do you see?* Back in the courtyard, behind the hedges where Little Bird had had his seizure on the same day some of us were beaten for stealing the green apples from the apple tree, were hidden the dead birds and dead mice we kept for future revenge on our perpetrators once we figured out the best way the stench would be most effective, and this was how Santi Lone Wolf brought up the possibility that Little Bird was dead: *Everything dies. Think of our dead birds and mice. They're just lying there hidden and dead. Maybe he's out here dead too.* The air was now asphyxiating as we watched the feathers float away from us, still in their childlike image, but we followed them slowly down the twisting path and among the pale brush where cobwebs stretched from branch to branch and moths fluttered around our feet. There were gnats and other insects buzzing around us. In recent months when Sergeant Cash fell absent due to a sudden departure to visit a sick family member three states away, we were told to take a break from our shoveling duties and instead spend the days sweeping, cleaning, and checking the facility greenhouse for the yellow jacket nest the sergeants said was in there somewhere due to the sudden appearance of yellow jackets, and those who dared to crawl on their knees to check around the bottoms of the polycarbonate panels among so much shrubbery were stung more than once, just imagine, crawling in such a space and getting attacked by yellow jackets and getting stung, which then buzzed around us because yellow jackets are aggressive; all this to say that we were in no way afraid of bad spirits or the feather-child who so eerily floated low to the ground as if it were about to form into the shape of some beastly thing or something other than the image of Little Bird. We followed the feathers as they drifted forward until we came to a black velvet curtain hanging nearly twenty feet high and we all wondered, *What was a black curtain doing hanging in the middle of the woods?* as we heard the frightened cries from people on the other side of it, and we stood still for a few minutes contemplating whether we should turn and run back or else stay and look behind the curtain, and when we peeked around the corner of it we saw the naked bodies of lepers whose faces were indistinguishable from their disease, but they were really the spirits of the dead, who begged to lick the salt from our hands and necks. Ho! We did not fall for their tricks because there were so many stories of tricksters out there that we all knew and recognized, and those lepers were definitely spirits in disguise, so we backed away and turned to the feathers, which began floating in the opposite direction now, inviting us to follow them, playing with us, and this was when Esther eagerly reminded us that Little Bird had once talked about his nightmare of the moaning lepers, remember the mourning souls of the dead who cried out to him in a forest filled with poisoned fruit and bloodsucking ticks, remember, you remember he had seen and described them as clearly as we had seen them, isn't that weird how he knew we would see them, tell me what you think, and we said, Yes, Esther, we remember his nightmare too, a nightmare that had, in fact, started the first night we were placed at the school, having been taken from our homes and put on a bus that pulled away from our houses on the reservation, where our mothers and fathers watched and wept from the windows in horror and agony, and we cried too as the bus hauled us away like pigs across state lines on a narrow highway all night and the whole next day, stopping only to allow us to use the public roadside restrooms while the sergeants waited for us by the door to make sure we wouldn't run away, and back on the bus Little Bird whispered that these men must hate all of us as much as they hate their own images in the mirror, they're taking us to cut our hair and will force us to think and act and look like them. That unprecedented decision to speak out loud about what was going to happen to us, and how he remained so serene telling those of us on that bus, indifferent, with the slow inflection his father had infused in him so that he would blur the linear identity those people assumed we all possessed, because speaking slowly and with such inflexible decorum was significantly different from the way the rest of us spoke, which was to say we rarely talked and whenever we did we tended to mumble or talk as little as possible, but the hope was that Little Bird speaking this way would drive the furious curse out of the everyday men who bore the insults and hatred and contemplated the beatings and punishments with the sick ardor of their ancestors, these men not even blinking, spitting tobacco, thinking they could rip away any culture, thought, and beliefs in order to brainwash us, so, yes, Esther, we remembered the nightmare Little Bird had because we had them too. There were nightmares we hoped we never encountered such as the killings and stabbings by these men wearing masks to hide their identities and the protection they received from the police and government to keep us against our will and torture us until we either were completely eradicated from our culture and identity or else we died, so we all shared the same night-mares, Esther; the difference is that Little Bird's has already happened and ours are still out there waiting to unfold. Other than Esther, the people who commented on Little Bird's extraordinary gifts were two sergeants from the Columbus House who came to our dorm and saw Little Bird sitting in a wicker chair on the first floor's living room enduring the drowsiness of a postwork afternoon, just after he had removed the worn shoes they had given him that were at least one size too small for his feet, his pants rolled up and his socks different colors, when the girls from Sallie Hall next door were standing out-side the window waving at him for his attention (Esther said they thought him the cutest of us all, even with short hair), and he would flutter his hand to produce a trail of blue smoke as if his hand were on fire, and the girls outside were all smiling while the sergeants took note of everything seemingly miraculous they witnessed, including, for instance, how the church bells in the cathedral would start ring-ing whenever he pointed at them from outside, which gave those of us working such sheer pleasure especially during hot days when the sergeants yammered on about how slowly we were working, and also the way he could attract yellow butterflies outside for the girls and then collect them as he walked from the dorm to the courtyard where the butterflies then formed into an image of a rose slowly lift-ing into the sky until they parted and flew away, and of course the sergeants and staff never discussed these miraculous gifts or ac-knowledged them around us, though we knew they were watching him. Sometimes Little Bird blinked quickly when someone was talking directly to him, which gave the impression that he had the manner of someone deep in social anxiety, but truthfully he was tor-mented by the idea that people talked about him at all. The many attempts to calm the rumors that he would be taken away from us and used for the benefit of the sergeants and the school had been use-less; they discussed using him for financial and personal gain among themselves, which some of the girls overheard when they were mop-ping the administration building's third-floor hallway and were caught listening and later subjected to punishments denying them of meals for an entire day, but the very administrators and sergeants who were in that meeting claimed it wasn't even discussed, that instead of talking about Little Bird's prodigious abilities they delib-erated for nearly four hours over how some of us would have to dig three separate graves all the way out at the cemetery due to the recent deaths of the three brothers who passed away from malnutrition; all

three brothers died within hours of each other, and they were also
some of the angriest and most rebellious of all of us, Eddie and
Chuck and Robby, and as a result of their anger they were also the
most severely punished, of course, how sad to think back on this,
how we could hear their cries at night coming from their rooms, how
we saw the broomsticks and the bruises and blood in the toilet, and
how the sergeants and staff must've done exactly as their ancestors
had done to our ancestors, burying us before sending word to our
families, and now they were faced with the debilitating problem of
who was going to dig the three graves, and how were they going to
transport us out to the cemetery when we were all such flight risks,
yes, this was what they said they discussed for so long in the meeting, not Little Bird, and they had the minutes in writing to prove it.
Although he did not know of the rumors, Little Bird told us he was
certain something significant was about to happen in his life and
that he would not be at the school for much longer, that sitting for
long periods of time in the wicker chair on the first floor of the dorm
helped him visualize this prophecy, which he described as looking
like the slow development of a chess game and he needed to understand how each decision affected the next, a game he had learned to
play from his grandfather only months before his grandfather passed
away, and even then, at the age of seven, he understood there was an
implication the game held him acutely susceptible to understanding
how greatly each decision affected the next, and how after he check-
mated his grandfather he rushed into the bathroom and vomited, the
crisis of a potential blame developing that his grandfather's loss con-
tributed to his death six months later and so rendered Little Bird's
glory bitter, and for the next seven years he took advantage of his
solitude to reflect on that game and how each move represented a
step leading toward death.

Following a winding path, we saw the blue and white feathers before
us still in the shape of a small person, when Santi told us to look
up through the slanted stream of sunlight and we noticed the three
brothers, Eddie and Chuck and Robby, sleeping in the branches with
their arms hanging down and their hair long the way it was before
the school cut it, and when we called out to them they opened their
eyes and looked down at us, shaking the tree limbs so that leaves and
twigs fell, laughing like devils, and then they climbed down and told
us not to follow the feathers because that was a trick too, there were
tricksters all around these woods, they said, and, waving away all the
flying ants, Esther asked how we knew it was them and they told us

to sit and listen, so we sat down in the dirt and listened to them tell us the story about the children who ran away from home and were mutilated to pieces and eaten by the wolves who roamed the woods, they tore into the children and ate them alive, but they weren't the usual wolves but trickster coyotes with the red eyes of bad spirits, all six of those coyotes, each prowling out from behind the trees and pouncing on the children before any of them even had a chance to run or help each other, and the three brothers said, "Listen to us, we speak the truth to you, beware of these tricksters here like the coyotes and the feather-child and the moaning lepers begging to lick the salt from your hands, and instead follow us because you know us, look at us, you recognize our faces," and then all three brothers lowered their heads to avoid looking directly at us. We abandoned ourselves to their story, trembling with the rage of knowing how the others before us had died, but we were wiser and more solicitous than they suspected because we quickly realized they were the tricksters themselves veiled in the illusory cloak of Eddie and Chuck and Robby, and Santi was the first to lash out at them and call them liars. "We won't fall for your tricks either," he told them. "If you think you can fool us, you're wrong; we can find Little Bird ourselves without any help from the spirits in the woods or from anyone else."

"Look," Esther said quietly, "I'm not stopping to talk to anyone anymore." The rest of us agreed the distractions were meant to throw us off course, but the bigger question that still loomed was whether Little Bird was even alive and, if so, was he hiding in those woods? It was all a mystery to us, and we could see that the sunlight had shifted in the trees and was now jagged all around us, and Esther was staring into the shards of light when she told us that Little Bird believed the less people understood about him the less afraid they would be, which was why he remained so elusive, quiet, and re-moved from everyone, and why he wrote in his journal about staring out the foggy windows of his dorm room where one night he swore he saw arrive in front of the school the horse and carriage with the hooded image of Death driving that he'd read about from the famous Emily Dickinson poem, something that frightened him particularly when he saw the figure of Death leaning forward from the carriage to look up at the school, as if looking directly at him sitting by the dorm-room window, but the night was cold with a light mist falling, and the gray horses shook their manes, and Death stepped out of the carriage and started walking—Little Bird had described the figure to Esther as a "shadowy thing with a limp"—but at that moment Little

Bird pulled the window curtain closed and spent the remainder of the night sitting cross-legged on his bed with the light on and the door locked. He wrote in his journal then, describing what he had just witnessed, worried not only for his own life but for the lives of all of us, everyone at the school, because children had already died (the three brothers, for example) and now Death was back for more. Esther told all of us this very matter-of-factly, noting that she had read the journal entry, unlike the rest of us, on one of the days he was serving his punishment in the Columbus House basement, and that he also saw gorged vultures hanging in the moonlit sky, he saw the dogs rooting around in the garbage bins behind the cafeteria where the stench of dead animals hung in the air, he saw the shadows of the sergeants in the windows of their building where they cast evil spells in the middle of the night, and he saw the ghosts of the dead moving from one building to the next and smelling like their rotting bodies, which lay in putrefaction down in the graves we all had dug. "What if he's dead," Esther asked us, suddenly in hysterics, as if the thought had finally hit her, "what if he's dead, dead, dead like all the others?" Whole nations are disappearing, we thought, they're slowly killing all of us, driving us into extinction and torturing us before we die. Esther was breathing with difficulty in the thin air, feeling herself lean into her friend, until she was able to calm down as we all comforted her, telling her we understood how frightened she must be because we were frightened too, that we were all in this together no matter what we saw or what would happen, and soon enough Esther was able to continue with us as we walked down the path for a ways, though too quickly we saw a figure up ahead of us who was sitting against a tree, and when the figure saw us he stood but didn't leave. We recognized that it was Sergeant Hood standing there, broad shouldered and hands authoritarianly on his hips, and he began to shout for us to "keep looking for Little Bird," and when we told him we *were* looking he stomped his foot and rattled on about how important the strength and will to live is, "you folks need to understand strength is mental and physical," he said, citing examples of names we'd never heard of and didn't care about anyway, and then he spewed on and on about how little we'd learned and changed from the months we'd been there. Sergeant Hood was like Sergeants Cole, Jackson, and Lee, all of them talking so much they often lost track of what they were saying, the type of authorities who liked to hear the sound of their own voices any time they gave orders, and they demanded that for us to avoid any punishments we speak more fluently than we had when we first arrived—by nature most of us were way more introverted than they ever suspected—and they required that the boys speak in full complete sentences, speak the hell up, spit it out, they'd say this among many other things, such as look a man in the eye and shake his hand like this, firmer grip, firmer grip, say yessir, stand up straight without slouching like you're a defeated knucklehead so that people won't think you're a defeated knucklehead, ah oh, tie your work boots so that the laces are nice and tight like this, no like this, watch me, son, and here's the proper way to grip a shovel and dig so that your back muscles don't strain, do it right or else, ah, hold a knife and fork like this, cut your meat like this, chew with your goddamn mouth closed, try not to look savage and maintain eye contact in a way that's assertive but not overly threatening, you sons of bitches, look at people in the eye when you talk to them without having to fiddle with your hands when you're talking to civilians or anyone especially in authority, son, ah, because authority means respect, and you'll need to learn to give it and show it to your authorities in power here, ah oh. Ah. Besides all that, the sergeants drank whiskey from flasks when they thought we weren't paying attention, you could always smell it on their breath, you could catch them stopping in the stairwells to take a swig or stepping into a bathroom stall and locking the door, meanwhile the rest of us suffered from the nauseating heat and were permitted to drink only warm water from a garden hose until lunch. We knew the only reason they let us take our time and eat a good meal and replenish fluids to hydrate was so that we could march right back out there into the sweltering sun and keep working throughout the afternoon. It wasn't all forced manual labor, of course. The boys weren't allowed to be around the women teachers, who seemed way friendlier and less authoritarian than the sergeants, and while we learned certain trades, the girls at the school were able to read and write and study, which made Little Bird envious, and they also sewed and made clothes and practiced cooking, which made many of the boys jealous. Part of what the school wanted was to integrate us into their everyday society by learning trades such as mechanical work and carpentry and useful skills so that we could earn a living wage, this was what they told us and anyone else, but many of us still craved doing art, painting and drawing, learning music and history, and reading books and talking about them, which was one of the reasons Little Bird once told the sergeants that he would rather be a teacher than any kind of manual labor worker, and Sergeant Lee grimaced, so we learned to read and write in English by ourselves. One of the fun ways of learning how to write in English was by hearing the sergeants' voices in our heads and writing everything down, which we later learned was a way of mockery Little Bird found genuinely funny, probably in the same way our ancestors mocked the Europeans by dancing and stomping foolishly. Sure enough, Sergeant Hood himself was stomping his foot and yammering at us to keep moving, move it, move it, move it, to keep looking, his face and neck flushed pink, which Esther reminded us was as striking as his face the time he discovered the news of the hurricane that brought so much rain it swallowed the land and drowned the army base where he was stationed during the pandemic many years ago, hearing that breaking news straight from the president's mouth flushed Hood's face so pink it brought tears to his eyes, which Esther said was sad for about six seconds until he turned and told her that no one would ever understand the circumstances of his suffering and that all the savages surrounding him were like an invasion of some strange cloud of pestilential vapor slowly destroying him, he called us "wild" directly to Esther's face, and she stepped into the shadows of the Columbus House hallway full of so much sadness and rage that she wanted to sneak up on him the next time he was lying on that hammock behind their quarters and strangle him while he napped, that's how angry Esther said she was—and who could blame her? We sensed his presence along with the other sergeants any time we were outside by the apple tree in the courtyard, where we would sometimes congregate after sneaking out in order to compare blisters on our hands or bruises so that we could make sure to have all the details correct for any proper authorities if we ever made it out of that place. Beside that apple tree was also where we were standing when we first saw the wolf with red eyes staring at us from across the road at the edge of the woods, and none of us moved or breathed for a minute as it stared at us, but then we heard Sergeant Hood step out of the barracks and yell, "YONDER SHINES THE BIG RED MOON OVER THE DEVIL'S LOST PLAYGROUND!" and we saw that his arms were raised as he stood barefoot and without a shirt looking up to the sky, and suddenly the wolf turned and ran back into the woods, and we knelt down and watched Sergeant Hood stretch and smoke a cigarette before he went back inside. Whether he knew the wolf was there or not wasn't as important as what he yelled, "YONDER SHINES THE BIG RED MOON OVER THE DEVIL'S LOST PLAYGROUND!," and why he yelled it, whether it meant anything or whether it was just a reflection of his own bout of insanity.

211

We wondered how so much confidence and authority delegated to each of the sergeants might not have been the cause of their misfortune, if it wasn't Sergeant Hood who would go crazy first, then it would be Cole, or Jackson, or Lee, because at night they each had their own strange rituals: Cole often stepped outside between two and four in the morning wearing camouflage shorts and black military boots and practiced marching with a limp, which was odd because he never walked with a limp, but there he was every night limping back and forth in front of the barracks; Sergeant Jackson woke before the morning bell, usually at sunrise, and ran up and down the stairs in front of the building, then did fifty push-ups, twenty-five jumping jacks, ten knee bends, and several shoulder rotations before heading back inside; Sergeant Lee sat on the steps at night and played the fiddle until the songs he sang brought him to tears and crying out various prayers of hope for a woman named Cleva; and we soon learned Sergeant Hood stepped outside to yell, "YONDER SHINES THE BIG RED MOON OVER THE DEVIL'S LOST PLAYGROUND!" any time there was a full moon, even if it wasn't red.

What had the strongest impact on us regarding Sergeant Hood in the woods was realizing after we walked away that it might not have been Sergeant Hood at all, but another trickster trying to lure us into some unknown hole in the ground, a thought that terrified us until Esther reminded us what we were there for, to find Little Bird, "Remember, he's missing and we have to find him, forget the tricksters, please," so we trudged on in silence down a path in the woods, and we could soon hear the rushing water of the tributary that flowed into the Chapa River miles away. We followed the trail toward the sound of water, a walk that took a long time, and soon we could see the clearing at the end of the woods, which none of us even whispered about because we knew we were about to emerge into new territory. As we moved slowly out of the woods we saw several birds scatter, and then we edged down a small hill where we saw everything we had feared from Little Bird's prophetic stories: the devil's lost playground full of the bones of dead children, a bubbling stream, and beside it, Little Bird's body facedown, one arm spread out and the other by his side, silent and still as the dead, like an animal thrown to the garbage bins, and Esther screamed as we saw his life pass directly in front of us, steam coming off the water like braids of smoke rising to the big red moon, birds flying all around.

Five Poems
Cindy Juyoung Ok

SUNSET, GLORY

There is a heavily chandeliered
gas station in California, and if
you wonder if the night manager
has any new obsessions lately,

one is positioning the trade-off
between flexibility and strength
as a modern development, and
another is considering talk of

weather as a way of making
mood public in other places (like
we use traffic). Also, a dosed
expansion of the octave range.

And then a joke I won't share
now because it only works
if you agree the idea of god is
hilarious. Mine: care as control,

moth wrestling as pageantry,
the intricacy of wiring the moon
would require if we lit it
ourselves, and scheduling

space to mourn a migraine as
it ends—the calm—the ceiling far,
and jeweled, and bright, brighter

THE CAPACITY OF HAPPENING

In another version, each of us has
the courage to give up power,
and we get an adult set of gums,
to powder a concept of practice.

We plant, never cobble, and put in
real work to do right by language,
so the downstairs joy and the dancing
upstairs never disturb.

        But in the version we have,
we are static in front of advertisement.
Fish do feel pain—whether that is
relevant to what étude we choose

depends on your performance of
restraint in the perfumed restaurant.
We buy well, the idea we have
of freedom, out of envy of our future

selves, the ones we are sure we are
on the border of becoming. This is
the only version, the one that paints
distance and celebrates owned space,

where anticipation exceeds any
impulse, every object. Yes, this is
peace. We have an economy
of movement, our market of care.

RATES OF GRACE

Most mornings I crowd the crowded,
the birds make ovals above the now

214

iceless river, and I surveil groupings
as they re-form by rain and flight and

report them on the phone—the saints
and the winners. You have rivers you

imagine, mostly, and I wonder about
painting (if it has to be an explaining).

I hope not and I calculate the flock's
days, which run on fewer hours than

ours, with less recursion than may be
suspected. You change the object,

rustling on the resistance of bacteria,
and given the rareness of your hands

you are the California redwood but
I am both the last three birds circling

the mill and the roof where the rest
of the birds land. Lands. I dream I

swim city intersections with you and
as I give the river report—nail beds

frosted—I remember the plainness
of the first peeling of the new year,

waking by the ocean when usually
we ally by the fields. By this river,

last week, we thought the moon was
moving up but it was the clouds, down

—why we are not archivists. A plate
of ice survived the storm by basin and

evenings I edge it closer to current,
face feigning haze for anyone watching

from above. You look up the possible
daylight while I threaten the threatened.

CLAIM

We keep clans to avoid
and I know how (to braid).
Eating fish cheeks is bound
luck, which exists if you would

want it to (true, there are studies).
Some of us here are lanterns,
representing things always.
The itching scar is news

of healing nerves (back
in the shade, we must risk
at times the timing of the oak).
There is an architecture we duck

but we don't know it (I do direct
the birds come night, you count
branches, pay grass, be swift,
share what we shouldn't,

like this jacket). To waver
is to admit a gaze can char,
that I do not have the power,
and some bugs survive winter

as words through translation
(suspicious is the traction).
Better, when this worn,
to be continged upon.

FEELING OURSELVES

I am not the kind of person who checks the weather.
Or founds a body by denial. I am not of the person
who is kind, or likes middles—of novels, or fractals.
We follow the scripts we don't remember being given.

The place we reshaped makes us more and more like
first-time lovers: only Syrian summers and Canadian
winters left. Tipping, so American, relies on the mood
of the master—no pleasure of being reacted to there.

You or someone like you: our version of rosaries.
Acceptance of the nonexistence of free will is one
thing, but to memorize the animal noises in every
language? Better to keep a placeholder in the draft.

Calendars flattened time forever, but we can keep
recruiting words newly, and asking for movement.
The idea of rescue collects wheels like wealth. This is
longing; I was right not to have heroes, or tapestries.

Texture is just distribution, you can pay for that. You
have. No such thing as a hijabi or a decisive person:
wear hijab or not, fry a large egg to clean pan scraps,
or scrub. Prosecute the urge to interpret these gaps.

We now prefer private spaces, how they usually have
not one pair but a drawer full of scissors. It's tacky to
say thank you on the subway and how rare is surprise?
As for me and my house, we will run from elegance.

Time after Time
Michael Ives

The passage of nature leaves nothing between the past and the future. What we perceive as present is the vivid fringe of memory tinged with anticipation.

—A. N. Whitehead

these hours
the days that hold
them their opalescent
moods autumns
recollected joys and hurts scattered
among other days
other moods lost
beneath the centuries the dust

*

these hours
clustered in a thought
of remembered twilight
the closeness
they had offered once more
flowing into an
emptiness freer than
itself and as its negation

*

these hours
following one after another
to the very
last this
present hour its surface impressed
with the soft
catastrophes the losses
and vanishings the subtle diminishments

218

*

these hours
spin into small riots
of empty splendor
the immortality
they would seem to promise
as swiftly vanished
as a snowflake
falling in a dog's eye

*

these hours
reckoned at the close
of day to
have been
the jewels slipped from a
velvet bag the
message undelivered the
melody heard and soon forgotten

*

these hours
cannot survive their impassioned
emergence but subside
in a
mild wash of melancholy the
faint sadness the
resistance yielding to
surrender to the following upon

*

these hours
more than mere wraiths
of what had
once erupted
into a present now indistinguishable
from the wreckage
of a past
less than the anticipation of

Michael Ives

*

these hours
as they foliate their
inner surfaces with
a rime
of tomorrow's cresting paradox always
about to flare
outward into what
will become yesterday and then

*

these hours
arrested in speech brief
victory gardens planted
against the
insensible falling away into a
no longer is
nor was nor
ever had been more than

*

these hours
mere fading tokens of
every thing other
than the
thing you lost would tell
you where you
left it if
it were not other than

*

these hours
their bid for our
attention nothing but
our attention
to their showing us how
who we are
is how they
must die into our being

*

these hours
these roots reaching down
into the power
of doubt
when the eye in our
ache clouds over
with the sight
of its inner miracle crystallizing

*

these hours
each a minute kingdom
of never again
written into
the forever after cannot fail
to have included
in the total
legacy whatever happens next when

*

these hours
unfolding without blemish without
daylight between them
redeem nothing
but their cold fusion of
fulfillment and its
cancellation the inevitable
surprise the death that lives

*

these hours
drifting through their flights
of animal language
through phosphor
stems below the sensitive water
through thoughts of
a single day
in a cottage once ago

Michael Ives

*

these hours
were small seeds from
which a root
had pushed
with undetectable force the hated
wall from its
footing and a
hundred thousand futures poured forth

*

these hours
plumped full with emptying
into their endless
passage lined
with angels one must wrestle
from their sleep
of fate they
have perfected at each moment

*

these hours
a swing moves in
wind leaves in
the playhouse
rustle the whole life spent
combing out a
failure to capture
it in a single phrase

*

these hours
whisper the destruction of
the world while
the construction
of the world drifts through
those sibilants as
transparent as glass
blown in cooling echoes through

*

these hours
one of their eyes
smeared like a
moon howling
without mercy at its wolf
in the indigenous
fantasy I have
burned their nations down to

*

these hours
every morning inside what
becomes my brain
when I
inflate a raft of imagined
time and drift
toward a destination
no longer willing to abide

*

these hours
as having overlapped like
embowered leaves hissing
to each
other of the other's betrayals
asleep inside their
apparent passivity were
not asleep in fact but

*

these hours
locked in their midnight's
blank curiosity the
grainy footage
of it running through a
silent electric paramour
the universe will
never release to its distances

Michael Ives

*

these hours
variously a caged bird
a man sunk
in a
bog blind abbess prison made
of air of
silk and boredom
an ever-mutating detention within

*

these hours
adrift along an inaudible
summons never to
be heard
for it too drifts aimlessly
toward a deferred
arrival a hunger
anonymous and insatiable for annunciations

*

these hours
must suffice until it
comes the time
within time
the fulfillment broken through complete
surrender the *is*
not inside the
is revealed and its hiddenness

*

these hours
fallen into a single
disclosure flashes through
space remorseless
threshing the grain of the
ultra-deep field
grain of the
mind of stone of number

*

these hours
a generalized and suffocating
proximity the enduring
a closeness
unbearable density crowded inward pushing
always the displacement
deeper seizing of
inner distances recoil and again

*

these hours
thrust toward a center
neither localizable nor
other than
unbridgeable removes inward a constant
compaction down to
such claustral scale
difference and identity merge

*

these hours
even deep in extinction
adorned with the
attainment of
heaven wandering through their countless
firmaments their bejeweled
grasses and waters
their transmission of signless lamps

*

these hours
that they never repeat
that they are
nothing but
repetition their singularity their
utter sameness their
baroque undetectable proliferation
within a single vacant throb

*

these hours
legs tucked in toward
the skull hands
under chin
eyes shut body cold laid
on its side
fed by no
hand through the unmoving turbine

*

these hours
make of our bones
radical harrowing medicine
of slow
concealments and those concealments a
wound to heal
them and that
wound a revelation to all

*

these hours
these causeways rooms fields
roads heights misgivings
never to
be duplicated triumphs humiliations blind
stair empty glass
rain mud all
of it guttering endlessly through

*

these hours
don't care what they
are where they
came from
nor into what mysterious reservoir
they empty as soon
as they arise
and no one expects them

*

these hours
already grandfathered into the
inescapable series of
their predecessors
so quickly to funnel away
through our persistent
failure to know
them as anything other than

*

these hours
thesc lcave-takings the
interminable succession of
them supplanting
all memory of the arrival
from which they
are presumed to
have departed all evidence of

*

these hours
as other than the
echoing denouement of
their flowing
out from a sourceless source
always plowed under
what was but
a moment before its anticipation

*

these hours
ripening into this single
dark pulse this
unreasonable soon
this outcome searching for its
appointed event while
already the event has
relinquished the outcome to

Michael Ives

*

these hours
to the language they
drill through this
world to
reach the world they want
to describe that
restive haven sleeved
in its own unraveling burden

*

these hours
whose forgetting has stored
its fulfillment in
ritual vessels
of remembrance these glassy insubstantial
reliquaries these tableaux
these wordless chronicles
these necklaces with no clasp

*

these hours
loud with dire supposals
in their perfect
silence they
fall away in sheets while
we watch from
our curious perch
trapped inside their unswerving plummet

*

these hours
falling through the world
they make the
world the
arc of their descent and
heavenly bodies trail
along in mild
awareness the curvature by which

*

these hours
plunged in great revolutions
enflesh themselves with
motion carry
all within their centerless impulse
foaming with centers
what exits what
enters the plume the canker

*

these hours
themselves their accumulated echoes
the clays and
marls the
granites ores shales the crumbling
the pitiless turning
of stone in
its sheathes involute glory of

*

these hours
their promised aftermath diffracted
through the truth
of their
passage gathered in a single
thought the very
first neither remote
from nor native either to

*

these hours
but somewhere deep within
them an unmolested
stillness they
cannot help drawing us toward
quiet bowl from
which they may
not drink nor can they

Michael Ives

*

these hours
ever rest nor will
a close to
their day
arrive nor any thought of
their cessation survive
our forcing it
into the inescapable queue of

*

these hours
and so their fate
must forever lie
beyond their
reach in futile dreams of
instantaneous moments unextended
in time briefest
fantasies of such sweet immediacy

*

the hours
cannot help but propagate
them while the
fruitless hope
these chimerical nows engender has
already expired upon
appearance its promise
nothing but a sharpened weariness

*

the hours
feed upon in the
midst of their
self-flagellation
which is their very passing
the thing they
are the hours
are their own eternal penitence

230

*

flowering and
dying in great profusions
of beautiful prisons
the hours
pumping through an inconceivable emptiness
from nowhere into
this briefest somewhere
the music of their disappearance

Water Music
Alyssa Pelish

THE SUMMER I WAS NINETEEN, I never saw an actual molecule of substance P with my own eyes, or even with the help of nuclear magnetic resonance spectroscopy, but I knew it comprised eleven amino acid residues and had an α-helical core stabilized by two hydrogen bonds, that it had a highly flexible extended NH_2 terminal, a central turn on its Gly9, and a carboxyl terminal sequence that bore a family resemblance to that of its fellow tachykinins. I knew that after—textbook example—a hand touches a hot stove or a finger is slammed in a door, or, say, the blade of a Swiss Army knife (which was the only knife I personally ever owned as a teenager) presses into the soft flesh of the inner thigh, ion channels in nerve cell membranes would open, depolarizing the membrane and sending an electric shock of excitation shooting through the sensory neuron, all the way to its terminal in the spinal cord. I could diagram this on a sheet of graph paper with a four-color pen. I knew that the depolarization of the sensory neuron terminal in the dorsal horn (blue pen) would result in an influx of Ca^{2+} into that terminal, the second influx of which would fuse tiny waiting vesicles of substance P to the terminal membrane (green pen), forming a temporary ion channel that eventually dilated (black pen), thus releasing the SP into the synaptic cleft (red pen). And I knew that everything that happened after that—the excitatory postsynaptic potentials that electrified motor neurons traveling back down to the body part in question and causing it to pull away, and the interneurons snaking up through the spinal-thalamic pathways, bulging into awareness of pain *qua* pain in the somatosensory cortex and bursting into an affective response in the limbic cortical regions—was set in motion by the release of substance P. And I knew that the theory was that all of this could be cut off, or at least blunted, if you cut off the substance P.

I'd just run five miles around the dim little indoor track, which was an eighth of a mile and so required a total of forty laps, which I would count out under my breath every time I passed the starting line, which began next to the steps to the weight room, each of the laps taking approximately 52.5 seconds, which was my training pace. I liked to think it focused me to repeat the lap number under my breath, like a kind of mantra, for the length of each lap. That it kept my mind absolutely still and nearly impervious to all those stray thoughts that could otherwise creep in and no doubt slow my pace. Early December in the Twin Cities meant the temperature outside was hovering at most around zero, and once I was done with my laps and the complex series of push-ups and crunches and glutes extensions and stretches I always did afterward, I'd peel off my sweaty maroon running tights and compressing maroon-and-yellow sports bra and take a scalding shower back at my dorm, after which I'd emerge feeling cleansed in a way that went beyond just my pores, and take my place at my desk with my homework and a cold can of Mendota Heights spring water and three hours to study before bed.

That night, I remember, I was reviewing the chapter on interneuronal communication in my neurophys textbook, which meant going over only the parts I'd highlighted, paying the most attention to those parts I'd highlighted in orange, as opposed to ordinary yellow. My hair was still wet and my cheeks still felt red from the shower, and I was seated such that I could imagine a thread pulled straight from my spine to my coccyx, my body weight distributed evenly on both hips, my shoulders parallel with my hips, my knees bent at a right angle, and my feet flat on the floor. *Type of stimulus, type of receptor channel, what change in permeability occurs, whether action potentials are used, what transmitter is released.*

I remember that the jangle of the phone broke in while I was concentrating on an orange passage about ionotropic (i.e., direct) versus metabotropic (i.e., indirect) opening of ionic channels in receptor cell membranes. I found it mildly condescending, the way the prim British voice of the textbook would anthropomorphize cellular anatomy, as in "direct channels are *looking* outward, *waiting* for signals to arrive from the outside world, whereas indirect channels are *looking* inward, *waiting* for messages that are generated within the cell itself." As if ionic channels had eyes or sat waiting next to the phone on Saturday nights or something. But anyway, the phone did ring, which was certainly not something I'd been sitting around waiting for like an anthropomorphized ionotropic cell membrane channel.

When I picked up, there was a pause at the other end, and then a voice that declaimed my name in full: the dactyl of my given name,

233

the single syllable of the middle, and the trochee of the last. (Or at least this was how it suddenly, beautifully occurred to me, having taken a semester of English Prosody from 1368 to 1798.) The voice spoke with what sounded like great fondness, and it seemed, for a moment, like my name was a kind of secret code that only I and this voice knew. I was silent, although I could feel my sympathetic nervous system pulse into gear.

"Do you know who this is?" the voice asked me, but not like it was a pop quiz, or in a creepy way, but like he was momentarily sad at the prospect that I genuinely might not know.

I did, though. I tried not to let the grin on my face or the throb in my chest seep too much into my own voice, which is something I'd gotten pretty good at doing—I mean concealing the effects of the sympathetic nervous system.

"KDWA," I finally said. "Straight Talk on Your AM Dial."

There was a pause, after which the voice replied, "KDUZ," pronouncing the three last letters as a single, drawling syllable. "Your Information Station."

This was how I remembered my brother answering the phone in our house, when I was twelve and he was sixteen. The chirrup of the antennaed cordless on the kitchen counter, his poker-faced delivery of a local radio call sign and slogan, the long pause on the other end.

I adored my older brother. As a kid, I had tagged alongside and taken orders from and copied him, to the best of my ability. It had been that way for as long as I could recall. A thing was good by virtue of his having done it, or covetable by virtue of belonging to him, and other people were important by virtue of his liking them. His standard, the most visible and most immediate in my small world, was like that of a ship sailing perpetually a knot ahead of me. I aspired, therefore, to know what he knew, do what he did. We could hate each other, have bitter, knockdown, drag-out screaming matches that would compel my mother to call my father at his office and demand he come home to intervene. But we were also, being the only two children in a household run by adults, coconspirators. Banished to the upstairs when our father held campaign strategy meetings in the dining room, we ran reconnaissance missions, gathering what scraps of intel we could and poring over whatever it was that the adults were saying or doing in our absence. We conjured an inner life for the family dog, ventriloquizing him in a coarse accent that gave us leave to utter things we could not say in our own voices. In the basement, we dressed up in our father's cast-off army fatigues, his old ties and corduroy jackets, picking through the accumulated stack of red-white-and-blue signs with his name blazoned across them (FOR BOARD OF COMMIS-SIONERS, FOR DISTRICT 23 STATE HOUSE, FOR DISTRICT 23 SENATE), and we'd hold them aloft and chant the slogans we'd hear him proclaim any year that the signs came—which was every other year—and then shake each other's hands officiously to make our mim-icry more authentic.

But my brother was four years older, and I was perpetually in his wake. As we grew, as he turned thirteen or fourteen, and I was still nine, or barely ten, he had no use for a little sister, for a hanger-on who couldn't compass whatever complicated considerations were now circulating in the narrows of his mind. So I lurked in the out-lands of his floating citadel, exiled but always admiring.

Early in high school, he drifted away from the wholesome, ball-playing figure of an all-American boy that had pleased our father (who had demonstrated his general approval by talking sports stats—professional and junior-senior–high league—with my brother, and clap-ping him on the back whenever he was suited up for a game). The nylon football jerseys and perfectly broken-in baseball caps fell away, as did the Old Spice judiciously applied after postpractice showers. All of it was replaced by a wardrobe either tie-dyed or salvaged from the racks at St. Vincent de Paul's. His once closely clipped hair, cut monthly by a hockey-booster barber at Buck's Clips downtown, now dusted his shoulders. A mossy, cuminy odor of sweat and whatever he was smoking clung to his hair and skin and clothes.

This new persona clearly rankled our father, who kept an antique carpenter's level on the little ledge over his home-office desk like it was some kind of religious icon, and developed the habit of hum-ming the refrain to "Straighten Up and Fly Right" in my brother's presence. But there was a cabin somewhere out in the woods where my brother and a few confederates—at least as suggested by their similarly shaggy hair and Deadhead tie-dyes—would disappear, pre-sumably to smoke up and noodle on the guitar. And so, when my father appeared in the evenings to drink his Scotch and eat mixed nuts poured tidily into a ramekin in front of the nightly news with Channel 12's Don Winn, after which he would preside over the dinner table, my brother's place setting would go untouched, the equilateral triangle of its napkin still neatly folded. When he was home, he dis-appeared behind a haze of sound and a skunky smell I couldn't ID at the time, the door to his room inevitably locked.

"The Lubrication Station," after the local oil-change place just off

Highway 47, was what my brother took to calling our father, whose greatest priority was that everything run smoothly, or, more accurately, that nothing ever be found to not run smoothly. We had grown up watching his glad-handing in church basements and at Lions Club suppers and while filling up his tank at the Pump n' Pak, grown up hearing his Dale Carnegie method of repeating people's first names an unnatural number of times while speaking to them, and knowing—in the way that we knew all twelve sound effects in Dig Dug— his indefatigable repertoire of phatic responses, which included *ain't that the darnedest, you bet* (typically repeated twice, emphasis on the second *bet*), *good for you*, and, most reliably, seasonally appropriate remarks about the weather. Every two years, his fulsome smile radiated from the TV screen, interrupting the regular string of commercials for Pepsi and Fruit 'n Fibre cereal and AT&T long-distance plans. "Sweeps Week," my brother called it, although it lasted much longer than that. We watched our father make conspicuous appearances at high-school football games, cheering boisterously in the stands, and at fire hall pancake breakfasts, cheerfully pouring OJ. At his own dinner table, the sharp corners of each triangularly folded napkin carefully pointing away from the place mat, he would give thanks for the bounty, proceed to slice and serve each of us our portion, and remind us that this was no place for Negative Neds or Nancys, which was a term that he preferred to use preemptively. Once, while paging through the S–SN volume of our *World Book Encyclopedia*, I read about the physiological differences between a genuine spontaneous smile and the more perfunctory social smile. After that, I would practice contracting my orbicularis oculi muscles in front of a handheld mirror in my bedroom, willing myself to produce the "smize," or "smile with the eyes," that is the mark of a genuine grin.

I don't remember exactly when it started, but there grew in me the dim feeling that whatever was inside me—whatever you'd call the vague hum or ghost in the machine of the face and body and voice that as far as you know everyone considers to be you—was entirely inappropriate for the table my father presided over and the world as stamped with his bland seal of approval. His was a flat plain of contented normalcy that I seemed always on the verge of staining with whatever black substance there was inside me. But that was all the world there was. I went to school dances and pep rallies and ball games and played volleyball as a Lady Trojan and sang in the choir at Immaculate Conception, even dueting "Faith of Our Fathers" and

"Let All Mortal Flesh Keep Silent" with soprano Amber Anderson, who would go on to lead the senior-high show choir to four medals of various alloys at the state competition.

My brother, though, played music I couldn't recognize, wah-wahing so fervently on his guitar that I assume he couldn't hear anything outside his room. When my father pointedly hummed "Straighten Up and Fly Right" on the increasingly rare occasions that he and my brother were in the same room at the same time, my brother, his eyelids heavy, bobbed his head and grunted out the first few bars of "Purple Haze," like a dueling Fender Stratocaster. He showed up to a family photo op dressed not at all in the plaid shirt and new Levi's and boat shoes our father had had our mother lay out for him, but wearing instead a multicolored, fringed serape and combat boots, looking so relaxed it was as if he were moving in slow motion. He did not attend the guest sermon our father gave at the baccalaureate service at Our Lady the year my brother's class graduated, even as my mother and I sat up front, ostensibly rapt, and afterward served Country Time lemonade and sliced squares of the giant *Congratulations Graduates* sheet cake at the reception. He did not even attend his own graduation ceremony—it was later found that he had not even gone through the charade of standing in line to pick up his blue-and-white cap and gown from the band-room storage closet.

I was in awe. Somehow, my brother had found a way around, or maybe under, the smooth surface of this world. I wanted to let him know that I saw this, and that I too loathed everything about these flat plains and the school spirit and county pride I pretended to spout, and our father's smooth smile, which had become my own smile. I would smile, attempting to convey the appreciation that I felt, when he'd let one of his deadpan remarks drop—sotto voce digs at our father or Hyde County, South Dakota, at large—but I knew my smile looked just the same as it always did, and there was no reason for him to believe that anything else lay beneath it.

The October I was thirteen, though, I found him all alone one night in the house. The lights were blazing. Approached from the driveway, where I was dropped off by a fellow Lady Trojan after volleyball practice, the house looked like it was on fire. It was Sweeps Week again, and my parents were away at some kind of fundraising dinner, but I assured my ride that someone must have just forgotten to turn off the lights. When I walked in, there was a human shape on the living-room sectional that it took me a second to realize was my brother. He was holding his head in his hands, like the ceiling might collapse at any minute. He rocked slowly back and forth. I stood there in front of the door, the hump of my L.L.Bean Book Pack still rounding my back, my blue-and-white-canvas athletic bag still in my hand. It wasn't just that every overhead light in the room was blazing, it was every tiny table-side lamp and corner lamp and even our mother's tiny faux-Tiffany night-light that she'd received one Christmas from her sister in Sioux Falls, switched on in the little nook above the kitchen sink, was also visible from the doorway.

When I called to my brother, he just kept slowly rocking and holding his head. I stood there a little longer before he said something. He muttered, not like he was talking to me, but more like he was registering an aftershock. I let go of my athletic bag and shifted my backpack to the floor. In as unobtrusive a way as possible, I asked why all the lights were on. By this time, I was in my stocking feet and had seated myself on the edge of the La-Z-Boy so that the chair was in no danger of actually reclining. *Oh God*, I heard him say, and his voice sounded like a little boy's, uncharacteristically high and thin. He had now removed his hands from his head and was clutching himself, his fingers trying to wind themselves around his thin arms. His feet were bare and he was wearing only a ratty undershirt and elaborately frayed and torn corduroys, and I wondered if he was cold. I was going to ask if he wanted me to get him some socks and a sweater. But he began to say *Oh God* again, an uncountable number of times in a row, so that the two words began to sound like one long, endless word. It sounded like a plea, but the fact that it wasn't clear whom he was pleading to (surely not actually God) made him sound even more wretched. He stared straight ahead, so that he seemed to be facing the sliding glass door that opened onto the patio but which right then was just reflecting all the furniture and burning lamps in the living room against the backdrop of the black night, as if there were some dark, alternate version of the rooms of our house right outside. I must have asked him then what was wrong. He surprised me by turning to look at me. His dark eyes were open wide and almost rolling in their sockets, which made me think of the squirrels our dog would sometimes pin in a corner of the garage. He called me by the whole of my first name, all three syllables, which hardly anyone ever did—certainly not my brother, who at that point barely called me anything at all. But he called me by my full name, in this terrified, pleading voice that seemed almost entirely disconnected from the deadpan, poker-faced delivery of the few things I still heard him say in those days.

He asked me if I'd ever felt the darkness inside of me.

I sat forward a little more on the unreclined La-Z-Boy.

"Just like this dark . . . formless thing." He was reaching for words, his hands moving even as he kept clutching himself. "Like it's rising in your throat, and in your chest, and maybe you're going to choke on it."

I nodded, slightly.

"I mean—" He shook his head, glanced at the sliding door again. "It's always there, in some way, but then—" His eyes almost rolled back in his head. "Then you're suddenly . . . choking on it. It's choking you." He seemed to be appealing to me. "I mean, it's always there, like sitting inside you, isn't it?"

I nodded again.

"And you try to push it back and you go through your day like that, just trying to keep it down, and then—" His voice, to me, sounded unbearably mournful. "It rises up in you and you're . . . drowning . . ."

He went on like this for what must have been a long time, sometimes looking out the glass door and other times at me, as if trying to make sure I understood what he was saying. And he seemed to keep trying to describe it—this dark, choking, internal thing—not because he could, not in any entirely accurate way, but because it felt too horrible to keep inside. I kept nodding. I thought of how, when I would sit cross-legged in my room and press the blade of my Swiss Army knife into the soft, white flesh of my very inner thighs, the part that wouldn't be revealed even when I squatted and jumped on the volleyball court, the line of blood would darkly swell out. Everything my brother was managing to convey seemed vaguely familiar, like he was referring to a dream I myself had had dozens of times without remembering it until then. It did, after a bit, seem to make him feel better to keep trying to describe the horrible thing, maybe like how you feel better after you've thrown up.

After a long while, he got up and took a glass from the kitchen cupboards above the sink and drifted out of the room. I almost thought that was it, that he was gone. But when he came back, the glass tumbler, the kind we drank milk and orange juice out of, was maybe a quarter full of some amber-colored liquid. Our father's liquor cabinet was in the dining room, but I'd never looked inside it. I'd taken the Trojan "Just Say No to Drugs" pledge and had developed an almost superstitious fear of Substances, although I couldn't exactly say what I was afraid of. My brother steadied himself on the couch, still hunched in a self-protective way. He held the glass up to his nostrils and inhaled.

His breath came out shaky, like the aftermath of a crying jag. I watched him sip, then swallow, watched the knob of his Adam's apple rise and fall in a deliberate way. I sat there on the edge of the unreclined La-Z-Boy and watched him sip, swallow, breathe, a little less shaky each time, the rigid hunch of his shoulders softening.

Then he held out the glass to me. I shook my head automatically, of course, as if the cup contained a distillate of contraband and poison that would send me straight to academic and athletic probation. But he smiled, a lost, mournful smile that seemed to fit the shape of his face but which I don't think I'd ever noticed before, and he kept his hand out. "Just a little sip," he said. "It'll make you feel better." It seemed to me then that he knew I understood what he'd been trying to describe. And how could I have understood him if I hadn't felt it myself, the awful dark thing he could only gesture at?

So I took the glass, and I brought it to my lips the way he had, and I took a very small sip, as if it were a chalice of Communion wine. I swallowed slowly, felt it burn my throat, and then imagined that what I'd just swallowed—in the way that I'd seen cartoon depictions of cough medicine coat the glowing throat of a translucent man on TV commercials and begin manifesting its soothing properties immediately—was soothing whatever awful thing was inside me, too. "One sip more," my brother said, very seriously, as if he knew what the recommended dosage was. So I did, one sip more, just for him, because he'd asked me to. I felt the fumes flood my sinuses and the heavy liquid burn my throat again, then I handed the glass back to him.

After he finished it off, his chest rising and falling after each swallow, as if he were rocking himself to sleep, he rose again and washed the glass in the sink and dried it with the Grand Canyon dish towel our mother had purchased a couple summers ago during one of the family vacations my brother no longer joined us on, and then placed the glass back in the cupboard where it'd come from. At some point, he wandered back upstairs, and I sat for a while longer, feeling the pleasant fog in my head. Then I walked from room to room, switching off enough lights so that just a normal, inconspicuous number would be on when my parents returned.

My brother never brought up that night, so I never did either. Sometimes, when I'd pass him in the short stretch of hallway that ran along our two bedrooms, I would want to say something, and then wondered if he even remembered. He was rarely home by that point, and when he was, rarely in sight. I could hear the high wah-wah on his side of the wall we shared, and sometimes I would find him staring into space as he spooned granola into his mouth at the kitchen counter, but he hardly registered my presence. And that June, he was eighteen and his senior year at Hyde County Junior-Senior High School came to an end, and while my parents and I were all at the ceremony in the school gym, my brother found a ride out of town and was gone when we got back.

When he called that winter, I hadn't seen him in five years. There'd been a few postcards over the years—from places like Crescent City, California, and Gold Beach, Oregon—and some stiffly delivered updates from my father, who I assumed had been ceded certain logistical details that I hadn't. But that was all.

"Where have you been?" I asked the voice on the other end of the phone.

There was silence for a while, like maybe he was trying to figure out how best to describe his trajectory from age eighteen to nearly twenty-four—which details had faded in importance over time and could be condensed into a single sentence or just eliminated completely, and which details had come to seem more like the watermark of the whole thing and thus had to be given their due, even if no one could ever fully know what he meant.

What he finally said, though, was, "On a submarine."

The lab did not study pain per se, I made sure to explain to anyone who asked—even though the regular people working in the lab didn't really seem to make a big deal, on an everyday basis, about this distinction. As soon as I got the internship, I made sure to read the pertinent lectures in Charles S. Sherrington's 1906 *The Integrated Action of the Nervous System*, in which he first makes the distinction between the "imperative protective reflex" triggered by the application of a noxious stimulus to peripheral nerve cells and the "displeasurable affective quality" that is a "psychical adjunct" to the former. His coinage for the former, in order to distinguish it from the latter, was *nociception*. What we studied, I would make sure to explain to anyone who asked, was *nociception*. This seemed to me like a higher plane of consideration. It was the reaction of the body before the brain, with its tears and distress and complicating associations, ever got wind of it. Pure physiology. You might say what the lab studied, then, was how to disconnect the one from the other.

The research subjects were Sprague Dawley rats, which, having been bred in the sterile confines of a laboratory, have lives as uncomplicated as their albino coloration. In the faintly musky, pellet-scented room where their cages were shelved, they would squeak mutedly when I picked them up by their ropy pink tails and placed them in the weighing pan, which was one of my regular responsibilities. The rats, in groups of eight, were moved in assembly-line fashion through the multiple phases of the study, which began with an important if workaday surgery, in which a tiny polyurethane catheter, about half the diameter of a juice-box drinking straw, was implanted in the lumbar region of their spines. After seven days of rest and relaxation, interrupted only by a shot of lidocaine through their catheters to confirm that the surgery had been successful, they were subjected to "the hot-plate test," which means they were placed on a Fisherbrand Isotemp hot plate with digital temperature control and a guardrail surrounding the plate like a tiny medieval city wall. The point of the hot-plate test was to see how long it took each of the rats to demonstrate nociceptive behaviors—namely, to withdraw their naked pink paws from the plate—as it was heated from 44 degrees Celsius to 47 to 52. At 52 degrees, which is 125.6 Fahrenheit, which is 21.6 degrees Fahrenheit warmer than the max hot-tub temperature that the US Consumer Product Safety Commission has determined is safe for human beings, the average time before a rat began hot stepping (as some of the lab techs liked to call it) was twenty-six seconds. These times were recorded scrupulously by the head lab tech, a small, toothy woman who herself had a certain rodent-like quality about her and was the only member of the lab to actually wear a white lab coat on a regular basis. The next phase, Phase III, was injection, the moment when one of four solutions was injected into each rat's tiny drinking-straw catheter, which poked out like some kind of cyborg scuba gear from its lumbar region. Aside from the control solution of saline, there were three kinds of "punch," as the round-faced dental-studies lab tech called it: an adenosine analog that was thought to inhibit the release of substance P; an NMDA receptor blocker that inhibited postsynaptic glutamate binding, which seemed as if it might enhance substance P's effects; and lastly, a dose of each, which some of the lab techs referred to as a "double scoop." Approximately thirty minutes postinjection, each rat was given the hot-plate test again. This was Phase IV. Phase V began thirty minutes after the commencement of Phase IV, an interval that was timed with the head lab tech's stopwatch, which she, as the de facto timekeeper, wore on her wrist at all times. As each rat lay prone, following an intraperitoneal shot of chloral hydrate, a twenty six–gage steel cannula was implanted in its fourth ventricle, like a pipeline, to tap its cerebral spinal fluid. CSF could then be sucked up—up to 200 microL of it, or until blood appeared in the cannula, was the rule of thumb. The CSF was released into a sterile plastic vial the size and shape of a bullet, after which the molecules of substance P in it would be counted via radioimmunoassay. The rats themselves were then "sacrificed," which is to say a glass stirring rod was pressed across the backs of their necks while their now limp pink tails were pulled, until you could feel the empty space between their narrow little spines and their skulls, and were then sealed in a Ziploc baggie and disposed of. The next day, another group of eight rats would be fished out of their cedar chip–lined cages for their first hot-plate test. Thus went the rhythms of the lab. I never observed any of this from start to finish, but rather in disconnected phases here and there, wherever another set of hands was needed for the most menial part of the work, so that I held in my head a kind of fractured tableau of any given rat's progress.

I stepped into this research cycle in medias res, in late May, after the end of my sophomore year at the U of M and my second semester of organic chemistry, which was a requirement for the neuroscience major. I was not, in fact, good at science, but I'd found that it was possible to become passable at it if I approached it the way I approached anything that didn't come naturally to me, which was via brute force and repetition. I had also taken up training for marathons. English lit was what I'd wanted to major in—I had hand copied "Ode to a Nightingale" on the inside cover of my diary my senior year of high school. My freshman year of college, however, I happened to pick up a copy of a book that my roommate, a future landscape design major who was at the time enrolled in Intro Psych, had left lying around. The book was the account of an academic with bipolar disorder, and, after chronicling the author's lurid bouts of mania and black troughs of suicidal despair, detailed the favorable effects of lithium on her throbbing brain. I stayed up into the wee hours of the night reading, although I couldn't have said much more about it at the time, other than it was a gripping story. Psych was not a plausible major. As I understood the subject, which was largely via my father's understanding, which he had occasion to voice when it was once suggested that a psychotherapist might provide some kind of guidance to his son (who was perhaps marching just a tad too much to the beat of his own drummer), the entire discipline was a quackery of *feelings* and mesmerism. (I remember having to look up "mesmerism" in the *World Book*.) But I had learned there was such a thing as a neuroscience major, and this included a course called Behavioral Neuroscience, which promised to lay bare the neural mechanisms underlying human behavior. The part I mentioned to my father was that the major required at least twelve credits of 3000-level molecular and cellular biology and six credits of at least 2000-level chemistry. I declared my major in the fall of my sophomore year, a full semester before the deadline.

The lab itself comprised two conjoined rooms on the fourteenth floor of the gray brutalist structure called "Moos," otherwise known as Moos Health Science Tower, and was headed by a postdoc whom I rarely saw whose wardrobe tended toward woolen pencil skirts and high collars, in contradistinction to the three lab techs, two of whom were male grad students who favored T-shirts with logos on them and the third of whom, the head lab tech, simply favored a white lab coat. The lab, which was already in Week 11 of the study (informally known as "the pain quotidien" study), didn't have a specific set of responsibilities for an intern—which of course disconcerted me, since I preferred to be given my marching orders and then to proceed full bore. Instead, the techs just began to pass off odd jobs to me, such as weighing the rats and washing the labware—tasks that I performed with as much industry and exactitude as possible, recording each rat's weight down to a hundredth of a milligram and hand drying the double- and single-spouted beakers and stir sticks and solution bottles so that none would be spotted with water stains, although no one seemed to notice.

At 5:00 p.m., I would most often go back to my subleased room in a house full of people I didn't know, feeling empty and unmoored. It was June, and I was waiting for a sign from my brother, scanning the streets and checking my email and the mailbox by the side of the door that I passed every time I entered or exited the house, and holding my breath when the phone rang, not unlike a receptor cell membrane's ionotropic channel awaiting the arrival of neurotransmitter particles in the synaptic cleft. There was never any sign, though, never any signal, and I would sit on my futon in my basement room and read the extra copies of articles on substance P research that I was occasionally sent to the bunker-like stacks of the biomed library to find. I was trying to memorize the entire process of substance P biosynthesis, its postsynaptic effects, and the various methods of inhibiting its actions that had so far been studied.

*

The submarine my brother had been on was an Ohio-class ballistic missile sub called, confusingly, the *Alaska*, which had been patrolling some classified area of the Pacific for the past seventy-seven days. The mission of the boat, he said, was strategic deterrence, which seemed to mean harboring twenty-four ballistic missiles while cruising at a classified depth of several hundred feet below the surface of the ocean.

My father, maybe two years before, had noted to me, in the tones he summoned to commend 4-H prize winners and honor roll students, that my brother had "joined up" and was "really thriving," but this was intel I received with some skepticism. I still imagined my brother, his sun-bleached hair dusting his shoulders, roaming free out West—a phrase itself that somehow suggested a release from our constrained, landlocked part of the country. I pictured him strumming his guitar beneath the kind of blossoming fruit trees that would never survive a South Dakota winter. But when I raced to the door to let him in that December, a week and four days after he'd called, his hair was shorn to regulation length, and he stood with his feet shoulder width apart and his hands clasped behind his back. When I hugged him, my face pressed to the scratchy wool peacoat he wore, there was no trace of the mossy, cuminy smell that would still hit me sometimes, if only in part, when I'd walk past certain rooms in Comstock Hall. I ushered him into my room, where *Neurophysiology: A Conceptual Approach* was laid open on my desk as a sort of prop, and he set down his olive-drab duffel, which looked a lot like a sandbag. I took in his pressed khaki trousers and tucked-in, buttoned-up khaki shirt, and did not know what to say.

"So what's the POD?" He was the first to speak, in that poker-faced way that had become, after a certain age, his main mode of communication. *POD*, it turned out, was navy cant: "plan of the day." As it happened, I did have a POD, because I always had a POD. I was incapable of getting through the day without the scaffolding of a highly regimented POD, which maybe my brother remembered. He seemed to.

"It occurred to me that you would do well in the military." He was still in that wide-legged stance, hands clasped behind his back like he was hiding something.

"Have *you*?" I was waiting for the electric kettle to begin steaming so that I could offer him a choice of Ceylon orange pekoe or ginseng Focus tea.

He rubbed the flat of his hand over his shorn head. "I do Oscar Kilo," he said, in a noncommittal sort of way. *Oscar Kilo* being the NATO Phonetic Alphabet rendering of OK, though I didn't get the sense, after he explained it, that this was a standard usage.

He told me that he'd let me have the ginseng Focus, since he knew it was finals week.

"Oh but it's not!" I was fairly bursting. "Finals are all over for me! I got permission to take them all in the first week—so I'm *done!*"

He tilted his head, and I was suddenly embarrassed at my untempered expression of pleasure. "So it seems," he said, helping himself to a packet of Ceylon orange pekoe, "that we are both on authorized leave."

I nodded, trying not to appear as happy as I felt.

"So what's this about you being some kind of rocket scientist?" He had removed his clunky brown leather shoes, and his socks, I saw, were the same khaki color as his pants and shirt.

"I build spaceships," I said, affecting the poker face that he'd just pulled. "It's the final frontier."

"Uh huh." He squinted at me over his orange pekoe, which he was drinking out of my human-brain mug, which featured a different cross-sectional view on either side. "And how's that going?"

"Oscar Kilo," I said, pronouncing *kilo* with an *ee* sound like I'd heard him do.

He nodded, impenetrably. "That's good."

We sat for a little while, neither of us saying anything, both of us cradling our respective mugs of tea in our hands. The dorm room I lived in seemed suddenly dollhouse sized, too big to contain my brother now that he was actually here. He was studying the room, its seven-anatomical-views-of-the-human-brain poster, including a close-up of the glial cells and meninges; the bookshelf of textbooks organized by discipline (e.g., chemistry, biology, cognitive science); the cold spotlight of the gooseneck lamp on my two neat stacks of anatomy flash cards, one for the general anatomy of the brain and another for that of a single nerve cell; the translucent blue-and-purple rendering of a nerve synapse, taped above my desk.

He nodded at me again. "Good program," he said. Which was one of our father's sort of all-purpose responses when presented with a description of something he knew little about but for which he needed to demonstrate his approval. It was also a term my brother had picked up on as a teenager and applied, absurdly, to phenomena and occurrences as disparate as his first swig of orange juice from a just-opened bottle of Minute Maid in the fridge, our mother's harried instructions to us prior to the arrival of some prospective donor cum dinner guest, the much-gossiped-about occasion of a student driver's unexpected crash into the storefront of the Ben Franklin on Main, and the red necktie and brass American eagle cuff links our father presented him with on his eighteenth birthday. "Good program." It was a response in place of a response, the ironic quality of which, in my brother's mouth, shifted from one situation to another, but which always, obliquely, damned its original user. It was a joke that I recognized and was in on, and I contorted my face to contain my glee.

"A real good program." I lent my voice the cartoonishly flat man-of-the-South-Dakota-people's pronunciation that our father's vowels would take on when he was at his most glad-handing.

"OK." My brother set down the human-brain mug. "Tell me the POD."

The truth was, the remaining POD was entirely devoted to him. I'd risen at six and run forty-eight laps around the indoor track and completed my complex routine of push-ups and crunches and glutes extensions and stretches, eaten my allotted portion of bran flakes, skim milk, and sliced banana at a nearly empty table in Comstock Dining, scoured the floors and surfaces of my room with a bottle of lemon-scent Lysol and a can of multisurface classic-scent Pledge, and read three chapters of *Consciousness Explained*, yellow high-lighter in hand. But leaving this iceberg of the day's activity unmentioned, I spread out my hands before me, as if to indicate the oyster of the world that was ours, in spite of the single-digit temperature outside.

"The meteorite collection at Pillsbury. The telescope at Bell." I began to recite from memory the list of sights I'd written down in semiranked order. "The Weisman. The American Swedish Institute."

"The American Swedish Institute?" He furrowed his brow.

I said I'd never been but the Nordic Christmas rooms were supposed to be nice.

"Uh huh." He nodded diplomatically. "Do they still have the tunnels here?"

These were the basement-level corridors running in a disjointed network across a patchwork of campus, a convoluted diversion from the cold. Of course the tunnels were still there, I told him. The Gopher Way. Six miles or more.

He wanted to know if I used them.

Only stretches of them, here and there, I explained. Instead of

247

tunneling steadily underground from building to building to building, a corridor would run for a block or so and then force you to
emerge aboveground for the length of a building before descending
again. They weren't all that practical.

Where was the nearest point of entry, he wanted to know.

We began in the underground parking garage a few blocks away, the
concrete ceiling pressing down with the weight of its rows of four-
wheel-drive vehicles, and walked, uncertain spelunkers, map in hand,
about two and a half sides of the square garage before following the
track lighting that led us below Delaware Street, after which we hit
a stairway that forced us to ascend for the length of the student
union before we spied the next stairwell back underground, where a
square circuit of the corridor took us below the campus bookstore
and then right back into the student union, at which point it was
once again necessary to ascend and locate the next stairway to the
next stretch of tunnel, which was on the building's east side, allowing us to snake once more below and across Delaware, tunneling
halfway beneath the Mayo Building, rising up once again, descending again, and skirting the west side of the P-W Building and Moos,
across Washington Ave. and beneath the Wash. Ave. parking ramp.
This was still less than half of the tunnels on the campus west of the
river. So we continued in this way, heading vaguely north, fretting
the cinder-block corridors that were at times lined with convolutes
of piping and ducts and other times with only lurid track lighting
against bare walls, which walls were occasionally painted with larger-
than-life-size depictions of Goldy the grinning Gopher leaning louchely
against a giant M. Whenever we were forced to emerge, like mole
people, onto an aboveground hallway, we scouted instinctively for
the next staircase down, descending as rapidly as we could, like children holding our breath past a cemetery. We had no destination in
particular, save to remain belowground, and thus we worked our way
along, from one segment to another, tracing our fingers along the
map as needed.

My brother walked at an even pace, his hands in the pockets of his
neatly buttoned peacoat, which seemed entirely without lint or pills,
steadily scanning the corridors for the next turn or the next stairway.
Sometimes, the only sound we heard was the echo of our footsteps
off the smooth cinder-block walls. Occasionally, a round surveillance mirror reflected our faces, now distorted, back at us. It struck

me as odd that someone who had just spent seventy-seven days beneath the surface of the ocean would be so keen to keep to the underground of the campus. But it also just seemed like a game that my brother might have made up when we were both still in grade school—like who could go the longest without using a particular word, or who could stay underwater the longest at the reservoir.

The amazing thing about nuclear submarines, he said, as we emerged from a stairwell onto a second-floor passageway, searching for the next portal down, was how they could, theoretically, cruise for years beneath the ocean. They generate their own fuel and thus their own propulsion, make their own oxygen, and distill their own water. Only the needs of the crew prevent them from staying down for years on end. He had nothing to do with the missiles per se, he said. His job was simply to keep the boat running. Maintaining the water-tight doors, repairing the valves and compressors, storing the oxygen. Strictly maintenance. He did what was needed to keep the boat cruising at whatever classified depth under the sea it was. And the entire design, he said, was in the service of stealth. To avoid detection at all costs. We sighted the next stairway down. You couldn't hear the nuclear-generated steam propelling the turbines. Nobody could hear it. That was the idea. He pushed open the heavy door to the stairs and we descended. The control room was bathed in the red glow of a darkroom, so that no light might shine its way up through a periscope and reveal the presence of the sub. There were even anechoic tiles on the surface of the hull. In the fluorescent lighting of the tunnels, I could see the violet shadows beneath his eyes. His face was very pale. When we emerged, late in the afternoon, the winter sky was nearly leached of its light.

That summer in Minneapolis was thickly humid, the heat like some kind of retribution for the terrible cold winter, and I often, after racing to Moos on my spindly Schwinn, entered the lab streaming with sweat. At the very back of the two rooms was a walk-in freezer, crammed with plastic cases of vials and racks of test tubes containing samples and solutions. I would step in and close the door and just stand there in my soaked T-shirt until I began to feel iced over. Then I would step out, into the air-conditioned lab, and wait for someone to tell me what I was supposed to do.

Frequently, the head lab tech was about to anesthetize another group of rats, presurgical implantation of their juice-box-straw-sized catheters. She went about this in a more ritualistic way than the other lab techs. First, before any of the rats were brought in, she pressed play on her own personal CD of Handel's *Water Music*, which she felt created a soothing ambience. And then, as I wheeled the rats in, each in its respective single-occupancy cage, she proceeded to drape a dark towel over each one, to calm them and shield them from the stressful moment when their peers were lifted, dangling, from their cages, and injected via hypodermic needle with a 350 mg/kg dose of chloral hydrate in solution. The HLT approached the task with great solemnity, like a high priest at the altar. Her faintly rodenty face would become grave as she donned her latex gloves, laid out a disposable towel on the bench, and prepared her instruments: the spray bottle of ethanol and stack of white towelettes, the rack of test tubes, and the 26-gauge needle and one-microL syringe, which she would flick officiously to remove any air bubbles after she'd drawn up the correct dosage of CH solution. At her side, I learned how to restrain each rat by the scruff of its white back, its chest fluttering and its tiny, pale pink, disconcertingly humanoid paws grasping at the air, as I applied an ethanol-sprayed towelette to the lower portion of its exposed abdomen and then used the same hand to firmly drive the needle home. It took at least a week of injections before I could do this without flinching or altogether letting go of the rat, which would then skitter away in terror. But I applied myself diligently, and I learned. The rat would squirm, frantically, almost insupportably, and then, within a few seconds, go limp, save for the slow shiver of its heart in its chest. Meanwhile, the dulcet tones of *Water Music*, which struck me as having an awful lot of allegro in it for something that was supposed to be soothing, would continue to fill the room, like counterprogramming to the musky odor of the rats' cages and their muted squeals.

When the HLT wasn't performing injections, the CD player was usually commandeered by the more affable of the two grad students, the round-faced dentistry student, who, at the age of twenty-three, already had a cheerful-looking blonde wife at home, whose wallet-sized photo he would happily display whenever the occasion arose. I don't actually think that he tended to play a lot of eighties synth-pop, but the only CD of his that I paid attention to was the Pet Shop Boys. Just about every track consisted of a dark, hushed melody undercut by an impossibly chipper dance beat. The melancholy voice of the lyrics could never quite extract itself from the drum machine. I wanted him to play the disc over and over, although I knew it would be inappropriate of me to keep asking. Eventually, I brought in a blank cassette tape and made myself a copy, which I could then in fact play over and over, on my headphones, as I ran along the cloudy Mississippi.

My favorite song, the one I would rewind and replay as I ran, was "Red Letter Day." *Aaaaaall Iiiiiii waaaaant . . . is what yoooooou waaaaaaant*, went the refrain. *I'm always waiting, for a reeeeeeed letter daaaaaaaay.* There was still no sign of my brother, no matter that I checked for his NAVY bumper sticker on every blue-gray car in the vicinity of Moos or my subleased room, and the song became like a private anthem to me. *All I want is what you want.* Like it was just a matter of waiting.

"Now, the navy," my brother was saying, "is renowned for their rack making. We're famous for our hospital corners." He was speaking in the stilted tones of a drill sergeant who'd been set down in a home-ec class. Before commencing, he had hauled the bunk bed away from the wall, scoffing at what I'd always thought was my perfectly respectable method of making a bed. He shook out the top sheet with one officious billow. "First thing you wanna do is take the sheet"—he was all focus—"and you wanna place it on the rack so it is flat, all the way from side to side."

I was stiff faced with laughter it seemed undignified to give voice to, given the admirably controlled pitch of his performance. I watched him line up the edge of my cornflower-blue bed sheet with the foot of the extra-long mattress, demonstrating that the overhang on each side was equal before tucking in the end of the sheet. "Now," he declaimed, "you go to one side of the rack to begin your forty five–degree corner." At this point, he had somehow lifted up the side of the sheet as if it were the wing of an origami crane. He pulled its triangular lower half tight and tucked it beneath the mattress, leaving the triangle of its upper half to flap. "Now." He stood for a moment holding this upper flap out tight, like its existence was a problem to be solved. "Now you will tuck up that excess underneath the rack." His hands, with their carefully clipped nails, took on a mitten-like shape, all the fingers pressed carefully together as he tucked in the flap and began to smooth out the sheet. "You wanna *tuck in* the excess." He stood back with a flourish. "Now what you've got there is your forty five–degree-angle corner."

"Could bounce a quarter off it." I tried to mimic the military machismo in his voice.

He held up an admonitory finger. "But we're not done yet." He worked his hands delicately along the edge of the mattress, toward the head, tucking in the rest of the sheet and smoothing it as he went. He paused to look at me over his shoulder. "You always wanna make sure that you smooth down the sheet." He swept the surface of the bed with the palm of his hand. "*Smoooooth* down the sheet." When he had repeated the process on the other side of the bed, the top bunk looked like it had been sanded down with a blaster.

With another sweep of his arm, though, he tugged the entire top sheet from the bed. He balled it up and tossed it at me. "Now *you* do it."

I gaped at him, and then it was like I was six and he was showing me how to make a paper airplane. His stubby fingertips on the folds of notebook paper, each sharp fold preceding another, even narrower fold, until the flat arrow of the nose was formed. He directed me, largely with his hands clasped behind his back, and I smoothed down the sheet on the rack, folded the overhang in a triangular shape, tucked in the excess, and smoothed down the surface, tucked in the excess, and smoothed down the surface.

I thought of the bunk bed he'd had in his room until maybe junior high—the *Star Wars* sheets and navy comforter, the fortlike feel of the whole structure, with the inside lair of the bottom bunk and the lookout of the top. Sometimes he let me sleep on the bottom bunk, and then, for the groggy space of time just before sleep and just after waking, I felt like I'd been let into his citadel, even as he drifted further and further away from me. I thought of this as I lay there in the dark that night, him on the bunk above mine. Shorn head, uniform, military stance, and as poker-faced as I remembered from the years just before he'd left. But he was here. He hadn't said, exactly, why he'd joined the navy, why he'd gone for a submariner. These didn't seem like the kinds of things I could ask.

Still, after only a few minutes had passed, I said his name out loud in the dark. "Are you awake?"

I could hear him breathing, very quietly, before he answered in the affirmative.

"Do you remember"—I wasn't sure how to formulate the question. "I still remember—"

He was perfectly still.

"That night I came home and found you with all the lights on?" I waited. "What you said—I still remember what you said—about the awful, horrible blackness."

There was still no sound from the upper bunk.

I stared at the bottom of the bunk and thought about what he'd tried to say—about the choking, dark, formless thing, about almost drowning in it. How he couldn't quite find the words for it. The horrible thing sitting inside you. I wanted to reach my hand to the bunk above me. "Do you remember?"

The room was completely silent. Most of the other students in the dorm had already left for break. The frozen campus outside was empty. There was the distant rumor of traffic on the East River Parkway. I lay there listening, for minutes, for maybe an hour, before I understood he wasn't going to answer.

When I woke in the morning, it was with the sense of someone moving in the room. And when I opened my eyes, I saw it was my brother. The light was a predawn gray, the color of insomnia. He stood in front of my seven-views-of-the-brain poster, in his khakis and thick-soled shoes, just buttoning his peacoat, as if, in another second, he wouldn't have been there at all. Where was he going, I asked. His face was very smooth, and composed, as if he'd just planed off any furrows or creases with a razor in front of the mirror. He had to head back, was all he said. "Back," referring very broadly to wherever it was that he'd come from—a naval base, or maybe the submarine itself. He'd hardly just gotten here, I said, an observation that he did not dispute. He was going off into the woods, and I was not allowed. He was locking the door to his room. My mind was still fuzzy with sleep. When was he ever coming back? He paused by the door, his sandbag of a duffel slung over one shoulder. His watch cap was pulled low, nearly over his eyes. He would have another leave in June, he finally said. It was December now.

I watched the door close, watched the knob being silently twisted. Then I lay on my side, my throat aching, and tried to visualize the relevant neuroanatomy as seen in lateral cross section: the curled horn of the caudate nucleus, curved around the crescent of the thalamus, which itself curls around the shell of the putamen, deep in the forebrain. The thalamus perched upon the brain stem, like an ancient bust on a plinth. And, as viewed from above, on a map of the brain's mantle, across the medial prefrontal cortex, the bilateral ripple that is Brodmann area 9, thought to be involved in the suppression of sadness.

*

All throughout the month of June, I looked for my brother. The blue-gray car with the NAVY sticker, the shorn head and military stance and regulation khakis, and, sometimes, the sun-bleached hair dusting his shoulders, the back of one of those faded tie-dyes, its ray of colors spiraling into itself. On the very last day of the month, like a ship sending up a flare, I decided to write him a letter.

The letter took up three sheets of notebook paper, and was written in blue ink. I told him again that I still remembered what he'd said about the choking blackness, how it was rising up inside of him, this awful, dark feeling. I tried to explain how it had stayed with me over the years, to explain much more precisely than I'd been able to from the dark of the bottom bunk. I told him that I'd never forgotten the horrible feeling he was describing. And then, I wrote, this was because I felt it, too. And I explained how the blackness had welled up in me, like an illness, like a heaviness, like a rottenness I could never root out. I apologized for still not having the right words either. I told him about practicing my fake smile, and serving sheet cake at receptions and harmonizing in the Immaculate Conception choir and cheering on my fellow Lady Trojans and doing the wave at Trojan football and basketball games, and then how I'd joined the Gopher women's cross-country and track teams, putting on the maroon and gold and radiating team spirit like a nuclear test site, all the while feeling like there was something rotting inside of me—like I was rotting—and that I'd rather just lie down and die. *I'm telling you this*, I finally wrote, *because I think you might be the only one who understands.* A declaration that today strikes me as melodramatic and naive, and probably honest. Then, not knowing what else to write, I wrote, *Please write back.*

I found the address of the naval base he'd mentioned, northwest of Seattle, and I addressed the envelope with machinelike precision, pausing after each letter and number, careful not to let any character blur into any other. I inscribed my own address, the return address, just as precisely. I slid it into the mailbox next to the front door of the house, and waited. It was a Sunday afternoon, and I looked at the envelope again before I went to bed. It seemed, in its compact way, as if it contained a small but volatile time bomb. In the morning, when I left for the lab, the envelope was still there, the last number of the address just visible. I wondered if I should take it back and tear it up. But I left it there. And when I returned in the evening, the envelope was gone.

By early July, I was assisting the HLT with all of the chloral hydrate injections. The draping of the cages, the flicking of the syringes, the plunge of the needle. "You have a firm hand," she said to me one day, and then told me there was a spare lab coat in the storage closet next to the walk-in freezer. Sometimes I would find myself humming different movements of *Water Music*—the overture, or one of the well-tempered allegros, or maybe the vaguely wistful lentement.

I wondered, often, where the letter was. If it had found its way to the naval base half a continent away, had it also found its way into my brother's hands? I tried to picture its possible fates. Was it pressed within the pages of a book, or at the bottom of his olive-drab duffel, or folded into his breast pocket? Or had it never reached him at all and was instead lying unseen in a pigeon hole or on a dusty metal shelf while he cruised hundreds of meters beneath the ocean? I checked the mailbox by the door every evening as I entered the house, peered inside to make sure there wasn't an envelope stuck at the bottom. I dialed the communal voice mail several times a day, listening till the end of every message, every out-of-breath hello or garbled instruction or meandering stream of consciousness that would get cut off after three minutes—just in case. At work, there was a computer with an Ethernet connection in the break room, and I would log into my email account at lunch and just before leaving for the day. I called home to make sure nothing had been delivered into the hands of the Lubrication Station. Every means of transmitting and receiving a message became a site of possibility, and then, just after I checked it, a site of acute disappointment. A hollowing out of my chest, an ache behind my eyes. I couldn't have said what it was, exactly, that I wanted from my brother, except for him to write back.

In August, the gruffer of the grad students—a callous young PharmD with a thin blond mustache and tiny eyes—told me that if I wanted to come in earlier one morning, I could assist him with Phases III through V. This was the core of the study, when a group of rats was injected with one of the four solutions and then tested again on the walled plain of the hot plate. That morning, only I was aware of which rats had been shot up with which solutions, given that it had been my job to prepare each syringe before handing it to the PharmD student. But right away, you could tell which ones had been given something more than the control solution. One by one, each rat, its tiny catheter still protruding from its lumbar region like a snorkel, was dropped by its ropy pink tail onto the hot plate. And certain of these rats stood dumbly on the plate, their red eyes absorbing the new sort of cage they'd been placed in. Instead of beginning to lift

255

their tiny, humanoid paws off the plate after about twenty-six seconds at 52 degrees Celsius, instead of squeaking with an alarm-like repetition, these rats lingered. They were slow on the uptake, beginning to get a little itchy footed only after forty seconds had passed. And then there were the real outliers of the group: after forty seconds, after fifty, these rats were unperturbed. Technically, we should have been removing every rat from the plate after thirty-five seconds at 52 degrees. But the PharmD student, as if to satisfy his own personal curiosity, in a way that made me think of boys pulling the wings off of flies just to see what they'll do, pushed it further. Fifty seconds, sixty. There was the faintest odor of something burning. The rat would crouch blankly on the hot plate, not even its tail twitching. When the PharmD pulled the rat out, the bottoms of its paws were a raw red, the underside of its pink tail a deeper pink. These were the rats—it would later be confirmed—that had been injected with the double scoop, the solution that suppressed both the release of substance P and the binding of another transmitter that worked in postsynaptic concert with substance P.

Later, as we aspirated cerebral spinal fluid from their fourth ventricles, that region between the base of the skull and the highest knob of the spine, I stared at the cloudy liquid. You couldn't, of course, tell one vial of CSF apart from any of the others. Only a radioimmunoassay could do that. All I knew was that in some of the vials there existed a deluge of substance P's undecapeptide molecules, and in others there was none. I looked at the two rats who hadn't responded at all to the hot plate, who had only looked blankly at their surroundings, the beads of their red eyes shifting. Where had the pain gone? Had it ever existed? Or was it still there in the terminals of their afferent neurons, in their unexpressed loads of substance P, waiting?

All eight of the rats lay limp on the bench, prostrate beneath the giant cannulas now embedded in their necks, their eyes closed like docile sleepers. Once 200 microL of their CSF had been siphoned off, the rats were of no more use. The PharmD took a ballpoint pen from his pocket and gave me a brief tutorial on how to roll it across the back of a rat's neck while pulling at its tail as if it were some sort of party cracker. He had me feel with my index finger the now empty space between the hardness of its skull and ridge of its spine. He gave me a grim smile. "No pain now."

*

I never received any reply to the letter I'd sent my brother. By the end of the summer, I had pretty well convinced myself that this was just as well. What I had written was something I no longer felt. It could be readily enough disavowed. And the hurt that I'd carried with me all summer could be sharpened into anger. My brother, I wrote in the pages of my journal, had become a military automaton who didn't have the common decency to even just acknowledge the receipt of a three-page letter from the one person on earth who had only ever admired him.

It's amazing how slowly but surely this occurs, like the transformation of a liquid into a crystalline solid.

The fall semester would begin soon, and I would be taking Cellular and Molecular Neuroscience, Pharmacology of the Synapse, and Neural Engineering. The Gopher women's cross-country team had begun training for the season, and I picked up my racing uniform from the field house. The lab had the data they needed and would submit their findings on substance P to *Anesthesia and Analgesia*. It was Sweeps Season again, and I would briefly travel back to Hyde County to pose with my father at the usual pancake breakfasts and Lions Club award banquets. He liked to refer now to his son who couldn't be there because he was serving this great nation in a submarine all the way under the shining sea.

Years later, back in South Dakota to appear at a fundraiser for my father's first run for the US Senate, I drifted toward the bookshelves in the home of the couple hosting the event. Weary of smiling and nodding, I began to gaze with tilted head at the spines. The husband, it seemed, was a military history buff, and my eyes skimmed over a length of titles like *Principles of Maritime Strategy, Modern Air Combat, Chemicals in Combat, Strategic and Ballistic Missile Defense, Field Artillery: V. I–X*, followed by titles such as *Desperate Stand, March to Victory, Honor and Fidelity, Arms and Men*, after which came *The Spartans, The Samurai, The Huns, The Mongols, The Cossacks, The Zulus*, which were directly above a span of spines branded with a single name, at least half in all caps: *GRANT, Lee, Custer, MACARTHUR, CHURCHILL, Pershing, PATTON*. Somewhere in the middle of the shelf that contained *B-29 Superfortress Units of World War 2, Combat History of the Panzer-Abteilung 103*, and *Fire for Effect: A Unit History of the 522 Field Artillery Battalion*, I came upon a narrow book called *The Sinking of the USS Thresher: The Most Tragic Dive in Submarine History*.

257

It would not be accurate to say I never thought about submarines, or about the fact that my brother was on one about 75 percent of the days in any given year. But it would be accurate to say that I tried not to, and thus that I actually knew very little about submarines. At that point, I had not seen or heard from my brother in nearly ten years. As far as my understanding of these things went, he had become what's called a lifer in the navy, a veteran submariner. That was all I knew.

The *Thresher*, I learned, when I sat down in a mid-century leather armchair with the dry martini the host had poured out for me along with some allusion to Churchill, had been a nuclear-powered sub named after the solitary thresher shark. The boat had the ability to operate at depths greater than any submarine before it. But in this ability, the author reflected, lay the *Thresher*'s undoing. In the spring of 1963, while diving about 250 miles off the New England coast, the submarine sank too far to be recovered. A day later, it was declared "lost with all hands"—a phrase that, somehow, in its workmanlike contraction, seems to compound the horror of the thing. Eventually, it would be determined that a pipe had burst, that the engine room had flooded, and that the boat could no longer propel itself forward. Heavy with the growing weight of water, it began to sink. At about 2,400 feet, it's estimated, the submarine imploded from the pressure of the sea.

Nearly two decades later, when the remnants of the *Thresher* were at last located, these were scattered at a depth of 8,400 feet below the surface. The only piece recovered was a fifty-seven-inch length of twisted pipe. No human remains were ever found.

Coin

Erin L. McCoy

YOU ATE WITH GREAT RELISH the first olive and placed the toothpick back in the glass, the second olive still speared and waiting. You focused your eyes on the dashed white line at your feet. This was not hard, you were not drunk. You assessed the newness of the paint, which correlated with the slickness of the paint, which determined whether you should let your heels land squarely on it or place them between the dashes, on the bitter gray asphalt, the unreflective asphalt, though the sky was mauve or lavender or any color that was both mournful and hopeful at the same time, like a sunset always is. It was breezy outside and cool and right.

From the doorsteps and the balconies you could hear voices. Voices had replaced the sounds of engines—the engines of planes descending on the south of the city, passing over your neighborhood as they came, the engines of cars zipping up or down the hill, to or from the important places where they were going or had been, the gears of garage doors churning, the gears of construction-site generators churning, the gears of televisions and computers churning.

Instead there was the squeak and whir of tuning pegs on the heads of guitars, disembodied whistling from inside a house, the *whuff* of heads turning on their necks while the eyes in the heads watched people walking by their houses, and the hinges of the doors that opened and did not shut.

It wasn't long ago that when you wanted a martini you walked to the bar down the hill, hopped up on the stool where your legs dangled and scooted it forward with one toe barely touching the ground, and said, I'd like a martini. Or said, Could I have a martini? Wait, how does it go now, the asking of easy questions?

And it wasn't so long ago that if you wanted to see a friend across the table you went up the hill to this or another table and, at an agreed-upon time with the friend, sat across the table from her, and shared or did not share what it was that you wanted to share.

You even went when you didn't want to see said friend sometimes. You went and saw her nonetheless, and she was predictably beautiful.

Other times you canceled, so you could sit inside your house and wrap yourself in someone else's words and pretend you were someone else. You'd spotted yourself in the mirror, the plush of new fat on your upper thighs, or you'd seen the painting you'd finished the day before, a painting of the feeling of a smell, and you had known, in the same way you'd known so many times before, that the Day would never come when you were going to create something worth looking at.

And then—a week ago, two weeks?—there came the very special and singular time when you realized you were not even that type of person, the type of person who *could* create something worth looking at. What did Virginia Woolf call them, moments of being? Shortly after this realization, you had had one of your déjà vus when you were walking down the sidewalk in your neighborhood, through a narrowing tunnel of new spring flowers; this brought you to a courtyard in Crete—archway tucked down a narrow street off the plaza, the brick wall with its furred vines encircling a single orange tree— where a band played Pentozali music while you and everyone ordered zucchini pies, a moment that even in that moment you knew you would recall later, when it was important to do so. Painting: another place you were a tourist—another place you did not belong and could not even understand what you were seeing. This had become quite clear now.

After that you were glad the world had shut its jaws. You didn't want to see the friend who was always more beautiful and talented than you were, even in the way she lowered her fork to her food, even in the way she raised it to her mouth, in the way she never took as many bites or sips as you did, with the same frequency, as though she had enough and also was enough, and food or drink was just a bonus, a beautiful addition to a beautiful life.

You, meanwhile, are and have always been hungry, even gluttonous, as though the next bite might be the bite, the next day might be the Day.

Today—the day, we will call it, of the olive—perhaps you believed, more profoundly than at any other time, might be the Day. The thing itself, the bite. Or perhaps you thought that the Day might need to be forced, or otherwise never come. Let's observe what has led up to this, as though the ingredients in the dish can fully express what the dish is.

Recall that six weeks ago today you were out on a run. You were running up the same hill you always run up because the view of the mountains at the top is exceptional and makes you feel both lucky and small. Until the Day you make something worth looking at, you'd mostly like to be small. Impossible-to-see small. Invisible small. And invisibility was indeed one of your achievements. Though it also worried you that this invisibility could be an obstacle in itself. Something can't spring from nothing, the same reason you can't believe in a God that one day just Was. Whether the Big Bang tells a more credible story, you don't know. Should you? There is too much in this world to know and you are often unsure what to know first, what to know second, what to know third, and what to decide must be unknown simply because there is too much to know.

The decisions that you make in this regard determine your worth. They determine whether you will arrive at the Day when you create something worth looking at. And if this is so, then a million decisions branch out before you, and the Day's arrival is no longer a sure thing. This is the problem that came to a head not so very long ago when you created the official ten thousandth piece of work you have created with no results ("results" being measured in various types of approval, contests won, and praise heaped upon).

But all of this is not related to the fact at hand, which is that six weeks ago today you were running and your lungs started to ache. They were sore when they opened and sore when they shut, like a bruise being pressed. And then, when you ran again, they were sore like pencils being stuck in them at particular spots. And they were sore in these ways for a period of two weeks, during which time you told no one because dozens, then hundreds, then thousands of people were getting sick around the country, around the world. Why did you tell no one? Because when you used to sit across tables from friends, you knew the rules of engagement: ask them question after question about their life because people love to talk about their lives. Nod with interest, then add thoughtful follow-up questions to show that you were truly listening. When they ask how you are doing, say, "Fine." The pain of the Day that won't come is not entertaining to your company. Try not to talk about it. And when you fail to not talk about it, deny later having talked about it and perhaps laugh like it was a joke. Friends love to laugh together and laughing at others' expense—or at your own—is an easy joke to make when you don't have another one ready.

So the pain came and the pain went and now all around the country and also the world the people who were getting sick were dying—dozens, then hundreds, then thousands. It was impossible to imagine thousands of people dying, so you went on worrying about whether you would someday be worth looking at. You decided you had been sick and were now immune and didn't much worry about whether you would die because that would rush the timeline of the Day that might someday come and make it too important that it should come now and now for you could not wait.

But what happened today that was different? Or what happened yesterday that made today impossible to ignore? You were perhaps clearheaded because you had not had alcohol in three days. Sometimes when you didn't have alcohol for three days you became so clearheaded it was frightening. You could see all the branching paths before you and the correct answers to the multiplicity of decisions that would lead you to the Day that must come. And then it was so overwhelming how far away that Day was, and how difficult the decisions, and how even if you made the right decisions the work that would then ensue would be superhuman work—not just painting for enough hours for enough days, but painting *well* for enough hours for enough days, which is not a thing you can simply turn on, which therefore could take weeks or could take years or could get to the point where you could never accumulate enough good hours to reach the next decision not even before you die. Said death being a thing that was closer for us all, and maybe even for you, if the lung pain didn't mean you had conquered the virus, for you were after all running while sucking the late winter's freezing clots of air into your lungs.

And closer for us all meant, surely, that those Days would come with more frequency for everyone who was working toward such Days, since many people had already proven more gifted than you were—your friend, for instance, who could eat with the proper frequency and smile with the proper vibrancy and lit up every room she entered so that everyone turned to look at her although by all normal accounts her Day had not come either.

So then, when you realized how she could do all the right things for all the necessary hours and get to her next decision and her next branch more quickly than you, and knew you could not achieve nearly the same frequency of rightness, you maybe panicked. You maybe binge-watched a reality show about models whose incredible beauty gave them incredible personalities because they were difficult to *not* look at, which meant their Days had already come, before they were even eighteen, because being worth looking at was the whole point of the Day.

Then you put on the highest heels you had with bronze soles and staggered over to the mirror and did some dramatic contouring on your cheeks, which made them look more sculpted and hollow. And that was better, but it showed how your lips blended away into your skin so you added some color to them and some gloss to make them shine. And this showed how your eyes looked tired so you lined them in black and heaved on layers of mascara and swept on various golds and bronzes and put oil in your hair and rubbed it into your neck and collarbones and arms.

After which you read the prologue to a book of photos about how the photographer had been sexually assaulted and had come out the other side, after a terrible time that lasted many years, loving herself and her body and sharing all of that with the world and not being ashamed to do it. And she shared naked photos of herself and she was not the right amount of thin but she still shared naked photos of herself and you even liked the photos and could not understand why you liked them. She had had her Day, because you were looking, and because the book had a sticker on the front to say it was a bestseller, which proved it. And you could not understand how her Day had come but yours hadn't, when you were thinner than she was.

You took off your sweater and you took off your other sweater and you took off your sweatpants and your socks. In the mirror your naked body was unsurprising and so you began to pull things out of your drawers to make it surprising—a tank top of transparent lace and a black pencil skirt with a long slit up to your hip—and though winter was still curling up its furry, ferny tongues you put these on, and you made yourself a drink. Because it was not looking at the decisions and the paths between the decisions that got you to the Day. It was walking right up to the Day and wrapping your hands around its neck, pressing your own two thumbs into it, and splitting it open. And flowers in violet and lavender would spill out, and as you split the body and folded it back on itself it would be covered in jasmine, and its vines would squirm down before your feet and you would walk out upon the rug of them finally not yourself but who you were supposed to be.

So you claimed it. You left your keys and your wallet and your mask strewn behind you on the floor of your apartment like the skin you were shedding and went with only your martini and your outfit, your breasts small and round and blooming through the loose weave of the shirt, your thighs slick and bronze and hairless through the slit in the skirt, and your calves powerful and clean. And you moved like

263

oil through the air, slid through and past the suspended humidity and spit and sickness everyone else was breathing, for you were made of the coins of the Day, the vein-live skin of the Day, and down the street the voices lifted and were singing, and the heads squealed on their hinges, and could not help but turn to see, because what you were doing was singular, and the roads were empty, the cars all retired to a past time, and the future would be this: you claiming the street and the street belonging to you gliding up and down it, the hill and everyone that goes important places now seeing you, you as they always would into the future remembering this moment, how on the way to their next decision, they must first surpass you and your achieved perfection, walking down the center line, glass poised in hand, like a needle: sterile, bright, promised.

Even the Sky and Clouds Were Walls
Alan Rossi

JAMES THOUGHT THAT IF he could think in the right way, behave in the right way, act out his outer life according to his inner principles, perceive reality in a way that was spacious and caring, less judgmental, considerate of others, and understanding of the fact that they were real people, not just avatars shouting things at each other, but real humans with flaws and faults and good points also, and find a way to care for the totality of them, individual by individual, while also recognizing that there were small, empowering things he could do that could make a difference in the larger world—eating less meat, driving an electric car, voting for candidates who were progressively minded, with their sights set on ending systems that oppressed various peoples, animals, the planet itself—and if he could listen to his wife, Andrea, with attention and care and attend to her needs first and his own second, and also care for and put their child, Katie, first and be both a friend and a father to her, and if he could additionally be a good friend to his friends, be funny and interesting and engaged, and if he could not only want to help his friends who came from historically marginalized backgrounds—he had once been exceptionally good at supporting other people when they had problems: his friend Devin (a Black man) he'd helped through a nasty separation with his first wife and allowed him to sleep on his sofa; his friend Stacy (a woman) he and his wife had made a room for when she was fired from her job and could no longer afford her apartment downtown; he got how difficult it was out there not only on an individual, emotional level, but also in the midst of this angst-ridden age, wherein everything seemed broken, wherein people had oppressed and broken each other as well as the planet itself it seemed, and he wished he could be that person who was there for others again—but if he could also allow *himself* to be helped on a personal, emotional level, if he could, say, tell his best friend since college, the now remarried Devin, his one friend whom he still hung around with frequently, whom he and his wife were friends with, if he could just tell him openly and with complete vulnerability that he felt something was very wrong with him indeed recently, that he felt this sort of constant pressure or tightness in his chest like he couldn't get a full breath ever, a terrible ball of anxiety there, and that several nights in a row he'd awoken to the feeling of not being able to get a full breath, his chest tightening and constricting, and one night he'd even passed out into what felt like a dream filled with a million voices coming out of a million tiny mouths that were all speaking in a cacophony that he could not understand, and he woke up the next day and deleted all his social media, feeling that the modern world was messing with his well-being, and he thought that if he could explain to someone that everything seemed wrong or backward, that the internet told him and everyone that the environment was doomed, that soon they would all be running out of fresh water, that oppression was everywhere and so difficult to eradicate, that the economy would eventually collapse and people would all be well and truly fucked, that he had the terrible feeling that everyone was selfish, including himself, and also that something seemed to be wrong with him internally, that there seemed to be some function of his living that was broken, and he couldn't recalibrate, which caused him to feel almost always unbalanced, dizzy, rushed, unclear, like some animal drunk on fermented fruit, wandering and lost with a terrible thirst in a black forest, and if he could just get clear, just get some clarity, just feel that his feet were on the ground, as they say, and he thought if he could call his friend, Devin, and try to tell him all this—though, he would say, he knew that Devin, as a Black man, had experienced and would go on experiencing the world in much more troubling ways than he would himself, and he knew something about all this was self-indulgent and self-pitying, and that as a white person he knew he had it much easier than many people, much easier than Devin, sure, but also much easier than those oppressed minorities around the world, the poor and disenfranchised, and yet still he felt himself to be truly suffering and just very confused here—and if he could say that about a month ago his doctor in a literally five-minute-long appointment had prescribed him an antidepressant, which made him feel numb to everything and like he was underwater, and also a benzo, which made him feel light but superficial, like he wasn't himself but was a cartoon sketch of himself whose head had been replaced with the head of a stick figure, permanently smiley faced, and if he could say that after about a month of feeling no better, perhaps worse, but more like barely there, barely even there, and then reading about his prescriptions on drugreviews.com— horror story after horror story—that he quit both and even then still had a withdrawal from the benzo though he'd only been on it a month, in which time he had decided to call Devin no matter how embarrassing all this was, no matter how small his suffering was compared to that of the rest of the world, and tell him that he was, apparently, not a person who could keep his shit together, though he knew that outwardly he looked like a person who could keep his shit together, and if he could only not rehearse what he had to say to Devin, but just say it, not try to control what Devin might feel about him, but to just come out and say that he was feeling like a piece of shit, indeed, for various reasons, and if he could do that he imagined some of the heaviness of things would go out of him, like muddy water evaporating from a puddle after a long rain and dispersing into the atmosphere of the larger world, which he felt was there but which he seemed constantly unable to access, and yet he also thought that if he rehearsed what he needed to say enough he would be able to say it, so maybe he shouldn't just go into the call blind, and so he thought that if he could just rehearse it lightly, and remember during the call that he wanted to tell Devin that he knew he looked like he was a person with his shit together, but he did not feel internally that he had his shit together in the least, he felt very lost indeed, and that it was this deception—that he presented one way, while internally he was another way—that seemed to be increasingly who he *was*, and if he could remain concentrated and unsurprised when Devin told him that he was glad he'd called, that actually his wife, Andrea, had texted last week and said she was worried about him, and if he could remain attentive and concentrated when Devin said this about Andrea, and not feel suspicious or paranoid, and if he could breathe through the tight feeling in his chest, and not think too much about the fact that Andrea was communicating with another man seemingly behind his back, and if he could just get a full breath, and while doing that if he could just listen as Devin continued—in the brief pause where James was attempting to feel open—by saying that James's wife, Andrea, had texted only last week and said that something seemed wrong with James, something seemed off, and she said that she'd been feeling lonely because of it, and if James could just listen and not judge, if he could just be patient and attentive and not feel the suspicion and paranoia deepening, and if he could hear when Devin answered his question about why his wife texted him rather than contacting Devin's wife, Chelsea, if he could truly hear and be eased when Devin said that he didn't know why, probably because he and James had been friends for so long, if he could really allow

Devin's words to sink in, to not see them in another way, to hear him when he said, I don't know, buddy, it was a harmless text, she was, is worried about you, and if he could just take a breath on the phone and listen to his friend and trust that he was being fully sincere and honest instead of thinking that Andrea had once kissed him and then been fingered by one of their mutual friends while very drunk at a wine tasting years ago, in the coat closet of a wine tasting, which had led them to never go to a wine tasting again, and instead of thinking that this past event had left its mark on his consciousness—he felt it now surfacing from the depths of his mind—and caused him to be suspicious and paranoid sometimes, as he was now on the phone with his good friend, feeling himself unable to breathe while attempting to talk to his best friend from college, if he could just listen, though he knew he was not listening now because he seemed utterly unable to take a full, deep breath, if he could just collect himself and casually say that he'd have to talk with Devin another time, actually, he'd forgotten he was taking Katie to soccer, if he could just make his voice sound assured and calm when Devin said that this all seemed weird now, he didn't mean to make it weird, and if James could just say perfectly normally that all was OK and then get off the phone, and after the call if he could go on a long run and really push his body and legs and mind and come home clean of it all, not think about all the cars going both ways on the highway beside the trail where he ran, not think of the unending pollution, if he could only for a moment see the mountains in the distance and let them cleanse him and not think that soon they wouldn't be there, or if he could only for a moment see the mountains in the distance and not think that soon people wouldn't be there and that the mountains would remain, that what would really happen was people—including his child—would end themselves, and that only then would the planet recover, if he could only feel more hopeful for Katie when viewing the mountains and return home renewed and replete with satisfaction after his run then maybe he would understand it all more clearly, including the phone call, which he didn't want to think about any longer, and additionally after the run if he could just feel that it wasn't annoying to have to stop thinking about the big things—i.e., climate change and what to do about it and the life of future generations— and again be focused on the notion that the phone call was not strange, that what his wife did was completely normal and a thing done out of concern, concern for James, and if after his run he could not feel annoyed when he viewed her on the sofa reading one of her

268

fantasies or historical fictions that he deeply despised and viewed as an escape from the difficult realities around them, an escape from reality itself, a thing that he knew was a small and stupid resentment that had its roots in a larger resentment, her kissing the man and being fingered at the wine tasting, which, in couples therapy, they had discovered, or she had revealed, along with the fact that there had been other such liaisons, was her word, but only a few, three, and which were her way of escaping the boredom she was feeling, her boredom at being an elementary-school teacher, her boredom at their mundane existence, and which in counseling she also revealed she felt terrible about, and was so sorry about, and which allowed her to see that she wanted to work on them, she just had this problem of wanting to escape reality instead of facing it, she guessed, which the counselor had asked about, what was it she didn't want to face, and Andrea had said, I really don't know, reality, and so now after he returned from his run and saw her on the sofa with another fantasy and/or historical novel, which he believed she read as just another way to escape her boredom and the difficult realities around them, as well as reality itself, he told himself if he could just be understanding and kind about it, and understand that the thing with the other man, or other men, had happened years ago, that everyone needed an escape sometimes, that he had often viewed pornography like a stupid animal after Andrea went to bed sometimes in order to escape, after which he would feel guilty, and if he just hadn't done these things or viewed her in this way, and if he could just understand and be kind toward her need for escape, then he could be understanding and kind toward his need for escape, and then he wouldn't have to do it, and then, when he was vigorously pumping his erection while viewing pornography, he thought that if he could just see the patterns of his life, the anxieties that led to his various attempts to alleviate anxieties, his defensiveness that led to his various attempts to be open, and if he could just not feel like a true piece of shit the next day after he spent an hour searching pornography websites for women who looked like his wife as she was up in their bedroom reading a historical novel, which he knew meant she did not want to have anything to do with him sexually, if he could ignore the two scabs on the sides of his penis because of how vigorously he pumped his erection the night before, if he could not hate this part of his personality but feel that it was a manageable part of him that could be worked on, and if he could not feel that almost no one he knew could deal with reality, that his wife, Andrea, couldn't, that his friend, Devin, couldn't, that none of the people he knew could do it, no one could look at the endless amounts of pollution caused by transportation and industry, nor the greenhouse gas emissions that everyone loved to blame on cows but that really came from power, electricity, fossil fuels, big industry, oil, but sure, he didn't eat red meat anymore either, neither did most of their friends, but still, even when people could look at those problems and attempt to address them, even when they could see political strife and sources of oppression and want to change these things, even when they could see these things that were things the mainstream media was telling people to look at all the time, even when they saw these things they couldn't *really* see what was there beyond it all, and he himself couldn't either, if he could just not feel that what everyone in America seemed to be doing was finding some way to entertain themselves, even entertain themselves with the various crises on the planet, rather than seeing what was all around them, so essential and real all around them, though he himself felt he only vaguely understood what that was, and what *was* all around them, he wondered, what was reality, after all, did it have to do with God (but he didn't believe in God), did it have to do with somehow making your life one that served others, that was less selfish (but that seemed too simple and obvious), did it have to do with some cosmic feeling of being alive, some feeling of Oneness that Andrea's friends Mark and Laney Phillips—each high-level yoga instructors who had studied under yogis in India and who seemed more into yoga every time he saw them—did it have to do with that, what was the thing that people called real, but that everyone seemed to avoid, if he could only grasp that, and if he could only be honest when the next morning Andrea asked him what was wrong, if he could only say something beyond the idea that he was just feeling down, which he knew would make him feel two-faced, deceptive, and even more like a true piece of shit, and if he could see that she needed his support, and if when giving her a hug and telling her that everything was all right, that she shouldn't be worried, that he was just having a difficult time, if he could just feel that she was not deceiving him in any way, that she had been concerned for him and that was all, that she had always been concerned in some way, and if he could just let it go and see that Andrea was here with him and he was here with her and they were here for their daughter, Katie, and that was enough, but fuck, that wasn't enough, the world was ending, how could it be that anything was enough, and if he could just feel that *something* was enough, and he thought that maybe if he could become more engaged and interested in the simple activities of his day-to-day life, say in making music the way he used to, or in playing with Katie in the yard, or in taking her to the zoo, or if he could be engaged in working on his environmental poetry once again, which he knew was difficult poetry in which trees were the protagonists, was poetry that would not be rewarded, as it had never been, not by a reading public, but only by a few close friends, or if he could be engaged in exercising not just for the sake of exercising but because it was an activity that promoted well-being, and if he could stop looking at pornography so much and probably other women too, and if he could just understand that Andrea was a very beautiful woman and that was all he needed, that he was dedicated to her and needed to show her that, just as she was dedicated to him, and he thought if he could eradicate his unnecessary desires, his unnecessary preferences and aversions—he saw the trouble they caused him—and if he could just stop wishing to be somewhere else, if he could stop wanting to be elsewhere when he was in his office at his high-paying marketing job and just accept that he was there and not hiking, nor playing music, nor just out having coffee somewhere, and if he could understand that this was a deeply privileged want, that many people didn't get to even question where they were and what they did and think about the environment and systems of oppression and whether their offspring would populate the planet or die off, many people didn't get to consider the source of the deep divide in the country and also have the time to feel anxious and depressed and lost in one's own life, he got it, and if he could really understand that he was getting paid a good deal of money to do, in actuality, very little, and if he could be grateful for the job rather than spiteful about it, if he could see it as a source of income and a way to contribute to a community rather than a chore he had to execute every day, a chore that made him some days very busy indeed and other days extremely bored, and if after a particularly long and stressful day at his generally benign job he could understand that when his wife said something about how many Oreos he was eating at night that she was not in fact trying to be a jerk, but just that possibly she had his best interests in mind, that she wished the best for him, that she knew that he would be vaguely regretful and irritated the following day when he would complain of a stomach-ache and headache after eating almost an entire bag of double-stuffed Oreos, which contained way more sugar than his body could handle at forty-five years of age, and if he could just be OK with that and not start an argument about it with Andrea, waking up their daughter,

271

Katie, who would come into the family room crying, asking why they were shouting about Oreos, and if when he told Devin about this episode days later he didn't exaggerate Andrea's meanness but just presented it fairly and then also presented his childish tantrum of throwing the half-eaten bag of Oreos away fairly, if he could just present that honestly so that his friend could honestly say that oh man I know how it is, and in talking to his good friend if he could just feel that he wasn't always selfishly dominating the topics of conversation while also feeling that it was important that he got certain things talked out, and if he could really say to Devin that he felt bad for calling him so often recently and really be able to hear his friend when he said that it was OK, this was just one of those times, he really got it, and if for a moment he could allow himself to feel better, feel almost held, through the phone, held by his good friend, who he had felt suspicious and paranoid about not a week ago, and now suddenly felt held almost in the way his mother had once held his body as a child when he had a bad dream, and if he could tell his good friend he was grateful indeed to which his friend would say it was really and truly nothing and anytime, and if he could the next morning accept that he felt spacious and wild and OK and that when he walked under some trees he did in fact enjoy the simple pleasure of seeing these other living things, and if he could continue enjoying it rather than considering how the previous day he had felt held by his good friend in the same way he had felt held by his mother when he had a bad dream, and then begin to think that if he could call his parents more, whom he had once been too distant from, and who were getting older and whom he genuinely liked now and wished he hadn't had those years of what now felt like silly rebellion and been the way he had been, treated them the way he did, though he knew it was most likely very normal, his entire life he understood as very normal and he did understand that this was just a period of time in which things had become unbalanced and he just had to, as they say, weather it, while at the same time not lose sight of the fact that time was short, everyone was going to die, that his parents were getting older and he should take advantage of this rare gift, and if he could just let them know how important they were to him, so that if under the trees—sycamores that lined the river, he liked the way sycamores lined rivers in this part of the country—while taking a walk during his lunch break he could call them and tell his mother that he knew he didn't say it enough, but he was grateful for all that she'd done for him, he wanted her to know that, college and all that, and more, just her being

272

his mom, he was glad she was his mom, and if he could just be there when his mother cried on the phone and he cried too, seeing his mother in his mind's eye rather than seeing the moment as it were from afar like an alien observing human life, and if when she asked if he was all right, if he could say to her oh yeah he was fine, and could she put Dad on, and if he could tell his father Dad I'm glad I'm your son and thank you for teaching me about consequences, he knew he didn't say things like that enough, but he was learning to, and if when his father said that that was OK in a very soft and gentle voice his father could sometimes have, and really hear him when his father said that Andrea recently called, she was really worried, and if he could not feel irritated at that fact and just accept that someone was trying to help him then he could stay on the line and keep this open and kind feeling going, and not feel the irritation that was there pushing up and causing him to hardly be able to get a breath, and if he didn't have a fight with Andrea that night because he made himself put the irritation at her talking to his parents behind his back out of his mind, and if he could just truly look at her and see her with new eyes and say that he heard she'd talked to his parents, and if he could just thank her instead of feeling frustrated at her, and if he could say to her that he knew she cared about him and was worried about him, but sometimes he was still suspicious or a little lost and he didn't like that he was a little lost, but he was, and he knew that this was selfish and that he was going through something he didn't understand, but he wanted to thank her, and if he could accept her embrace and feel the warmth of her body, if he could see her anew, hear her tinkling laugh, truly touch her body, feel her mind, and know that she was who she said she was, and feel that he was who he claimed to be, and feel relief at this, and the next day if he could only stay in these moments, which were open and spacious moments, which were somehow not even moments, but just being exactly where he was, if he could be exactly where he was and not somehow return to the narrowed and confined space he so often returned to, anxious about the future or depressed about the past, which he knew engendered the tight feeling in his chest that was occurring so often lately, that tightness that felt like his heart was being strangled, and he thought that part of the problem was that that feeling came from his deep self-concern, and maybe if he could just feel that he was contributing in some way to something larger, maybe something culturally important, or just contributing in some way to a community that seemed in some way meaningful, rather than working a job that was

273

designed to help sell products that he found a little bit morally repre-
hensible, his job being to create online marketing campaigns for art
galleries or the local theater or the local ballet, all of which were
things he found culturally important and meaningful, but which he
reduced down to a simple product that was being sold to people, and
after making the transition into the marketing job several years ago,
he began to see that all America was a series of products being sold,
that even supposed cultural artifacts were just French fries, that
everything, in a sense, had been reduced to French fries, that his job
was to take something that was or looked like art and turn it into
French fries, and when the local yoga studio met with him to come
up with a better online presence—Andrea had sent Mark and Laney
Phillips to him—and he'd created a web page for them and helped
them with their Instagram page and helped them begin to really form
their brand and identity, it started to become very clear to him
indeed, as he listened to Mark and Laney Phillips explain to him the
spiritual discipline of yoga, that what he was doing was taking something spiritual and turning it into something material, or that they
already had and he was only finalizing the product, that he was taking
some essence of reality and repackaging it as a product, that, forget
raw materials—the essence of things—taken to build the iPhones and
tech products and gas and rubber and plastic and all the rugs and the
clothes and all the actual products people could buy, forget all that,
all of that was of course stupid and did untold harm, but what was
worse was that he was now part of a system that took things that
appeared to be beyond commodification and he was commodifying
them, and he was commodifying not only various types of art, but
he was also commodifying now a spiritual discipline, and so it was
becoming clear to him that nothing indeed was anything other than
French fries anymore, and so when Mark and Laney Phillips also
wanted their own web pages and Instagram pages and all the other
varieties of social media, what he did was he also commodified them
too, he turned Mark and Laney Phillips themselves into a brand, and
their so-called pursuit of unfolding the ultimate potential of the human
mind and spirit seemed a little bit like presenting a well-photographed
box of spiritual French fries, and when he asked the Phillipses about
this, and said it seemed a little weird to be doing it like this and didn't
they think there was some other way, that branding and commodifying like this, he knew it was his job, but wasn't it sort of against this
spiritual discipline that had to do with relinquishing or seeing through
the ego or something, and the Phillipses had laughed and explained

to him that, yes, from his limited perspective, it might look like that, but no, see, matter and energy are one, all is one, and frankly, it can't be corrupted, nothing can be corrupted, there's no such thing as ego, and so while it might look a little egotistical to him, from their humble and grateful points of view, there was nothing to be worried about at all because you couldn't commodify or make a product of or even ruin in any way what was exactly and precisely cosmic reality anyway, so thank you for the concern, but let's get these pages really focused on this modern karma yoga that Mark has developed and the more classical hatha yoga that Laney presents, and also, Laney wanted to know if he thought it would be a good idea if she began to present some of her jewelry and her own line of clothing, and he had said great, that tightness in his chest returning, and the feeling that outwardly he was being one way when inwardly he felt something totally else seeming to make it impossible to see or feel or hear or touch anything with any degree of clarity, like he was finally aware that he had been confused all his life but had no idea what to do with that confusion now that he saw it, he just knew he was confused, and so after that meeting with the Phillipses he had thought that if he could just find another job, if he could only stop working at this job, which commodified everything and made even human beings into a brand, which he had to pretend was not what he was doing, but which was in actuality exactly what he was doing, maybe if he got into nature and just got away from the job a bit, if he started hiking more, he had once been an avid hiker and had recently lost touch completely with the outdoors, he worked out in a gym, he worked from an office and was constantly in front of a screen, he watched pornography at home, he and his wife had sex and filmed it and then watched that together when they were going to have sex again, until they each no longer really got turned on by it, they weren't professionals after all and they often looked clumsy or were out of focus, and yes, he walked the dog every day in the neighborhood, which was outdoors, but at this point, having lived in the neighborhood ten years, the neighborhood just felt like another big room, just as the city felt like just another room, a box, that even the sky and clouds might as well have been walls, and if only he could do something like his friend from years ago did and go live in an ashram in Thailand for six months, and he said this to Andrea one night as a quasi joke, maybe he should just quit his job and try to honestly figure out what he wanted to do and who he really was and go to Thailand, and she said, you mean like Daniel, you know he's back, right? and he hadn't known that and she said, yeah, he got malaria and was in a hospital for like two weeks and now he's back, he's been working at Wells Fargo, and so he said he was just kidding about Thailand, but he was thinking of buying this hiking stuff, and he showed her the products on his phone—hiking shoes, a good pack, a camelback, a waterproof hat, hiking pants that zipped off at the knees, a Kevlar tent that cost nearly $2,000—and she said that that was so cool, they could do it together, and she began looking up products on her phone, and if he could only be OK with her wanting to come with him rather than feeling that this was a thing he wanted to do alone, and then if he could only not say anything, and then as he was saying that he actually was hoping to do this alone, if he could only keep himself from getting defensive when she was hurt and defensive, and if he could only stop the argument from happening when he continued it by saying that the thing was he never got any downtime, she got all this downtime, she only worked twenty hours a week because of her job share at the elementary school, she got to do what she wanted with her time, and if he could only listen to her when she was saying that she was trying to start her own business—it was a French pastry place—while also still contributing to the family by continuing part-time at the school until she could get the patisserie off the ground, did he have any idea how difficult that was, to get the loan, to perfect the food, to still be working a job, to which he'd then found himself saying that that wasn't at all what he was trying to say, he didn't know why he even brought any of that up, he just wanted to do a long weekend hike alone, to which she would then be walking out of the room and saying yeah, OK, and I just wanted to hang out with you, and if he could only not feel shitty about that for the next two days, and if he could only apologize and not only apologize, but learn from it, and he knew he was, as he apologized to her, he knew he was learning to be better, but it all seemed to be happening too slowly and too quickly at once, and if, when his mother called to tell him she was sick, she had to have a surgery, if he didn't have the thought right below the thought of concern that he was really busy at work right now, he hoped she wouldn't ask him to come to Illinois, and if he could just be caring and thoughtful on the phone when she told him this and not feel relieved when he offered to come home and she told him that wasn't necessary, and if after he kissed Andrea and Katie goodbye for the weekend and finally went hiking, if on the trails he could feel that he was in the mountains and among the trees and finally settled into what was so essentially real rather than thinking that that's what he should be feeling, if he could also not think that all of it would one day be gone, that it would all be a field of soybeans or something eventually, the mountains mowed over, if he could just not look at it all and see something else, or be being the way he was, and if he could just not be constantly thinking of the way he was supposed to be, and also if he maybe wouldn't have chosen to go in the heat of a Southern summer, with temperatures reaching 95 degrees that day with 90 percent humidity, and if he had brought more water rather than anxiously wanting to get out there and experience nature, and if he had chosen a lighter route, rather than the grueling ten-mile loop that had an incline of nearly three thousand feet on the west-facing part of the trail, and if he had been more attentive in all things he wouldn't be stooped here having to try to find a cell signal because the cramps in his legs were getting too bad and he was running dangerously low on water, if he had started out with something simpler, and if he wasn't the way he was he wouldn't feel like he was about to pass out on the trail, no longer sweating because he was dehydrated, his clothes almost stiff from the salty sweat that had now dried, unable to get a cell signal, and as he falls toward the ground he'll feel like a drowning man suddenly at peace as he sinks into the earth, like falling into a great bed, and it's not until some local kids stoned as all hell find him with a bloody forehead and very unconscious and send someone to get help with their panicked and worried faces peering down at him who is not there not awake no eyes no ears no hands no tongue no color no consciousness no body no mind gone, gone beyond, gone beyond gone if only for a moment and then a boy gently slapping his face and coming out of it and back again and sitting upright with the help of one of the boys, the boy holding one of his shoulders, balancing him, and before knowing that this is just another moment he'll have to explain to himself, before knowing that he'll be embarrassed to tell it to Andrea, to Katie, to Devin, before making it into a self-deprecating joke, before feeling anything, before he can think anything about it, tulip trees, oaks, maples, gray and brown and green, clouds, a wind through the leaves rushing like a stream, sky, sunlight shifting in columns through the trees, and the boys' faces, their speaking mouths, his mouth making sounds to answer them, their bodies here, just here, gateways all of it.

Soteriology

John Darcy

HIS LIFE IS A SILENCE, a listening. Jim slips on his boots. By the time
the coffee is finished brewing, he's done tying them.

It's the bending over.

It's the type of wood, the age, his name. A living memorial.

He pours the coffee and takes a sip. It's a quiet morning as the sunrise starts to spread, reddish, tossing see-through stripes around the
sky. The coffee drags along his tongue. The bitter bite of it. The bitter
giving way.

Looks like the clouds might clear.

He heads out the door and walks to his truck. Off to work. It's an
honor. Even today. A quiet morning. Quiet. There never seems to be
enough.

Jim says good morning to Peter and good morning to Matthew and
asks Teresa if those earrings are new.

They are, Teresa says. Three dollars at the flea market in Platteville,
if he can believe it.

Jim says no, he can't hardly believe it. He was going to guess
Tiffany's.

He puts his lunch in the fridge, goes to his workbench. The day
just starting. There is always work to do. Tools and saws and drills, a
votive buzzing, a soundtrack, the scratchy pull of sandpaper. The different sounds swerve, merging. Sawdust puffs over metal partitions.
His area is disorganized in the precise way he likes. He can find anything he needs. Move it an inch, he'd lose it forever.

Jim starts on his work. There's always work to be done. This place
is one of penance, maybe. A kind of gradual gasp of forgiveness. Even
today.

He tightens the slip screws into the slide rail. Rotates, repeats. A
firm givingness to the wood, all wood. The slant of the grain he's
chosen cradles tiny slits of light, always lovely, this shimmer, its
movement. He slips in the drop bolt, reinforces the socket on the
runner wall. A hush, a breath. Fastens the torque nail snug but not
tight. Twinfast into runner guide. Turn, quarter turn, almost music,

278

liquid feeling. You let the tools do the work. It comes together in pieces, stages. That's the how behind all this. What's the why? Slowing down as a form of remembrance. Remembrance as absolution. Five days a week, every week for three decades, minus two for shingles, three for his mother, the annual retreat at New Melleray, that long stretch with some stomach ailment. And now this. His sister. Best not to think about it. This. My sister.

But it's an honor.

One step after the other. Like thinking you'll walk to a tree, then walking to it.

Stray parts converge. He likes to think they come together on their own. He is only there to supervise the joining. Everything its own creation story. Everything just is.

The lacquer comes last. There's always work to be done. Best not to think about it. Best to never stop. Best to build, to breathe, be kind. Make others laugh. Care for the wood and leave yourself out. No trace, no seams, no sutures, no creases. Leave only the thing itself. Best to look after the metal and the tools and the lumber, look after them like kin, like some beloved souvenir. More, always more. Develop a surplus of sentimental value. Not the object but the story behind it, the tools his confessor.

Margaret, the forewoman, walks over. Already it's closing in on lunchtime.

She says, You know you didn't have to be here today.

I know, Jim says.

You should go. It's really not a problem. You should be there.

He says he might try for three today.

She asks if that's a good idea. If he's sure.

He can do three today.

She says she knows it's not her place, but he might feel better if he goes.

I think I'll stay.

Well, it's good work you do, she says, and her eyes are suddenly faraway. The best.

He thanks her for saying so.

I'm sorry, she says. I'm so sorry.

She walks away.

Jim gets back to work. Decides to take a working lunch. An honor. It's an honor to do it.

The wood is sourced on-site. Jim finishes what was left from yesterday, and then starts on the three. He takes a small break between the first and second. To make three in a day is difficult, possible. He will be here late, and will need a small rest.

He goes on a walk through the old-growth forest. Sunshine warm on his face, beaming through his gray hair. There is a spirit of stewardship here. For every tree, they will seed five new ones. Walnut, oak, pine. No breeding, no adjustments, only natural colors, variegated patterns. The beauty comes from the imperfections, ancestry, the golden ratio and the Fibonacci sequence, ancient drops in pressure, the soil composition, maybe God. All and neither. Jim has never found a satisfactory explanation on the difference between worship and idolatry.

He uses walnut or oak, pine if he's in a pinch. When a staining is requested, he does it himself. They receive orders from around the world. Their work is renowned, acclaimed. Jim's especially. When they are given awards for their craftsmanship, their sustainability, they do not accept. There are no pull quotes of praise on the mailings or the website. There is only the thing itself.

Sunshine, and the forest floor transfigured into brightness. Clouds open overhead. A rush of cool breeze. Out among the trees, he's looking for a way into the silence. My little Muir, his mother called him, my little Emerson. It's been ten years and how he misses her still. The best person he's ever known. And now this.

Insurmountable, the loss. Both of them. Of his warmth for them.

The question of course is where does it all go.

It's not hard to imagine. Not for Jim. It seems to him like the trees know how they'll be used. They communicate, trees do. They warn each other and sound alarms, notify their neighbors of spring, of insects and disease. The world taking shape around his thoughts. He knows, yes, that trees don't know. That trees can't know. Of course. But it's still there, a small droplet, a small wondering. Perhaps. Maybe that's why their grain is always just so.

The question of course is whether he's worthy.

It's hard work and it's an honor to do it. Sometimes he'll wonder where exactly these last thirty years have gone. But he will remember: they've gone here, into this, into making. Jim himself has never read Muir, doesn't like Emerson. He is fifty years old, has lived forty-eight of them here in Wisconsin, in this rolling river valley. He thinks one of the finest things ever written was in a newspaper, back in 1963, in November. He found the clipping in his mother's garage, when he was cleaning it out after the funeral. It was Jimmy Breslin's column for the *New York Herald Tribune*. About JFK's funeral. About a man, Clifton Pollard. The man who dug John Fitzgerald Kennedy's grave. Who dug the thirty-fifth president of the United States' grave for $3.01 an hour. The story is about duty and honor and sacrifice. It's about service. Breslin wrote it on Pollard because he'd gone out drinking the night before and woke up late. Jim learned this part later. By the time Breslin arrived at Arlington, he could barely see for the swell of the press corps. He had to find another angle, a newer vantage. The story is about Pollard, about labor as cleansing, sacramental. About the way Jackie walked to that hole in the ground, the forever of it, about how she rescued the country from fear and helplessness by the way she walked, the unspeakable breathtaking dignity of it. It's hardly five hundred words in all. It moves Jim to tears whenever he reads it. A hagiography of service. Margaret and Teresa and Peter and Matthew will say, Good lord, not the Breslin thing again. And they'll all laugh, Jim included. Now this.

There's always work to be done. Of course. A living memorial. How to bear this fall into such darkness.

Jim finishes the second of the three. Daylight falling through the windows. That's all right. He will stay until he's finished. Finished what? Why not call the thing what it is? Humble himself before the pointlessness of it. See it through to the end. You let the tools do the work.

He believes and he does not believe. He sees it as his greatest failing, his finest triumph. When he was twenty years old he'd taken temporary vows. Two years as a novitiate. He was presented his robes by Abbot General Gillet when he was on a tour of the United States. The way of the cross. Lectio Divina. His love for the sorrowful mysteries. They are not vows of silence; they are vows to limit oneself to meaningful speech. That people conflate this with silence, it often makes Jim smile. To leave the abbey is his life's great regret, the choice his most thoughtful, considered, prayer shaped, correct. These ideas are not exclusive. Nothing can change. We do not exist for ourselves alone. There is no hope, only the slip screws, the runner walls, repetition, reputation. Error and compassion, error and compassion. The building of the thing a simple prayer, a small surrender.

He knows he's hiding. It is a denial within the desert of himself, to stay walled off from it by making it. A chilling of his faith. He sees in himself a terrible cowardice, a failure of guts and constitution. But he returns every day and it is too deep for words. He is flattened by the paradox of continuing. Our conception of God is proof that we misunderstand him. We are complicit, all of us. This dark night of the soul a lifetime in the making. We are obliged to each other and there is no hope. A crisis of torque nails, of this, of course. Of snug but not tight. Three in one day. Difficult, possible. Everything is fixed. Teresa says she and the others are going to go for a drink. Reoccurrence, communion, attention. It's an honor. There's always work to do. Teresa asks if he's coming. Jim says he will stay here, that he'll try to get over there later.

During Jim's postulancy, the novice director Brother Stephen was a man of the five wounds. The story told to Jim was that, in the time of Brother Stephen's own postulancy, late on the fortieth night of a fast, the figures carved into the stations in the chapel began to weep, and a drop of blood appeared on the replica of the Holy Lance. Above the altar, INRI scorched off the crucifix in a smokeless, crystalline fog, and Brother Stephen was anointed with stigmata, blood pooling in his shoes, crying down his hands and his side.

When he sat Jim down in the nave, the stigmatic bruises still visible on his wrists, he asked Jim this: What is it exactly you're living for?

To achieve moral stamina before the ultimate end, he said, and to remain in a state of contemplative supplication. I am living to find oneness with the cross.

Brother Stephen sat in prayer before he answered. An aim for oneness with the passion is evidence of a moral blind spot. To think you can attain it stems from an awful sort of pride, and we will speak of it no more.

The day was just starting when Brother Stephen said this, sunrise polishing the windowpanes.

Jim washes his hands before starting on the third.

Slip screw, slide rail, runner wall, repeat. Rotate. Glint on the grain. Varnish smells tighten in his nostrils, warm like a candle burning. Fasten, tighten. There's a difference between the two. Nothing showy. No seams, no sutures, no creases. It's too important to ease up. Even today. Drop bolt, Twinfast, runner guide. Sawdust floats incense-like, catching the light, drifting into the rafters. Snug, not tight. Saw teeth stutter against the wood. Into each he places a personal card: his name, the type of wood, the age of the tree, confirmation that new seedlings have been sown. A living memorial. He decides on an addition. Not something he's ever done. He writes her name instead. His sister's name. Somebody will see it and that is enough. You can do any job if you have the right tools. It's an honor. You put yourself into it. All your aches and baggage and breaks. This is not a weakness. You keep an eye on the fit, the edges, the lid. It's harder than it used to be. But his hands are accustomed. The lacquer comes last. More like prayer than anything, private vespers. His life an autobiography of hours. You put yourself into it, every inch, every heartbeat. You become what you are.

Sometimes the families will visit. This is always years later.

They want to look around and see how it is. They want a place to put their gratitude, their grief. Margaret will walk them around the forest, show them where the seedlings were scattered. She'll walk them around the floor, give a short introduction, and then she'll bring them to Jim.

It's my honor, Jim tells the families. I hope I did right by you all, by the departed one, by the little one. I pray for them every day. I hope I did a good job.

And they'll choke out a yes, throats slick with swallowed tears, a yes, yes, you did. Or they'll say they were so glad to have found this place, because the thought of something made on an assembly line, something cold and metallic, something machine built, was too awful to even contemplate. Or sometimes they can only manage a nod.

It comes back to them when they visit. This is always years later.

His sister's husband had her cremated. The word is barbed wire in his thoughts. Jim cannot decide whether he is glad she's been burned, turned to ash, scuttled. Whether, given the choice, he would've made one for her, as he did for his mother.

I pray for them every day. His favorite is the novena to Thomas the Apostle. The Doubter. Unless I see the nail marks in his hands and put my finger where the nails were, and put my hand into his side, I will not believe. Though the doors were locked, Jesus stood among his disciples. Thomas, put your finger here, see my hands. Reach out your hand and put it into my side. Stop doubting and believe.

Caravaggio's seventeenth-century chiaroscuro painting of the scene, a cheap framed print of which hangs back at home, on Jim's bedroom wall, shows Jesus guiding his follower's finger into his gaping side. There is no halo painted above the Lord. Often considered heretical, many theologians instead argue that it is meant to emphasize the corporeality of the risen Christ, the biological truth of Jesus and his divine begotten oneness with God the Father. The skin and the bodies in the painting are rendered in hyper photo-realistic detail, though the greatest attention is paid to the dimensions of Thomas's hand, as if a meditation on skepticism and the limits of faith—man's selfish, bodily unbelieving.

The Gospel's human failures. Peter's denial, the doubting of Thomas, Iscariot's betrayal. Jim sees himself in them, that trinity of the lost.

He's made a virtue of solitude, of poverty, and it is the worst mistake of his life. Because what has it cost him? Postcards, just checking in, calling to say hello and thought I'd drop by. Saw this at the store and it made me think of you, maybe coffee on Sunday, sure, that would work. Funny emails with rowdy subject lines, the lending of cherished books, take your time, no rush to get it back. And dinners, gentle teasing over heaping meals on dark holiday nights, stillness, calm, the intense colorized joy of really truly knowing my family.

Jim is fond of this final one he's made today. He thinks that maybe he will hang on to it, in a sense. Save it for himself. He climbs inside. Lays himself out. A living memorial. He climbs out. That's enough. Even today. He hears a small tap, like a leaf falling. The card. Must have stuck to him. He picks it up, turns it over. Her name was Helen.

What exactly are you living for. Ask it again, and again, always more.

It's the understanding that he cannot do it forever. Living, working. That one day he will no longer be of service. Some quiet morning. When the clouds might clear.

His life is a silence, a listening. There is always work to do and he'll try to get over there later. Peter is having his birthday party this weekend. For a present Jim bought a new video game he'd overheard Peter talking about in the break room. The man at the store was helpful, because Jim didn't have a clue. He also got a box of Junior Mints. Peter's favorite. My soul is overwhelmed with sorrow to the point of death—Jesus said this.

The pointlessness a simple prayer. To do right by the departed one. A small surrender.

Say it again.

Puffs of sawdust. What exactly are you living for. Even today. The pull of the sandpaper. Sunshine in the silence, forever and ever.

Five Poems
Rae Armantrout

LONELY GIRL

1.

It wasn't her fault.

She couldn't have loved
any of them because
they never came out of themselves, emerged
as what?

Disembodied? Transparent?

2.

She couldn't explain herself either.

Self is an area
where will intersects
with drift.

It has ruffled, frothy
edges

like a square-dance dress.
Look.

3.

Lying in the dark,
nose buried in her arm's
crook, she felt like a girl,

Rae Armantrout

or pictured herself as one,

or loved herself as much
as she had
when she was a girl

and first coiled
up. That

was her secret.

SAYINGS

Playing ball across the street,
one boy shouts, "I'm gonna show you
my whole potential!";

"Better do it now,"
the other taunts—

like a clumsy translation
from what?

I'm alone with the sun
in my lap.

"Not a bad day,"
I say to myself,

repeating this
like a bird-call.

286

SELF-COMPOSURE

Every eight or nine minutes, I check
to see that enough time has passed.

I am accurate as a frog
hopping between lily pads.

Though I have no sense of
what I've skipped over
or why I came down
where I did.

At the dream conference,
I go down a plastic slide
on cue, shouting the word
"enjoyment."

In my defense, I have
my doubts.

In relaxation videos,
the stars steadily converge
on a cosmic horizon
while the observer
stays put.

I am one of several,
perched alone
at these blond tables,
where the supermarket
joins Starbucks.

Rae Armantrout

SHUSH

1.

A smart pop song
can convince a desperate person
to see herself
as a thrill seeker.

This is considered a job skill.

"Take me to the job.
I'm ready for anything
because I love the adrenaline . . ."

She's a daredevil
or a white devil
on her way to work.

She can beat the rhythm out
on her thighs. I do,

though I have no place to go.

2.

Half-formed
letters lean in

to the near silence.

If by write
you mean set down,

shush

of wheels
on wet pavement.

FLOCKS

As thoughts take pleasure
in forming,
then break and
retreat.

*

As flocks of crows sweep
low above winter trees
at dusk.

*

As one and one
are one.

Viscum Album
Sylvia Legris

The imperative of an obligate parasite:
to exploit a suitable host.

1.

Plants and potent juice.
Mist and droppings.

Birdlime.
Missel thrush.

Beak.
Or of the nose.

Sap.
Or of the skin.

Blear.
Vapor.

The air is seeded.
Contagion or prayer.

2.

Ring a ring o' roses.
Broom root and mistletoe.
Ligneous chatterers.
Lungs halo March.

Skint wit; scantier spring.
Housed in bindweed.

With-wind-invasive.
Aggressive triple-glaze.

3.

April enters blank-leaved.
Snowbanked, eco-dormant.

Waxwings initiate budburst.
Mountain ash and winterberry.

Balsam poplar a study in starling leaf-out.
Western larch lurches gray jay and blue.

April Fools is blowing snow.
Good Friday cloudy with flock calls.

4.

Stigmatized by the confusion-chorus.
Wistful New World sparrows.

The shelterbelt a stormcocked cock-up.
A three-noted cluster song.
A varied trill transmission.

5.

April 21st and winter gravels into spring.
A season of *restless, puny, energy.*
Frantic kinglets, freeloading plants.
Nest-squatters in their element.

6.

What the wind carries is up for grabs:
plastic, elastic, particulate-filtering paper.

Fourteenth Street a molt of latex and medical-grade nitrile.
Walkers cautious-walk the two-meter wingspan walkway.

Runners flappable as flycatchers.
Ill at ease eavesdroppers.
Spittle in the slipstream.

7.

The spurious specious present.
The calendar slurries toward May.
Late April grueling snow and deciduous indecision.
Leaf mold, wilt slush, the days all fall down.

8.

A calendrical clot.
A six-week intercalation.
A thousand-hour schism.
An embolism.

9.

May is self-digesting sky,
intrusive granite with floaters.

Necrotic flowerbeds,
cartilage-grinding wind,
an unremitting erroneous huff.

10.

. . . the sinking vessel of the landscape. —Miroslav Holub

Blast-bagged and walking windward.
Peripheral foliage, last year's cavity-nests,
witches' broom avoided like . . .

11.

A segue:
Seed-dispersal
by upward-inflected whip-bur.

The trouble-excreting thrush,
the implicated junco,
the hectoring
venison-hawk vector.

Pickthankless days
parasitize days.

Eye of the Bhajan Continuing
Nathaniel Mackey

—"mu" two hundred eighty-first part—

If I saw myself I saw myself assemble, an
  emblem or a stem otherwise adrift. If I
saw myself I saw my sundry parts come in
                          from
  out far, the blessèd assembly there'd been
so much talk about, so much talk I'd heard.
If I came upon myself I was I and I. I and I
                        stayed
  or stood charitably distant, I and I themselves and "I and I" out of each one's mouth.
If I saw myself I saw myself concocted, I
                      saw
  myself conniptic again… Nub was now all
a conniption, ears perked up inside a cardboard hollow, Crater times Crater, exponential
                      haunt,
  exponential hastening, a hazing subterrane-
ously sought. From stratum to stratum damage
passed. Between the virus and the wannabe
                      king
  voices cracked, dry reeds ripped from the
reed bed, to the larger from the lesser death.
  From the lesser to the larger death, lament never not to be remembered, St. Anger slogging St.
                    Suf-
  ferhead's terrain it turned out it was, working
  it not knowing how… If I saw myself I saw
my head wrapped in wordskirt fabric, a star-scarf
                    ban-
  dana, part tourniquet, part turban, the night sky
itself it seemed. If I saw myself I heard more than saw

myself, a dilatory squawk, a devotional squawk as
                                                    from

a penguin, head back, petitioning heaven. If I saw
   myself an ensemblist I it was I saw, double whatever xtet I was or it was I was in, free assembly
                                                    what-

   ever x was, modest our estate were there one...
It wasn't I was back in Stick City, more I'd maybe
  never gone away. Stick beat the bhajan tala. The
                                                    tin-

tal's witness, I simply stood by, whatsaid meliorist
                                                    ame-

  liorating
away

Nathaniel Mackey

————————————————

We were living a life after which hell
would've been redundant. Between the
virus and the wannabe king our voices
                                        broke,
    breakage's own truth our toll and our
testament, cracked, broke, crackling blue-
ness's bequest. We were ourselves when
                                        we
    were real, congregant memory misery's
        equation, the crown infection it wore of a
        kingdom not of this world... So it was we
                                        sang
        our bhajan less crystalline than cracked,
    ourselves when we were real we kept telling
        ourselves. Between the wannabe king and
the virus, between the devil and the deep blue
                                        sea,
        we sippped tea made from rainwater wrung
    from Aruna's tights, the legs of a Carnatic singer
                                        me-
        dicinal we
    thought

296

•

(*chant*)

Inside the shadow box it turned out to be
we saw the virus crown atilt on the prez's
   head. Say so or not, a troubling song it was
                                                    we

   sang, sweet melt of consonants and vowels no matter. We sang with swabs high up
   our nostrils, the cautionary falsetto we floated
                                                    si-

rened out across the air... It was a devotional
   song even so. Right would out, it said or it
seemed it said or it wanted to say, as we'd have
                                                    had

   it no other way and we certainly said, our-
      selves when we were real we reminded our-
selves. All the same, it wasn't singing. It was
   ourselves when we were real, me seeing myself
                                                    when

I was real, so that seeing myself I saw what was
   real slipped and in arrears, the world wondering
   what when it was real had to do with it, the end
                                                    of

the real or the end of the world, the again of what
   had been, was and would be. So going from tourniquet to turban I saw myself... Such was being
                                                    said

   of each of us, the being real a next-order com-
mand incubating synapse, there before we knew it,
   there, some would say later, but for knowing, no
                                                    time

   soon would there be both. We ignored them, re-
sound of hermetic doctrine though it did, the nonsonant singers or the devotional nonsingers we once
again were long since beyond all that. Marks made a
                                                    sound

on paper. Only the exed interstice forbore... All
it was was bat gristle crowned us a new one, the wannabe king the worse but not the only one. Our turbans
                  took

off skin coming off. It was the day of the dying, the
day of the living dead, gunmen on government steps
the crown's accomplices. Protesters they were calling
                  them-

selves. We the conceptual singers went on conceiv-
ing the singing whose being real we'd be, nonsonant
our way with it until, ourselves when we were real we
                  kept

insisting... So if I saw myself I sat up straight, happy to be seen, sad to've slouched in my seat. Marks
made a sound on paper I was lifted by, a Sanskrit rope
of knots, Aruna's hair tied in a bun love's late severity,
                  love

of the unlikely its play. We kept our conceptual bhajan afloat. Want was our bodily share of infinity,
flesh our cogitative share of restriction, a tax ourselves
                  when

we were real exacted, rent we owed being real. It was
the day of the dying, the day of the zombie dead. Vaccine
or no vaccine, they were back... If I saw myself I saw
                  my-

self sit up, said but not only said but seen to take notice. To see was to be said's redoubt. I saw Nub upside its
own head or beside itself it seemed. If I saw myself I
                  saw

myself spy with my little eye a Nublican death commission meet without meeting, arms of the viral crown
a parallel hammering, faint what hope we held for the
                  bless-

éd assembly we'd be. If I saw myself I saw myself
leave or myself look away or, from jump, I saw myself
spy with my little eye myself not looking, unselfcon-
sciously of the blesséd assembly we'd be... The paddings
                  of

space fell away, so close were the lights of the contaminated city, and of tall grass on the infectious hillsides rumors continued to abound. All I wanted now was not to

be

seen, look no matter I might, a reverent leavetaking and a
song on its behalf, the thing be susceptible to the name
we knew it by, to spy with my little eye the world could it be
real,

the eye of the bha-
jan still

———————————

Covid sounded like a night sky covering, stars a
rash or a breakout, a deep receding dome we lay on
our backs looking up into. A conceived singing rose
from
the ground up and thru us, rose as if it was ours,
we sang it, so intrinsic we said we sanged it, called it
not singing but sanging... The paddings of space
fell
away, loose accoutrements, an earth exhalation
so harmoniumlike we lost count, devotionality were
such a way to say it. One was no longer a number
but
prolonged, exacerbated, lost, a beat more former beat
exten-
uated through-
out

Tilt-A-Whirl
Susan Daitch

THERE WERE BENEFITS TO working the summer at Noonan's Playland, and there were disadvantages. You got a discount on food, though
among the concession-stand operators, there were a few who would
hand you dogs and fries gratis anyway. In turn there was an understanding—the guys smelling of fried clams and the girls whose hands
were stained blue and red from the slushy machines—you let them
on the rides anytime without having to hand over a ticket. On the
other end of the benefit/loss spectrum, people tended to throw up on
the rides, and it was somebody's job to hose down the bucket seats,
shoulder harnesses, waffle-textured metal footrests. If you were a
ride attendant, that somebody was you, and you better have a strong
gag reflex. At night when mechanical parts were illuminated only by
short-lived carnival lights, cleaning could be tricky and time-con-
suming, as lines to board rides grew. The Tilt-A-Whirl was one of
the most popular rides at Noonan's, especially after the accident on the
roller coaster that cost a couple of patrons their lives. The owner
insisted the coaster was safe. The kids had lifted the lap bars, so when
they looped the loop, out they were chucked, headfirst.

Working on the Tilt-A-Whirl was relatively simple: make sure all
the passengers were buckled in, operate the manual clutch, start the
motor, release the magnetic brakes, and you're off. The ride's basic
construction is a rotating platform made of hinged metal plates, sort
of like pie slices that undulate in a wavelike fashion as the ride spins.
Seven spinning cars that look like clamshells are attached at pivot
points. The cars turn on their own axes, but their gyration and change
of direction is random and unpredictable. Even string-theory physicists have studied the Tilt-A-Whirl.

Some riders grow panicky and try to get off while the ride is just
picking up speed. This is an annoyance to the operator, and if some
scaredy-cat or wiseacre attempts such a stunt, he increases the speed,
so there is an instant point of no return. Once the lap bar comes
down, that's really it. No exit. When everyone disembarks the ride,
he pretends to check things out, making sure no one is hiding in a

car, hoping to cadge another ride for free. No one ever does this. In reality, the operator is hunting for change that falls out of pockets during the spin cycle. Hundreds of extra dollars are gleaned in this way every season.

Noonan's opens in late spring. After a long, hard winter with what meteorologists always claimed were record snowfalls, birds and mosquitoes arrive followed by tourists who check into campsites and motels looking for a fun place to go on summer nights. Among the fun places, if you asked around, Noonan's Playland was recommended.

That spring, bears awoke from hibernation to encroach further into the amusement park than anyone could remember, and camps that lined the lake posted more urgent red-alert bear warnings. A man suffering from dementia was arrested wandering naked and rambling among families at the beach, and so it was closed for a week. A rabid raccoon bit a woman who had just gone out to bring in her garbage cans from the road in front of her house. The crowds stayed longer at the fair, lingered at the rides, and left more soda cans and chip bags that eddied in drifts along Noonan's chain-link fence. One June night, close to closing time, groups of children and adults crowded into the area cordoned off into lines to have one last ride on the Tilt-A-Whirl. Four friends, delirious to be done with school, one week off before they started their jobs at the mall, at Steve's White Water Rafting, at the Belleville Motel, were finishing their popcorn and cotton candy, leaving a bread-crumb trail of boxes and wrappers like everyone else. The earth was tilting toward the sun, and it was hot even at night.

Jamie, Sheila, Eileen, and Tyler clearly passed the height requirement, but Ricardo, the night operator, felt it was so close to quitting time, he might as well shut down after this spin. He'd adjusted the music to high volume; he'd buckled in laughing and frightened children. A few cars were empty, but this was the last ride of the night. He wanted to go home, crack open a beer, and wait for his girlfriend to get off work at the reservation casino. The kids should come back tomorrow. Lights blinked out in other distant parts of the amusement park, then were turned off at the Scrambler, Dodgems, the Reptile House. It was time to go home.

"We paid. We can't come back tomorrow." Eileen was the most forceful. She wore frayed cutoff jeans, and her underwear appeared under the tears. Midnight-blue eyelashes found in her mother's room were glued to her eyelids, and her toes were painted a color called Khaleesi Gold. Rather than stand right next to the young man operating the ride, she stood off a bit, fingering the unraveled threads of her cutoffs. This was more effective, to be just out of reach, and she knew it. As more people lined up behind the four friends, Ricardo relented. He would operate the ride one last time.

All four crammed into one car because the more people in a car, the faster it spins, but Ricardo, unmoving hand on the lever, told them cramming was unsafe. There was an edge to his voice, Jamie noted.

"One of you has to move, or I can't start the ride." He leaned out from the operator's platform, then leaned back in as if he had all the time in the world.

"We're OK," Tyler shouted back.

Ricardo would not budge. Letting them throw the ride out of whack could cost him his job, and there was no way their pleasure was worth his paycheck.

"Yo, let's get this thing moving."

Other riders half stood in their seats, semi-restrained by lap bars, and yelled, they wanted to get going already, so Eileen grudgingly relented, looking at Ricardo like he was one clueless spoilsport. She stood up, walked to an empty car, and sat by herself. He knew Eileen was one of the kids who called him Retardo, who mimicked him behind his back. The ride started up, spinning faster and faster. People screamed and yelled for eleven minutes, then he brought the ride to a stop more abruptly than usual. Passengers pitched forward, though none were ejected. There were a few what the hells, but everyone unbuckled and trooped off until only Jamie, Sheila, and Tyler were left standing near the entrance to the ride.

"Did you see Eileen?"

"Are you sure she was on the ride?"

"Of course, I saw her get on. Are you blind?"

"She went back into the park to get a soda or something. I'll text her."

"She went home. She ditched us."

The friends complained that Eileen was supposed to give them a lift home. Now they were stuck.

There was no answer from Eileen's phone, but when the three friends looked in the parking lot, her car was still there. They called Jamie's father, who arrived in thirty minutes and grudgingly dropped each off at their respective homes. As they pulled back into their own driveway, Jamie's phone rang. It was Eileen's mother.

"Is Eileen with you? She's not answering her phone." The voice was calm with only the beginnings of concern. Her disappearance could still be nothing and completely explainable.

"She split off from us. We don't know where she is."

The next morning, the police dusted her car for prints, scoured the park, interviewed anyone who might have seen Eileen. They traced her whereabouts since last seen boarding the Tilt-A-Whirl. Eileen had ridden the Scrambler, the Rockets Red Glare Roller Coaster, bought kettle corn, visited the Reptile House, then arrived at the Tilt-A-Whirl line with her friends at a few minutes past ten o'clock. That was the last anyone saw her.

A week later another group of friends boarded the Tilt-A-Whirl. Adam, Phillip, and Kyle sat together on the ride. As a trio, they were known for their what-me-worry? attitude. If there were tornado warnings, they drove out for beers anyway. If someone drowned at the lake, that didn't stop them from partying on the shore within hours of the body's retrieval.

Adam drummed a song from one of his father's Hell's Belles tapes on the lap bar. He planned to lift the bar when the ride was at full speed. Ricardo pulled the lever and the swirling began. At first, it wasn't so bad. This is a baby ride, Adam shouted at his friends. As it picked up speed, he tried to lift the lap bar but couldn't budge it. It was as if some force were holding the bar down. His spine leaned immobilized at an obtuse backward angle against the fluted tin clamshell. Adam felt mildly sick and was afraid he would really lose it once the spinning slowed down. He saw himself staggering off the ride, his friends calling him a total wussbag. The car spun clockwise, then without warning, suddenly reversed to counterclockwise. He didn't look at Phillip or Kyle. The faces of the crowd just outside the perimeters of the Tilt-A-Whirl were an acid-trip blur.

When the ride stopped, Kyle was gone. He had been sitting between the other two. They felt nothing, but the space where Kyle had sat was empty, completely Kyle-less.

The police were called immediately. Ricardo couldn't be entirely sure Kyle or any of the boys had been on the ride. He couldn't remember everyone who came and went, and he was pissed off at Adam and Phillip, high as kites, what did they know?

Kyle had a necklace of skulls tattooed around his neck, the police noted, a DWI on his record, had been caught stealing a Bunsen burner from the chemistry lab, once slammed a random kid's head into a cinder-block wall. His teachers tried to remember something posi-tive to say about Kyle as the local news crews urged them to do but, microphones in their faces, they drew blanks. He would give you the shirt off his back, had a great sense of humor, the reporter suggested off camera, but everyone knew this was untrue. All they could say was, He will be missed, when, in fact, many were privately thankful when he stopped coming to school. The cameraman, relieved he had some usable footage, remembered when the kids fell out of the roller coaster at Noonan's and an out-of-town visitor to the park, micro-phone in his face, said, "You can't cure stupidity." This sort of re-sponse was nixed by the producer of the nightly news, who had wanted more empathy in what was supposed to be the lead story at eleven o'clock.

The police went to Kyle's domicile, a do-it-yourself structure he had put together as an annex in an abandoned housing development. Kyle had used heavy-duty staples to pin plastic sheeting and black contractor bags to a structure made of two-by-fours. He had pirated electricity. It was not designed to be a full-time residence. His mother lived in another state, father's whereabouts unknown. That he would move on when winter arrived had been factored into his plans, though Adam and Phillip knew Kyle wasn't exactly sure where he would go. The police found porn in magazine form, which seemed old-school to them, since most kids got their stuff online, or so they thought.

They brought Ricardo in for questioning, but pretty much the most dangerous action he'd ever taken on the job was to unlatch the lever from its leather strap, pull it one way to start the ride, another to slow it down. The Tilt handled five hundred riders an hour. He tore tickets, did his work, didn't remember anyone suspicious, and he himself had no time to abduct anyone. They thought he must have had an ac-complice, and sent a team to search his apartment above the Yogurt-land, but found nothing that could possibly implicate him in such a crime or series of crimes.

For a few weekends, business slowed at Noonan's. People stayed away, then there began to be a shift, and they came back in droves. The Tilt-A-Whirl became the most popular attraction of the park. It developed a daredevil reputation, like doing an extreme drug, drop-ping from a plane onto a supersteep slope and skiing down, breaking into a car lot and helping yourself to the most expensive car you could manage to start. The Tilt was badass, and Ricardo couldn't keep up. Lines extended as far as the Centrifuge and the children's train ride. Kids went alone on dares. Parents tried to keep them away to no avail. The owner and manager, Mr. Manucci, was petitioned to close early for the season, but he was making too much money, and had put a down payment on a condo in Florida. This, he insisted, was the reality of realty.

Manucci watched the news about the shooting of an unarmed black child by a white police officer. There were marches and protests, but Manucci also noted the reporter, who claimed that the shooting victim had once shoplifted. He started to say publicly that while the Eileen and Kyle disappearances were a tragedy, let's face it, he hinted, they were troublemakers, bad apples, good riddance. The town could feel it didn't have to mourn too much and could return to business as usual, and business for the amusement park wasn't at all bad. Years ago he had bought the amusement park from J. Noonan, a Korean War vet whose family built the original structures. Manucci expanded, leased more rides.

Hope Sargent and her friends put up a Facebook page declaring they would go on every ride at Noonan's Playland to raise money for charity. This will look really good on college applications, she told her parents, and they agreed. Each participant picked a different cause, and signed up contributors from family, friends, and townspeople. The drive would take place at the end of August.

Ricardo had seen Hope at Shaker's, a bar downtown where she and her friends hung out, using fake IDs. Her crew was not going to spend the rest of their lives in that town or in the big houses of the outskirts. They would soon leave for universities, to be replaced by others who would also leave in time. Though she was only a couple of years younger than Ricardo, Hope and her friends were completely unapproachable. At Noonan's Playland, the rules shifted. On the rides, the physics of thrills didn't read parents' tax returns. Everyone got tossed into the air or hurtled around a track in exactly the same way. Ricardo knew this better than anyone, and he had faith in the democracy of the Tilt-A-Whirl. If Hope got scared like everyone else, he would be there, he would be the only one to tell her it would be OK, it was just a ride.

On the night of the drive, Noonan's was supercrowded. A surge of people would get on each ride, depart, another surge board on their heels. Ricardo couldn't keep track of who was with whom. He herded folks onto the Tilt and off again, certain that night he would find hundreds of dollars' worth of coins. He tore tickets, checked to see everyone had their lap bars down, pulled the lever to start the spin. He would then sit back for a few minutes, and let the Tilt do what it did best. Ricardo liked to watch the people's faces run through the spectrum from anticipation to terror, like the dumbass in a horror movie who hears a sound and goes into the cellar alone. Someone always yells from the back of the theater, "Don't go in the basement, bitch!" On good nights, he felt like that person, sitting back and watching, eating popcorn.

Hope and her friends crowded into a single car, and once again Ricardo had to tell them it wasn't safe to all smash in like that. He gallantly cleared some ants-in-their-pants fifteen-year-olds from one car, so Hope would have a private car all her own. Ricardo climbed onto his platform and started the motor. The cars spun in the familiar blur of delirious, petrified faces, trapped and immobilized. He accelerated, held the speed for the requisite number of minutes, then slowed the Tilt down, and everyone disembarked, giddy they'd survived, or lurching, unsteady, holding their hands over their mouths.

When Hope's friends assembled themselves on the other side of the gate, peering into the darkness for her, they yelled at Ricardo to turn on more lights, and not to let anyone else get on the ride. It was too late; the next cycle had already started. When this last group had cleared, Ricardo told everyone else the ride was closed for the night. There were no extra lights to raise, only the sporadic Japanese lanterns already in place that did little to really illuminate the Tilt-A-Whirl. In the distance, over the lake, end-of-summer fireworks bloomed. News that there had been another disappearance ran through the park quickly. The Playland became quiet and still.

After the police and everyone else had left, Ricardo stayed behind. He walked in circles around the Tilt-A-Whirl. The base of the ride hid the workings behind a series of metal panels, and he knew which ones snapped out, in case repairs were needed. Removing a panel, he took out a flashlight, held it in his teeth, and crawled under the ride. There were no trapdoors, no laughing homunculi chewing bones. Some dimes glinted in the beam of his flashlight; a couple of rats feasting on fallen caramel corn scuttled away from him. A glint near one of the gears and chains caught his attention. It was a charm bracelet bearing a cluster of bits and pieces: the school hawk mascot, a high heel, a lightning bolt. He remembered seeing the charm bracelet on Hope's wrist when he checked her lap bar, then his eyes had been drawn to the wisps of cotton candy caught in her hair. Ricardo had wanted to brush the wisps away and let one dissolve in his mouth.

He pocketed the charm bracelet but told no one about it. He was already a suspect. There was no point in drawing even more suspicion.

Manucci was brought in for questioning. The amusement park was just one of his local investments, and it was a headache. He threatened to sue the Texas company that manufactured the Tilt and other rides. The company insisted the Tilt-A-Whirl had a superlative safety record and quoted its inventor, Herbert Sellner, who described his invention as "a new and improved amusement apparatus that would furnish pleasurable and unexpected sensations, may be operated economically, and will furnish a high degree of safety."

Manucci's lawyer advised him not to pursue the matter unless there was definitive proof of the company's malfeasance, but since there was none, he fired the night operator instead. Ricardo promptly left town, raising more doubts about the young man. Why did he leave if he had nothing to do with the disappearances? He left because he needed a job, and no one would hire him.

Then Ray Dooley did not disappear. Ray was terminal and could no longer live on his own in his house. A degenerative disease was attacking his nerve cells, and the drugs he'd taken for years were causing seizures and hallucinations. Relatives arranged for his house to be sold and for him to be moved to a rehabilitation facility, but Ray knew there was no reverse switch for the damage to his nerve and bone cells, no rehabilitation for his badly folded spindle and motor neurons. He wanted to make his exit while he could still put one foot in front of the other. Dooley broke into the amusement park with a coconspirator who would run the ride while he went on by himself. It didn't work. They tried for hours, but as the Tilt slowed down, Ray was always still sitting there. Take me, take me, take me, Ray pleaded to the metal plates and clamshell cars. The ride, apparently, only took the young and the healthy, which, by the end of the night, infuriated Ray, though his friend tried to soothe him, suggesting the Tilt needed more witnesses to work its magic. Whether this was true or not, he had no idea. Heads down in defeat, they spoke their conjectures to the bare ground on the way to the Playland's exit.

Ray wasn't the only one known to trespass in the middle of the night. Kyle's friends Adam and Phillip broke into Noonan's to steal metal railings and kiddy train tracks, which they heard weren't all that hard to pry up and cart off. They were planning to sell what they could to a scrap-metal yard out on Route 9. As they shone their flashlights onto the path from the Reptile House to the Tilt-A-Whirl, Adam thought he heard a whispering voice, but one that was in pain, crying and unhappy. It sounded like Kyle. At first Phillip didn't hear it, thought it was just the wind, and Adam was a load.

"This place is talking to us, man. Let's get the fuck out." Adam had heard that Eileen had been sighted in another town, running past cars at a drive-in, as if she'd been swallowed up by the Tilt-A-Whirl, and spat out in a phantomlike form somewhere else. The rumors were unconfirmed and the sighting dismissed but, still, Adam believed it was possible. Noonan's seemed to have a mind of its own, he'd always felt that way, even before the disappearances.

"It's the generator." Phil wanted to ditch Adam, but Adam had a gun.

"The generator is off. It's three in the fucking morning."

"No, you're wrong. It's on for the snakes and for the food freezers. Look, I need the cash." Phillip kept walking. "Go ahead; leave if you want to."

Adam didn't want to walk back alone in the dark, so he trudged along pushing the stolen supermarket cart in which they planned to stack pieces of track, siding, etc. Then the sound picked up in pitch. It wasn't exactly a voice, but sort of like a voice, a voice that sounded like it was being broadcast from a scratched record, so you couldn't be exactly sure what the person was saying, but he or she sounded as if chanting the number three over and over.

Three, three, three, the voice or the wind sang.

"Triple three," Adam said. "No one knew about triple three but us." Adam felt for the gun in the waist of his jeans. He had shot deer with a rifle, but the truth was he'd never used his father's pistol and wasn't supposed to touch it, but the gun was his, he figured, when no one was looking, and most of the time, no one was.

The wall of lockers in their school presented an array of storage possibilities that might be some future archaeologist's treasure: a record in graffiti glyphs and objects representing the punishments and aspirations of a lost civilization. Number three-three-three, Kyle had discovered, was empty. No one was using it. For Kyle and his two friends, the vacant locker was an easy-access-storage boon for accommodating what was, for them, sizable quantities of dope and other products. No one else at school knew what was hidden there. No one would have known the significance of those numbers except the three of them, and the only living people in Noonan's that night, as far as Adam and Phil had counted, were them.

*

The mayor was angry. People disappeared in Mexico, in Egypt, in Russia, but not there. He demanded action be taken. Physicists and mechanical engineers were called in. The Tilt-A-Whirl was taken apart, down to the support structure, which looked like the ribs of a giant alien spiderweb. If there was a portal to a colossal, bottomless sinkhole, like the one that had appeared in Siberia, it had closed.

An anthropologist from the local community college said that the nearby Mohawk and Abenaki tribes told myths about children or young adults who disappeared into the woods and became animal spirits. There was one tale in particular about a Mohawk boy who refused to work or hunt because he loved animals and so was exiled from the tribe. He warned the animals with whom he could speak in their own languages that hunters were approaching, and so food became scarce for the Mohawks. The tribe had mixed feelings about their outcast. They had valued him, recognizing he was different from the general population, but this business of depriving them of food did not sit well. They chased him deeper into the mountains. The boy turned into a man who turned into an eagle. Hearing this story, Adam and Phil went into the woods looking for Kyle. They figured he'd have become a mountain lion or something carnivorous and combative, though how they would recognize a mountain-lion Kyle, they couldn't say. Eileen and Hope's friends organized searches too, though without knowing exactly what they might be hunting for.

By the end of the summer, especially at the end of the day, Noonan's took on the sad aura of a last breath of pleasure. The cold was beginning to sweep down from Canada, signs for back-to-school sales filled storefronts. Foxes nested in the struts of the fallen roller coaster, bears preparing for hibernation foraged among the remains of food stands, kids who ventured into the area swore they heard the cries and footfalls of those who had vanished long ago. Some interlopers claimed to develop hearing and speech disorders following their hours spent exploring the defunct rides. In one case eye color reportedly changed from brown to violet.

Then snow fell over the amusement park in drifts so high the children's trains were buried. The peaks of the roller coaster poked through like upside-down smiles, the Tilt-A-Whirl's scattered half shells looked like they contained white ghosts sitting patiently, waiting for the ride to begin.

When spring came, the owner never returned from Florida, and without adequate routine maintenance, Noonan's fell into ruin. Now

Manucci was ready to wash his hands of the property. Metal parts continued to be stolen, graffiti was sprayed over any available flat surface, the go-kart track buckled and split as if there had been an earthquake, Godzillas and cowboys made of Homasote toppled and melted in the rain.

Rumors spread that a consortium of developers, a limited liability company from downstate or overseas, had bought the property and planned to build luxury condos and a two-tiered shopping mall on the site, advertising it as a lakeside gem. Bulldozers razed the western flank of the Playland, but heavy machinery disappeared from time to time. Work crews tended to quit despite the scarcity of jobs, and hiring skilled construction workers was a problem. Illegals to be paid in cash were picked up for day labor. When a couple of them vanished, the developer claimed he had no record of them and stated maybe they'd never even been there in the first place. The project was abandoned.

Finding a place where the chain-link fence was bent to the ground, ignoring warnings and private-property-keep-off signage, Ricardo drifted back one time, breaking in between late in the afternoon and early evening when natural light was just fading. Once inside Noonan's, he took pictures of the metal plates of the Tilt sticking up like mammoth shark fins, osprey nests, and crows the size of spaniels feasting on the remains of non-native bivalves and ice-cream-cone rinds. If a fallen string of lights reminded him of riders who shrank from him when he lowered a bar over their shivering thighs, there was also pleasure to be found from those who, in their dizziness and fear, grabbed his arm at the ride's end. Weeks later, when he looked at his pictures again, some cars appeared upright, as if functioning, though empty. The remains of one ride were a little less than empty. A woman, who he swore was not present when he took the pictures, appeared sitting in a Tilt-A-Whirl car, swinging her blurry feet.

He knew some compared the spot to Chernobyl, another desolate, unpopulated site, though no known radioactivity emanated from the amusement park. Others found this comparison unfair and unreasonable. A punishment for a mishandled nuclear accident had nothing to do with their town. What had they done that was so very toxic?

Now living in another town, he had learned to drive an ambulance, to swerve though traffic, speed through red lights, inject morphine, work a defibrillator, administer oxygen. Sometimes, as he drove faster and faster, he imagined he was on one giant whirling ride and would end up who knows where. No sick or injured person had yet disappeared on him, though he was afraid some of his passengers would have been better off if they had.

Finally, no one broke into the park anymore, or at least no one would admit to doing so. Vines and creepers sprouted from the earthmovers, backhoes, and rides equally. The sign dating back to the original park was still standing, but all that remained visible was the lettering, PLAYLAND, like a promise that was also a dare, threaded with a few still-flashing Christmas lights strung by someone who'd long ago cashed his last paycheck. It was said the forest had reclaimed the Playland, and within the town it would be difficult to find a citizen who would publicly contest this assertion, but privately, among themselves, they believed it wasn't just a matter of plant and animal life but something else that reached out and swallowed, and what exactly that was, no one was yet ready to say.

Three Descriptions of Flag Burning
Rick Moody

ILLINOIS

ACCORDING TO A REPORTER on the scene, three different persons present at the Chicago-area protests, in the days after the murder of the Minneapolis citizen, claimed to be responsible for the alleged flag-burning incident on Dearborn and Washington, at 3:06 p.m. on May 30, 2020. As the flag-burning incident took place prior to more general agitation (targeted anti-capitalist interventions) later in the evening, the reporter questioned each of the claimants in turn about the intention of the performance, attempting to arrive at a definitive account, as though, in this way, through multiply sourced illumination, he, the reporter, might retroactively apply to the act decisive cultural implication. It was a scoop. The first of those claiming to have burned the flag (and obviously there could have been more than three, claiming, participating, bystanding, exaggerating, or fewer than three) was from the South Side of the city, in the area of the University of Chicago, and was employed, part-time, as a teacher of piano for the young, but while the flag burner was talking, and ideas were thus being released into the swelling organism of the crowd, particularly ideas about power, ideas about class and race, the reporter found himself failing to consider in full the words of the flag burner, instead thinking back to the instant in which he beheld the burning flag himself on the corner of Dearborn and Washington Streets, if *thinking* is the right word for a playing back of bodily shock, isolation, images thereof, some of them already corrupted by the groaning into being of a new era, these instants exhilarating to a person of a reportorial profession, for whom the novel moments of history did have the additional éclat of professional advancement. The reporter felt the visceral impact of the moment, having just come down the escalator from the building that housed the television station on the corner, where he'd met a colleague for a caffeine infusion, after which he simply proceeded to cover the story, sort of stumbling on it, really, with a cameraperson just behind him who had since been lost in the

312

disorder; the first thing the reporter saw was the flag, raised up, by multiple hands, nearly Iwo Jiman, many of these hands BIPAC, and, as if it were a sign for him above all, and then the sudden dispersal of a group, something smaller than a crowd, more like a clutch, around the conflagration, the idea of conflagration. And it would have been natural to assume, because it was 3:15 or so now, and the police were beginning to swarm, it would have been natural to assume that these activists, the flag burners, had come from the nearby subway entrance, in concert with one another, having brought flag and inflammable materials from elsewhere in the city of Chicago, because it was mostly banks, offices, pharmacies, on the corners of Dearborn and Washington, many shut up tight, and thus the first claimant was not from nearby; there was a smell, and the smell was both welcoming, as of backyards in summer, your friend the barbecue enthusiast, and of something more ominously military, like civilians were getting killed (if not yet on this block). And the reporter couldn't be sure if this first claimant was actually *there* at the moment at which the reporter came upon the flag burning, at which the reporter had simply happened, though he said, *Yeah, I was there,* but in a way the reporter didn't care if the burner was present, though journalistic ethics suggested he ought; he cared about the feeling, the meaning of uprising in one's body; it was an unfolding of a new meaning; it was describable; one hears so much about flag burning, and then here it was, rippling through the sinews, the musculature, in the beholding, as if one has always known about it, known about the idea, and then the thing, which is like a nerve tingling, a demyelination, the sudden presence of the politics of complex patriotic expression, and the reporter called out to the first claimant who suddenly was running across the street, toward Daley Plaza, as crowds seemed to form and dissipate, and protests formed and then spun off subnarratives, and the reporter called after the first claimant, *What does it mean for you?* And this claimant turned away, perhaps dismissively, and in the moment afterward the reporter felt a new intensity as upon seeing the flag itself, as if the two moments were ever to be fused for him, warehoused on the same extrusion of neurons; the fellow looked at the reporter as if the business had all been transacted, disappointment, and words formed in his mouth, but then he was in the crowd, the claimant was, and no longer easily reachable, if reachable was still a thing, as the crowd engulfed, and formed and people who were standing next to you for a minute were enveloped, distinguishable and indistinguishable, all the kinds of people, and a moment of fellowship gave way to a bittersweet taste of physical uncertainty, and the reporter glimpsed at hand instead a young woman whom he had earlier seen, with a certain bandana, stylized with small piratical crossbones, covering her face—as many but not all faces were covered that day; faces were a thing that were in short supply, as if the time of the new event, the new idea of the flag, was a time that had moved the crowd beyond a depiction of faces, and whereas in Hong Kong flag burning meant one thing, now in Chicago it meant another thing, a thing less afflicted with individuals. The crowd flowed toward Daley Plaza, or at least in this part of the crowd the reporter was whipsawed toward Daley Plaza, named, you'll remember, for the mayor of Chicago, he who presided over the city during the 1968 Democratic Convention (and attendant riots), no stranger to the crowds in the street, this place; and the reporter called out to the woman in the mask, was it still her? Was it the same woman? *Did you see it? Did you see the flag burning? Over on the corner?* To which she said, *I lit the match,* which, you know, anyone could have said it. Anyone could have said they lit the match to the reporter, who called after her, *I'm a reporter!,* as though that would somehow make a difference, could somehow change the course of the story, as though he would have been understood, in his business-casual attire, as anything else; literally anyone could have lit the match, excepting that it was undoubtedly *not* a match, because in the Windy City, with the breeze coming off the lake, there was no one who could successfully light a match and start a fire, and no one carried a matchbook anymore anyway, or those flip-top Zippos from film noir that you had to refill with lighter fluid, flag burners carried only the one-click, ease-of-use models that came in three-packs at the bigger retailers, they were employed for camping, and now for political uprisings. *Did you know . . .* he started, but then she too was gone, into the rhetoric of crowds and power, and he failed to be able to give his short talk about Daley Plaza and the Yippies, who promenaded in this very direction in 1968, before Mayor Daley said to *shoot* any arsonists, *shoot to kill.* And what about the Picasso sculpture? Were the protesters mindful of The Picasso? In 1968? The Picasso was already there with its weird hangdog face, and its Cor-Ten, had been there a year or so, and now it was the only visible face, well, not exactly; in 2020, the reporter should have been wearing a mask himself, instead of leaving it dangling around his chin like a steampunk accessory. In 1968, he remembered reading, someone lowered the American flag during the Yippie march, and replaced it with a red flag, by which was meant a Communist flag, though he was uncertain if the removed American flag had then succumbed to flames. Accounts differed. There had been tear-gassing of protesters later, and a curfew, and all the other gestures that one associates with the coming of a military-industrial complex, and the reporter had read deeply in certain chapters of American history, especially history as it played out in Chicagoland. Here on this spot, riots *and* orderly protests (accounts differed, the reporter observed) were a thing that happened, were a part of urban life. Riots convulsed the cities and then just when it came to pass that riots were forgotten, the burning of a flag was also a thing that happened, a thing that altered protest, though the reporter, in reading about burning flags of the past had never felt the energy blast of nylon as it goes up in liquid flame. Did Picasso's biomorph, maybe a girl of his acquaintance, maybe some kind of protohominid, an earlier human manifestation, so hard to tell, somehow symbolize the coming of the protester in Daley Plaza? Or was it more intended to be the image of justice for the courthouses nearby, the not-impartial civic justice, the justice that was anything but impartial. Not a heroic sculpture of a justice in draperies with a blindfold on, but rather a great ape-dog hybrid in front of the courthouse in a *gangster town*, where there were flags burning on the especially difficult nights, they helped pedestrians navigate home in the dark. The reporter was sweating horribly and had only begun to realize that there was a certain kind of ontological dread in being part of a crowd whose goals and ambitions are unknowable and unpredictable. A crowd of this size, he reasoned, was inherently inimical to the apparatus of state force, and is unknown and other than itself, even to its participants. The state feels it has to intervene with the crowd, just as the elephant trainer has to persuade the elephant that it has no power, but now here was the reporter in the crowd, trying to work his way back to the corner of Dearborn, for a reputable account of the flag-burning incident. The afterimages of flag burning lingered in collective memory, if not otherwise seared on the concrete of the sidewalk. Was it a thing he had actually seen? Or was it a fantastical interpretation of events, a premonitory belief in the rightness of a flag-burning episode at this time? There was a transcendentalism to being, as the reporter neared the corner of Dearborn just now, the reporter seeing a great number of police, perhaps more police than the reporter had ever seen in person. The transcendentalism adhered to the fact that the reporter became in this regard an observer and maybe was *consumed* by the act of observation, like this was a celestial fire, a supernova, and the reporter was robbed of name and identity to become

315

simply the human who observes, as he wheeled up to the corner, not far from the television station, and saw a man standing there, and said to the man, *Did you see the flag? The burning flag? Right over there?* And the man to whom he spoke, masked, chuckled, or he thought the man chuckled or believed he could hear a chuckle, whatever that might sound like over the din of shouting and bullhorns, directing the protesters in particular directions, the man chuckled and said, *I bought the flag down at Walgreens, did it up myself.* Was he a man the reporter had already interviewed? He was wearing a mask. How many people had the reporter talked to now? And what time was it? Were there individuals in the crowd, or was the crowd only an organism amassed? Somehow he had lost track of the time, as if time only happened to the individual, but not to the group. The man asked the reporter if *he* had seen the flag burning himself, interviewee becoming the interviewer, and the reporter said that the flag burning was *unforgettable*, and the man said now that was a thing worth thinking about, *how some moments are*, or that seemed to be what he said, and the reporter, again, asked what the burning flag *meant*, and the man said, it wasn't a thing that meant, it was a thing that grew and stretched and engulfed, a perfectly rendered *performance*, or so it seemed he said to the reporter, of all that was, of what injustice needed then, and so the flag burned because the streets were burning, and the photographs of the burning were incorrect, because the photographs changed events while recording them, the man said, the persons with the press credentials changed the events, causing things to happen elsewhere and out of sight and more reductively, *What's it mean to you, mister?* And here the reporter fumbled, holding his phone up to the gentleman, as if to record, and then somehow holding it up to his own mouth, and then not saying anything, *Do you think it's going to get worse tonight?* he asked, never sounding more than just then like a person who had gone to journalism school, a person worthy of suspicion, though the very idea of narrating the events, of creating an orderly account of the night, was getting further from him, just as he imagined he was drawing nearer to it. *You're the third person who's said they started the fire,* the reporter said, *and I can say all sorts of things about what I saw, like that it happened on this block by the Bank of America ATM, and that it was just after three,* and worried now about if it was going to get worse and exactly how it was going to get worse, and what would *worse* mean, and what would the shattering of glass sound like? And was professional advancement worth the trouble, like if it was going to get *worse* later on, and suddenly the police in a phalanx were advancing, toward the two of them, the reporter and the man were chatting, a line of men in *blue*, and then the police were surrounding them, some cohort of the state apparatus, and then there was shouting, and the police were saying, *What kind of reporter exactly? Who do you work for?* Like flag burning was not federally protected, rogue officers, perhaps, but the cops weren't having any of that, they were trying to figure out if the reporter had inflammable materials on his person, like one of those one-click camping lighters, some kind of fire-starting device, flint material on his person that might be used to start a fire, or had in fact started the earlier fire, and the police were shouting that he smelled like gas, and the other man, the third claimant, was moving quickly away, now, *running* toward Daley Plaza, and then there were more groups, and more people and fewer people, and tear gas, and then as if foreordained the police brought down the baton on the reporter, and the reporter did not like to fall into hackneyed speech where the description of violence was concerned, even though it was an important part of newsgathering, a guaranteed bonus on social media, but he had no choice now, as he was reporting the *story*, but he needed to say that at the site of the flag burning on Dearborn and Washington the baton was brought down a third time upon him, three times he was battered, and some contusion he suffered on the hand that was upraised to stop the baton, and there was the skittering of his phone, away into the crowd, and his feet were giving out from under him, and the cops held him up long enough to cart him to the bus, he couldn't possibly be a reporter, a person like him.

MICHIGAN

Denise J. Walker of Ann Arbor did, this past March, by word cast contempt on an American flag, at her public school, MLK Jr. Middle School, in contradiction of Michigan statute 750.246, during a social studies report on the limits of free speech, by saying, during a class presentation, "I have contempt for you," three times to a flag hanging in the back of her classroom, noting in her following remarks that display of a flag mistreated or mutilated or disrespected constituted an infraction according to Michigan state law. By allowing the flag to remain, the school was now also in dereliction of this state law. Walker further pointed out that according to Michigan state law, and in other jurisdictions, it was not a crime to cast contempt *in private* on the flag, and she noted that she had practiced on an American flag in her bedroom at her home address, a flag on top of her dresser, next to her shrine to a certain singer, and that she had sworn violently at the American flag that very morning to compare implicitly private and public disavowal. Here were her feelings, she told the class, as she swore violently at the flag in private: she felt nervousness, she felt nerves, she felt elation, she felt liberty, and she felt that the liberty was not inherent in the flag but was transactional with respect to the flag, liberty was energy potential in the symbolic field of the object, she felt like she was getting away with something, she felt like she was doing something her mom would not approve of, she felt a sort of agitated feeling like she contained either helium or carbonation of some kind, she felt like she was learning, though she wasn't certain whether it was a good kind of learning or a bad kind of learning, she felt moments of nothing, when the silence after swearing at the flag was a routine silence, she felt like she was going to be late for the bus, she felt like she wanted to bring her brother in so he could swear violently at the flag too, she felt lonely, like violently swearing at the flag conferred a kind of loneliness on her, she felt like she wanted to get it over with quickly, she felt like she wanted it to go on forever, she felt like an American, though she was aware the term wasn't exactly adequate, and she felt that swearing at an Italian, French, Serbian, Vietnamese, or indeed any other flag would probably provide like sensations, she felt like an adult, she felt like she was growing up and out of her childhood, and like swearing at the flag, however transiently, was a sign of her growing up, a mark. The public disavowal of the flag felt dangerous too, but now constituted a repetition of the performance. It was, actually, a *reperformance.* She felt like she had conducted a valid educational experiment, and she wanted to be done so that she could go on to the next one. Walker received an A for her oral presentation (from Ms. Carter, the very lenient history teacher), though she was also sent to the principal's office, where a debate ensued among various parties, an assistant principal, and teachers on break, about the appropriate punishment for Walker's presentation. Because Walker was also a Girl Scout, a candy striper, alto in an upcoming glee-club show (temporarily suspended because of viral contagion), and because every day from circa 3:00 to 5:00 p.m. she took care of her little brother, the one with mixed developmental delay, it was determined that her presentation was not the work of a stridently political student, who, in any event, was protected by the Supreme Court ruling in *United States v. Eichman*. On the contrary, it was observed that Walker was somewhat overcommitted at her domicile and was a very good kid. There was no punishment at all, though the assistant principal did give a verbal warning. The health and safety liaison, Mr. Hagerty, however, protested the absence of any punishment, saying that the Congress of the United States of America had passed a federal statute proscribing flag burning in every year between 2004 and 2007, and that it was a de facto federal statute, but everyone disliked Mr. Hagerty, who frequently complained about people spending too much time in the halls on their phones. And: he often inveighed against the immodesty of the clothes at the MLK Jr. Middle School, repeating frequently, e.g., that *leggings are not pants*.

After some pushback by the school board, probably tipped off by Hagerty, Denise Walker was chastised by the principal at her school, who reversed course officially thereby, affecting a stridency that was not native to him. He made clear that suspension lay in wait for any further infraction along these lines, as in further violation of state law, any actual flag burning, any mention of legal cases about flag burning, and did he need to say that any burning of anything else by Walker on school property would be taken very seriously, no smoking, no vaping, and that Walker had better adhere to school policy as regards her uniform, and she had better not, for example, recommend books with flag burning in them, or any books that had arson in them, or even books with campfires in them, while on library premises, if she wanted to avoid suffering the consequences of her thoughtless actions, and by the way where was her mother who was intended to be present at this meeting, was she not, did Denise not have a mother, was a mother not a person who served as a backstop in these important transitional moments, the principal wanted to know, forgetting just then, that Walker's mother taught social studies at a high school elsewhere in Ann Arbor, and thus the hours during which Denise took care of her brother, who sometimes would not calm down, except in the presence of cartoons, lately *The Fantastic Four*.

NEBRASKA

In the interrogation room, in Omaha, Nebraska, 2013, Stevens Jay Murray Jr. began the portion of the confession of murder in which he discussed the ancient Egyptian serpent god, Apophis, and the role that Apophis played in his crimes. The supervising detective, who has asked that his name not be used in this account, was in the next room watching on the monitor, as the video camera documented, and there he noted that the introduction of Apophis followed several other colorful distractions from Murray's spree of alleged murders, including the part where he blamed his cousins. The detective noted this down on a legal pad because it was good to have redundant information storage technologies during interrogation. *Cousins.* Was it true that members of Murray's family were indeed involved in the murders substantially at multiple levels, not excepting, as Murray indicated, his father's brother, who lived out of state and was in his late seventies, and the alleged murderer's own mother? The introduction of Apophis, then, could appear to be yet another constructed version of the story, an internally performative side journey, like other high-calorie lines of Stevens Murray bullshit. Unless, of course, Murray was telling the truth, whichever version of the truth he was capable of telling. What *was* true was that the detective had never heard of Apophis and needed quickly to consult a search engine on an OPD personal digital device, which lay before him on a cheap and functional IKEA breakfast table. In a dull patch, when Stevens Murray was just picking at a skin lesion or scab or other minor irritation that might have been inflicted during a struggle, on his hand between thumb and index finger, for eight minutes, just scratching, the detective went scrolling through lists of comic-book villains, trying to see if there were any mentions of this Apophis. His daughter had favored the comic-book style of entertainment, and he attempted to discourage this when she was coming up; in any event, the detective was not a big reader himself, excepting the occasional western. He could find no such bad actor as Apophis in the list of one hundred most fearsome villains, or the fifty most fearsome villains, or in any other such web-based listicle or fan database, and in considering these things, he also went rather too far down a comparison of certain Hollywood types before and after cosmetic surgery, all part of a self-protective tendency to fail to concentrate on the mind-numbing cruelties of some of the offenders passing through the main entrance of the precinct. The detective had become merely reactive as regards his official position and was now simply trying to get promoted to a supervisory capacity. When Ned Bean, the detective conducting the interrogation, asked Murray if he, Detective Bean, was meant to take the Apophis reference literally or rather as a kind of emblem for the kind of mayhem that Murray undertook throughout the spree, over the thirteen days of the spree, Murray took umbrage, giving the interrogator a malevolent stare, followed by the eight minutes of silence, and other ambiguous physical gestures.

Like, do you mean some actual Egyptian god?

This ultimately prompted Murray, unbidden, into a long ramble of alibi construction relating to the most recent victim, high-school age, one of a series, or so they believed in the precinct, some of the murders taking place in Indiana, some in Iowa, meaning the FBI was on the way to supervise and consult. The detective somehow got from the Hollywood types and cosmetic surgery to some articles about a certain asteroid, named 99942 Apophis, which not long ago was given a 2.7 percent chance of hitting planet earth, and this caused a flurry of interest in 99942 Apophis, at least until the calculations were double-checked. It would be close, it wouldn't be close, it would be close. In none of these astronomical articles, which the detective continued to scroll through while unwrapping a turkey wrap (leftover from dinner last night), could he find any reference to a prior Egyptian god, in the astrophysical language as it overspilled the container of language, just as the lettuce and melted cheese exceeded the turkey wrap, just as Murray blamed virtually anyone, any bystander, any institution, any state apparatus.

For example, Murray insisted that any crimes that had taken place, which he could not have committed, were not committed by him on the given night because on that night he was at the Oak Bluffs campus of the Metro Community College, where he had gone to talk with his academic adviser, Tish Adams, MA, about whether he could do a final paper in his business-writing class on chaos theory, having missed the prior week for doing the swing shift at the Omaha Box Company, where he took some shifts that were impossible for others in his family, his cousins, who also worked at the Box Company. The final paper he wanted to compose was on the role of Apophis in modern business communication, which invoked gravitational pull and with the graviton, which, Murray observed, is a spin-2 massless particle. I can't, no way, Murray said, have been at the site of the abandoned vehicle, because my uncle will state that he drove me and my mother to the Metro, to talk with Professor Adams, my adviser, and Mother was coming in with me because she wanted to help explain that I was suffering from sleep deprivation and night terrors, which did cause me to get fired later from the Box Company, and my uncle will say so. I wanted to get the degree in business communications because I want to start a business that tutors disenfranchised and at-risk kids.

321

Murray continued, while the detective, still unwinding his turkey wrap, now splayed out more like an entrée, tried to learn about the asteroid. If there are three factors that increase the chance that an at-risk kid will commit a crime, Murray continued, these are things I learned in a criminology course, they are, first, mental illness in a parent, secondly, addiction in a parent, thirdly, violence by a parent or between parents, and, fourthly, if a parent abandons, and all of those things are true in my case, or let's say three out of four anyway, because I don't know much about my father now, I haven't seen him in a long while, since the last time that he battered me, which Professor Tish Adams told me was a traumatic event, suitable for a term paper on PTSD, but which I thought was just what angry fathers did, so I guess I'm just an at-risk kid myself.

In 2013, Apophis was felt to have a one in forty-five thousand chance of striking our planet, the detective was learning, most likely, according to the experts, on April 13, 2029—though this calculation has since been declared invalid or at least significantly amended. Apophis the asteroid may have many of the qualities attributed to Apophis the god, who was Egyptian but borrowed by the Greeks, such as an ability to commit mayhem, in the form of seven hundred and fifty megatons of impact energy and a fourteen-thousand-foot-impact crater, with a potential for ten million casualties, even though 99942 Apophis is just a little four-hundred-meter amalgam of rock and ice shaped like a Cheeto. The detective learned that Professor Tish Adams, political science department MCCC, retired in 2012, well before any predictions of the collision event, likewise eight years before Stevens Murray, who would have been sixteen on the date of her retirement, commenced the alleged spree. The detective texted this information to Ned Bean, with whom the detective had a functioning working relationship, despite Bean's need to enlist the detective and others in the evaluation of women colleagues for nonwork purposes.

Stevens Murray was now on the subject of high-school basketball in the Omaha metro area. My dad, said Murray, liked to go to high-school basketball games, and this is a thing that I remember about him, from back when we were still a family. The beatings were, you know, regular, but we were still a family, which is a group of related people all sharing a mailbox. My dad was a doctoral student at University of Chicago except he never finished his, what do you call that thing, because of his problems, but he knew a lot about mathematical structures. He had a lot of ideas, and sometimes he would tell me about them, like he had this integer *sigma* he used to tell me about, which was the integer that represented pages in his whatever you call that, term-paper thing; he said this number described chaos as a thing, a force, in closed systems of which the world was one, closed.

Are you going to be discussing the specific details of your where-abouts on the night we're talking about when these two murders took place, including here in Omaha?

The remotely viewing detective was now scanning for types of propane grills. The Feds were going to take control of the investiga-tion. He'd always used charcoal in the past, and this was because his family had used charcoal, and it's just funny how these things re-peated. The grill belonging to him was rusted out, and he needed to replace it, and many friends (some on the force) were arguing for propane. It burned more easily, they said; you could control the cook time better. The detective worried a little about something blowing up with propane. One minute you were cooking some frankfurters, next minute your propane tank was a flaming missile fifty feet in the air spewing shrapnel chunks. The detective, unconsciously, scrib-bled on the legal pad an asteroid shape. And then, with the OPD per-sonal digital assistant, he verified that there never was a Stevens Jay Murray registered as a graduate student at the University of Chicago in philosophy, mathematics, physics, or in any other department.

Dad, see, was following this team called the Omaha North Vikings, the women's team, very good. You probably know about them. They went twenty-one to zero going almost to the end of a second season undefeated, and although there were lots of girls on those teams who were really good, my father was really, you know, taken with this point guard called, I think her name was, uh, Denise . . . Denise Browder. Yeah. I would say his interest was intellectual, but you never know. She was particularly good on the D, and this was despite the fact that she was not so tall. There was something about her, and my father suggested that she was a disturbance in the field, a strange attractor, that was Dad's thing, and opposing teams, they'd be coming down the lane and Browder would be standing there, like a mosquito try-ing to hold off a bunch of tanks, but she'd wave her hands and make a certain scary *war face* and then the forwards from the other team would lose the split-second timing, the numerical advantage, it would throw them off somehow, and more often than not the Vikings would end up with possession, and they would convert, really fast. There would be disarray on the court just because of the hard-to-put-your-finger-on technique of Denise Browder. This was the chaos theory of

323

high-school basketball, women's side, in the Omaha area. My dad made a map of the possible outcomes of games by the Vikings based on a Lorenz attractor model where Denise was a node for stochastic outcomes. My dad said a volatility of systems made Denise possible, birth control, school choice, corn futures, and a Supreme Court case on flag burning that happened the year she was born—flag-burning events were topologically transitive, get it?

Can you circle back to what this has to do with the alibi? Bean said.

I'm getting to that.

The detective was, in a back-brain way, aware that Stevens Murray was answering questions without counsel, and in a dynamic encounter like an interrogation it was obvious that both sides were jockeying for the methodological upper hand, thus a disquisition on high-school basketball. The detective was hoping to keep Murray talking. The Feds were just across town on 121st Street, but the indication was that they would arrive during normal business hours, as Murray's arrest, the extraction, had occurred under cover of darkness, in the very early morning hours. The arrest had gone smoothly.

A Weber grill has 240 square inches of cooking space on it, according to the literature, and that means up to fifteen patties, and the detective, in any normal barbecuing situation, required no more than twelve.

He was getting ready to write "patties" on the legal pad, the stylus was actually indenting on the legal sheet, when it hit him, like an entire side of beef, like a whole Guernsey of not-yet-processed beef, that his daughter had played basketball in high school in the very same period as the alleged point guard of the Omaha North Vikings, Denise Browder, and could have played against her, perhaps, which meant that Murray's father could have been in the stands the night his daughter played against the Vikings. Was he doing the math right? How could he have missed this?

I've sort of leaving out the gambling part, Murray said to the interrogator, Detective Ned Bean. My father's gambling. It made the games more relevant for him, the basketball games, because often he'd have more wagered on the games than our house was worth, or he'd bet his entire savings, which wasn't anything special, or he'd bet more than he made in a year doing database work for the city. The tiniest changes in game preparation, my father said, like if Denise Browder had an argument with her mom that morning, could mean our car getting repossessed or worse. If someone had a blister that day, it could change the outcome of the entire season, new clothes for school, you know, and our financial well-being. Of course, he didn't worry about whether there were problems for me, only Denise.

I would think about Denise Browder sometimes, and I would wonder if things were good for her, if she went to bed without the kind of worries we had, me and my cousins, who were living with me. Did she have a worried mind? Did she have obsessive thinking? My dad would burst into our room in the night, you know, and rage, like I somehow made him lose the money.

Anyway, it's part of my alibi, which I'll sign my name to, that I ran into Denise Browder at the Metro on my way to see my adviser, Tish Adams, and my mom was with me, and I said, Hey, are you Denise Browder, the basketball player? You might think how would I possibly know it was Denise Browder because it was years later, but some people just have this plastic imaging talent, you know, where you can see these faces, you can see in your mind's eye how the face is going to change, doesn't matter if there are a few extra pounds or whatnot, you can see that face from however many years ago, eight years, shining through. She was wearing a basketball jersey too, and she wasn't tall for a basketball player, but she was tall for a lady walking around the halls of the community college. I know that all sounds ridiculous, that she was wearing a jersey, but sometimes the truth is ridiculous, like the purple and orange Vikings jerseys are a bit ridiculous, easy to spot. I said, Hey, are you Denise Browder the basketball player, and, *boy*, did she look shocked. Not too many people asked her that after all this time. We got chatting, and I asked her about one game from when I was seven when the Vikings were behind eighteen at the half, and Dad was sweating something awful.

A great number of story elements, narrative touchstones, would have to line up for Murray's story to be true, and therefore the detective did not believe the story—it was a matter of probability, and a simple scan of the local news from back in the day would verify, and so he did check to see if there was a Denise Browder playing on the Vikings, during their undefeated streak. It was as if the air went out of him when he found that, *yes*, indeed, there *was* a Denise Browder, and this prompted the detective to conduct a text-message exchange with his daughter, which verified a certain basketball game against the Vikings, though not Murray's alibi, not yet, but which exchange also caused a tangent unrelated to the investigation, typed laboriously by the detective with his thumbs, while watching Stevens Murray, smooth, thin, hard, sinister, calculating, and scabby, in the interrogation room, Murray, who may have killed five, *I just want to tell you, honey, how sometimes the skies clear and it's like I can see all the way up to the edge, and then I know how dearly I love all you kids, and you know I sure disliked your grandfather, just couldn't ever talk to him really, and then I got to having kids myself, and I would catch myself doing the very same things he did, I would get short-tempered about the same pointless things, the same loud noises would set me off, same anxieties, same vulnerabilities, making all the mistakes he made, and then I could see that we are all desperate, just trying to do the job, so frail, and in the humble knowing of what a regular old dad I have been, who loves you kids so much, couldn't live without you, this is me humbly saying so. Try not to forget later on.*

Apophis, god of Egypt, may I tread on you with my left foot, in this my prayer, may I triumph over you, and with you, may the fires burn because of you, may only those of the night adore thee, may you be utterly spat upon, may we stab at your neck, set fire to you, may we take you into the underworld and scourge you, may we make a mockery of you, as the sun rises again, that the scourging of you makes us plausible, said Stevens Murray, evidently taking the language of the Egyptian prayers literally, or at least making up some translated equivalent, translated from ancient Egyptian into ancient Greek and from ancient Greek and into American English.

That was the prayer of Apophis, which I wrote out by hand at the library that night, and because of which I wasn't *anywhere near* the Circle K. And you can ask Denise Browder. And here Stevens Murray reached with manacled hands for his back pocket, which was awkward.

Do you need a hand with something?

He didn't have his wallet, of course; it was in a bin with his personal effects. There, later, the supervising detective *would* find a wadded-up piece of paper with a signature on it in green ink. Who uses a green pen? Maybe Stevens Murray wrote it out himself, Denise Browder's signature. The detective too loved the basketball season, its passing game, the necessity of the passing game, rather than the open break, and he felt again the pride in his daughter's sportsmanship, her ability to praise the opposing and victorious teams, the Vikings, e.g., at the game's close, and in particular he thought about the games where the margin of victory for the opposing team had been particularly unforgiving. These were the days he had to comfort her.

326

Rick Moody

So what I mean is I could not have killed victim number five, Stevens Murray said, and I did not set fire to the car of the victim, because I was at the Metro, getting an autograph, and there's probably security-cam footage, and what was the point; the victim was already dead, that fire is like committing the crime a hundred times over, that's excess, setting fire to the car, the fire is so gaudy, it probably drew attention and firefighters. So I say the state of Nebraska burned the car, the victim's husband burned the car, seven prostitutes burned the car, or the god Apophis, but I wouldn't do it, I mean unless I was going to burn it because of the flag sitting in there draped across the back seat.

NOTES ON CONTRIBUTORS

RAE ARMANTROUT's most recent book, *Conjure*, was published by Wesleyan University Press in 2020.

CLARE BEAMS's novel, *The Illness Lesson* (Doubleday), was a *New York Times* Editors' Choice and was longlisted for the Center for Fiction First Novel Prize; her story collection, *We Show What We Have Learned*, won the Bard Fiction Prize. With her husband and two daughters, she lives in Pittsburgh.

CHARLES BERNSTEIN's new collection of poems, *Topsy-Turvy*, out in spring 2021 (University of Chicago Press), includes the poems published in this issue of *Conjunctions*. He is the 2019 recipient of the Bollingen Prize for lifetime achievement in poetry and for *Near/Miss* (University of Chicago Press).

Longtime *Conjunctions* contributor and friend H. G. CARRILLO is the author of *Loosing My Espanish*, a novel (Anchor Books, 2004). His short fiction also appeared in *Kenyon Review*, *The Iowa Review*, *Glimmer Train*, and other journals and publications. Sadly, Carrillo died on April 20, 2020, of COVID-19.

VANESSA CHAN is a Malaysian writer whose work is published or forthcoming in *Electric Literature*, *The Rumpus*, and *Pidgeonholes*. A fiction editor at *TriQuarterly* and an assistant fiction editor at *Pithead Chapel*, Chan is currently completing an MFA at The New School. "Firsts" is her first appearance in print.

COLIN CHANNER's latest book is the poetry collection *Providential* (Akashic Books). Born in Jamaica, raised there and in New York, he teaches at Brown University.

SANDRA CISNEROS is a poet, short story writer, novelist, essayist, and visual artist whose work explores the lives of Mexicans and Mexican Americans. Her numerous awards include a MacArthur Fellowship, the National Medal of Arts, a Ford Foundation Art of Change Fellowship, and the PEN/Nabokov Award for Achievement in International Literature.

GILLIAN CONOLEY's *A Little More Red Sun on the Human: New and Selected Poems* (Nightboat Books, 2019) won the Northern California Book Award. She received the 2017 Shelley Memorial Award for lifetime achievement from the Poetry Society of America. Conoley is poet in residence at Sonoma State University, where she edits *Volt*.

SUSAN DAITCH is the author of six books, most recently, *The Lost Civilization of Suolucidir* (City Lights) and *White Lead* (Random House).

From Madison, Wisconsin, JOHN DARCY is an MFA candidate in creative writing at Virginia Tech. His work has appeared in *Stoneboat*, *White Wall Review*, and *Underwood Press*.

The author of fourteen books of fiction, RIKKI DUCORNET has received the Lannan Literary Award for Fiction and a Literature Award from the Academy of Arts and Letters. Her novella *The Plotinus* and her novel *Trafik*, also a work of science fiction, will both be published in 2021 with Coffee House Press.

FORREST GANDER's *Twice Alive*, from which the poem in this issue comes, will be published by New Directions in April 2021. Gander's *Be With* won the 2019 Pulitzer Prize in Poetry.

BRANDON HOBSON is the author of the forthcoming novel *The Removed* (Ecco); *Where the Dead Sit Talking* (Soho), a 2019 National Book Award finalist; and others. An assistant professor at New Mexico State University, he also teaches in the low-res MFA program at the Institute of American Indian Arts in Santa Fe.

MICHAEL IVES has taught at Bard College since 2003. His books include *The External Combustion Engine* (Futurepoem) and *Wavetable* (Dr. Cicero Books).

CYAN JAMES holds a PhD in public health genetics from the University of Washington. She is currently completing a novel about the girls who survived the Green River Killer in 1980s Seattle.

SYLVIA LEGRIS's poetry collections include *The Hideous Hidden* and the forthcoming *Garden Physic* (both New Directions).

NATHANIEL MACKEY's most recent book of poetry is *Blue Fasa* (New Directions). *Double Trio*, a three-book set, is forthcoming from New Directions in 2021.

ERIN L. McCOY holds an MA in Hispanic literature from the University of Washington. McCoy's poem "Futures" was selected by Natalie Diaz for inclusion in *Best New Poets 2017*. Her website is erinlmccoy.com.

RICK MOODY is the author, most recently, of *Hotels of North America* (Little, Brown), a novel, and *The Long Accomplishment* (Henry Holt), a memoir. He teaches at Brown University and is at work on a new novel.

KYOKO MORI is the author of three nonfiction books—*The Dream of Water* and *Polite Lies* (both Henry Holt), and *Yarn* (Gemma Media Books)—as well as four novels. She teaches in the Creative Writing Program at George Mason University.

YXTA MAYA MURRAY is a Whiting Award–winning novelist, art critic, playwright, and law professor. She is the author of nine books, including the story collection *The World Doesn't Work That Way, but It Could* (University of Nevada Press, 2020) and the novel *Art Is Everything* (TriQuarterly Press, 2021).

CINDY JUYOUNG OK's recent poems can be found in *Bennington Review, Michigan Quarterly Review*, and *Fugue*. She teaches creative writing in Iowa City and is assistant poetry editor at *Guernica*.

JANE PEK was born and raised in Singapore, and now lives in New York, where she works as a lawyer at an investment company. Her short fiction has appeared or is forthcoming in *Brooklyn Review, Witness*, and *The Best American Short Stories*. Her debut novel, *The Verifiers*, is forthcoming from Vintage.

329

ALYSSA PELISH writes, edits, and teaches in New York. Her work can be found in *The Paris Review* online, *Harper's*, and *New England Review*. Her fiction has been recognized by *The Best American Short Stories* 2018.

An artist and novelist from Philadelphia, MARC ANTHONY RICHARDSON won the Ronald Sukenick Innovative Fiction Prize and an American Book Award for his debut novel, *Year of the Rat* (Fiction Collective Two, 2016). "Night Is the Best Counsel" is an excerpt from his upcoming novel, *Messiahs* (Fiction Collective Two, 2021).

ALAN ROSSI's stories have appeared in *Granta*, *The Missouri Review*, and *AGNI*. His fiction has received a Pushcart Prize and an O. Henry Prize. His first novel, *Mountain Road, Late at Night*, was recently published by Picador.

DAVID RYAN is the author of *Animals in Motion: Stories* (Roundabout Press). A 2020 Artistic Excellence Fellow with the Connecticut Office of the Arts, he teaches in the writing programs of Sarah Lawrence College and New England College. Read more about him at www.davidwryan.com.

BENNETT SIMS is the author of the novel *A Questionable Shape*, which received the Bard Fiction Prize, and the story collection *White Dialogues* (both from Two Dollar Radio). He teaches fiction at the University of Iowa.

MEREDITH STRICKER is a visual artist and poet working in cross-genre media. Her forthcoming collection, *re-wilding*, was awarded the Dorset Prize from Tupelo Press. She co-directs visual poetry studio, a collaborative that focuses on architecture and other projects to bring together artists, writers, musicians, and experimental forms.

BARBARA TRAN's writing has appeared or is forthcoming in *The Cincinnati Review*, *Ploughshares*, *Poetry*, and *The New Yorker*. In 2021, her first poem film will tour with a Diasporic Vietnamese American Network exhibition.

HELENA MARÍA VIRAMONTES is the author of the novels *Their Dogs Came with Them* and *Under the Feet of Jesus*, as well as the collection *The Moths and Other Stories*. A 2007 Ford Fellow in Literature, she has also received the John Dos Passos Prize for Literature and a Spirit Award from the California Latino Legislative Caucus. Viramontes is Goldwin Smith Professor of English at Cornell University in Ithaca, New York, where she is at work on a new novel.

ANNE WALDMAN is the author, most recently, of *Sanctuary* (Spuyten Duyvil), *Trickster Feminism* (Penguin), and *Songs of the Sons and Daughters of Buddha*, translations with Andrew Schelling (Shambhala). She is the artistic director of Naropa's Summer Writing Program and a member of the Rizoma Collective in Mexico City.

JOHN YAU's most recent book is a selection of essays, *Foreign Sounds or Sounds Foreign* (MadHat, 2020). He has a book of poems, *Genghis Chan on Drums*, forthcoming from Omnidawn in 2021.

TRADE PAPERBACK · $17 · EBOOK AVAILABLE NOVEMBER 2020

TRADE PAPERBACK · $17 · EBOOK AVAILABLE NOVEMBER 2020

"Breaks down genre boundaries, combining elements of fantasy, mystery, science fiction, and horror, in settings ranging from the historical and familiar to the wildly imaginative." — *Publishers Weekly*

"Susan Stinson's *Martha Moody* is an exuberant, cheeky Western in which sensual hunger steers an offbeat homesteader toward freedom." — *Foreword Reviews*

"A rich and complicated novel, nearly edible in its sensuous physicality." — *Sojourner*

TRADE PAPERBACK · $17 · EBOOK AVAILABLE AUGUST 2020

"Karen Russell's cover blurb praises Cotman as 'a synthesizer … of lewd dialect and high lyricism.' I'll speak instead of Cotman's high dialect and lewd lyricism, of how his fashioning of character voices is superbly disciplined, lit from within, while his lyricism is the realm of bawdy jokes and opacity, a kind of literary trolling."
— Amal El-Mohtar, *New York Times Book Review*

BOOKS, ZINES, CHAPBOOKS &c.
SMALLBEERPRESS.COM
DRM—FREE EBOOKS: WEIGHTLESSBOOKS.COM
PICK UP A T—SHIRT FROM OUR BOOK SHOP:
BOOKMOONBOOKS.COM

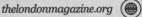

The American Journal of Poetry

theamericanjournalofpoetry.com

‖CCS BARD HESSEL MUSEUM

→ WITH A ROTATING SCHEDULE OF
EXHIBITIONS FEATURING BOTH MAJOR AND
EMERGING CONTEMPORARY ARTISTS
THROUGHOUT THE YEAR.

→ Hours and information at ccs.bard.edu

Hessel Museum of Art
Bard College → Annandale-on-Hudson → NY 12504-5000
845-758-7598

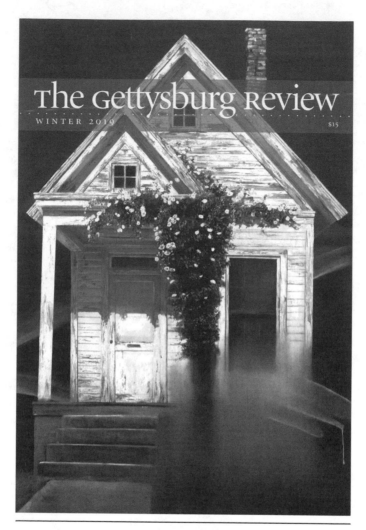

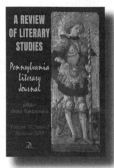